THE LIBERATION OF

Marguerite Harrison

THE LIBERATION OF

Marguerite Harrison

—— ★ ——

AMERICA'S FIRST FEMALE FOREIGN INTELLIGENCE AGENT

—— ★ ——

ELIZABETH ATWOOD

Naval Institute Press
Annapolis, Maryland

THIS BOOK HAS BEEN BROUGHT TO PUBLICATION WITH THE
GENEROUS ASSISTANCE OF **EDWARD S.** AND **JOYCE I. MILLER**.

Naval Institute Press
291 Wood Road
Annapolis, MD 21402

Library of Congress Cataloging-in-Publication Data
Names: Atwood, Elizabeth Ann, author.
Title: The liberation of Marguerite Harrison : America's first female foreign intelligence
    agent / Elizabeth Atwood.
Other titles: America's first female foreign intelligence agent
Description: Annapolis, Maryland : Naval Institute Press, [2020] | Includes bibliographical
    references and index.
Identifiers: LCCN 2020009877 (print) | LCCN 2020009878 (ebook) | ISBN 9781682475270
    (hardcover) | ISBN 9781682475300 (epub) | ISBN 9781682475300 (pdf)
Subjects: LCSH: Harrison, Marguerite, 1879–1967. | United States. War Department.
    Military Intelligence Division—History. | Espionage, American—Germany—History—
    20th century. | Espionage, American—Soviet Union—History—20th century. | Soviet
    Union—Politics and government—1917–1936. | Spies—United States—History—
    20th century. | Women intelligence officers—United States—Biography. | Intelligence
    officers—United States—Biography. | Baltimore (Md.)—Biography.
Classification: LCC UB271.U5 A88 2020 (print) | LCC UB271.U5 (ebook) |
    DDC 327.12730092 [B]—dc23
LC record available at https://lccn.loc.gov/2020009877
LC ebook record available at https://lccn.loc.gov/2020009878

♾ Print editions meet the requirements of ANSI/NISO z39.48-1992 (Permanence of Paper).
Printed in the United States of America.

28 27 26 25 24 23 22 21 20   9 8 7 6 5 4 3 2 1
First printing

For *Andrew* and *Michael*
Wishing them many happy adventures

CONTENTS

PREFACE

MARGUERITE ELTON BAKER HARRISON was born into a wealthy Baltimore family during the Victorian era, when a woman's status was determined by her family and her life revolved around her husband and children. And so it was with Harrison—at least until her husband's sudden death in 1915 upended her world. For the next ten years she sought solace from her grief and freedom from societal expectations, first as a newspaper reporter and then as an international spy. At the time she entered the Military Intelligence Division, American women could not vote for fear they would be corrupted by the unseemly business of government and politics. Nevertheless, Harrison's missions took her to dangerous streets in postwar Berlin, across frozen plains of Russia, and, ultimately, to the fetid cells of a Bolshevik prison.

In the numerous books, magazine articles, and newspaper stories that Harrison wrote about her adventures, she never mentioned that she was America's first female foreign intelligence officer. This accomplishment was not something she would have found noteworthy because, for most of her life, Harrison was an ambivalent feminist. She did not publicly champion women's suffrage, birth control, or equality in the workplace. Raised as a woman of privilege, she saw no reason to advocate for women's rights. Wealth and connections opened doors. She founded a children's hospital, worked as a newspaper reporter, and became an international spy with the help of family and friends. Only when she approached the age of fifty and founded a society for women explorers did Harrison embrace the feminist label and become a champion of women's equality. Even so, after she remarried in 1926, she quit the foreign service and ended her solo adventures in order to support her husband's acting career. When Harrison died in 1967, she left it to a new generation to fight for women's rights.

I first heard about Marguerite Harrison soon after I started work at the Baltimore *Evening Sun* in 1988. As someone who entered journalism just a few years after Bob Woodward and Carl Bernstein helped bring down a president, I found the idea of a reporter working as a government spy disturbing, even scandalous.

As I learned more about the Baltimore socialite turned reporter and agent, I became intrigued by this unconventional and controversial woman. I discovered that she grew up in Catonsville, Maryland, the community where I live, and that she held a life-long fascination with Russia, the country where I researched my doctoral dissertation and met my husband. While I could never identify with her privileged upbringing or zest for reckless adventure, Marguerite Harrison and I shared many of the same interests.

In 2016 I resolved to learn everything I could about Harrison. This task was complicated by her having left no diary and few personal letters. Few of her intelligence reports have survived. In many cases the only accounts about events in her life are those she revealed in her autobiography, *There's Always Tomorrow: The Story of a Checkered Life*. In her memoir she recounted growing up under the restrictions imposed by a domineering mother; her happy but brief marriage to a Baltimore stockbroker; her work at the *Baltimore Sun*; and her decision to become a spy at the end of World War I.

But digging deeper, I discovered that Harrison was less than forthcoming about many aspects of her life. At times she either misremembered or intentionally misstated events and circumstances, including the extent of her involvement with U.S. intelligence services. She hinted at her need to be circumspect when she told readers that she recognized the risk of espionage: "If I succeeded, my efforts would never be publicly recognized. If I failed, I would be repudiated by my government and perhaps lose my life."[1]

Harrison portrayed her intelligence work as a brief interlude in her career as a writer, but I uncovered evidence that her spying lasted much longer and was more involved than she revealed. Files in the National Archives show that she sent reports to the U.S. Army and State Department throughout her travels in the early 1920s. Most surprising was the discovery of a note scribbled in the corner of a letter revealing that a 1925 documentary she made with noted filmmakers Merian Cooper and Ernest Schoedsack was a cover for a spy mission to the Middle East.

The archival records gradually began to reveal a picture of Harrison very different from the image portrayed in her writings. Records show that Harrison's linguistic talents and familiarity with Europe persuaded officers in the U.S. Army to hire her as America's first female foreign agent. Although women had spied during the American Revolution and Civil War, Harrison was the first to be dispatched overseas because of her knowledge and skills. She performed so well, she was entrusted with some of the nation's most sensitive missions. She was among a handful of spies sent into Berlin to collect information on political and economic conditions while peace negotiations were under way in Versailles. With the rising threat of Bolshevism, she gathered evidence against suspected Socialists and Communists. She was dispatched to Russia to locate American prisoners and to collect information on the viability of Lenin's government. And she was the United States' eyes and ears in Japan, China, Siberia, and the Middle East where newly emerging American industry sought a foothold. The fact that she accomplished these missions when many Americans still believed women should not involve themselves in the sometimes dirty business of government and politics is testament to both her talents and the vision of the men who trusted her.

Yet I was unable to completely penetrate the veil of secrecy that still shrouds Harrison's life. Records of her U.S. spy missions are incomplete, especially those pertaining to her travels in the Middle East. In some cases I was left to surmise her intentions, given scant information of whom she met during her travels.

Many questions also remain about her role as a double agent. She wrote that she was forced to provide information to the Soviet political police in exchange for her freedom in 1920. Seeking the truth, I traveled to Moscow, Russia, where a Russian translator helped me read her prison files. The documents provided new details of what she told Bolshevik authorities about American spy operations, including information she provided on other British and American agents, but they do not answer whether she continued to give information to Russia after her release.

Her words and actions often were contradictory. She helped catch Communist journalist Robert Minor, who distributed propaganda to American troops in Germany at the end of World War I, and she provided reports on suspected Bolshevik agents when she left Russian prison in 1921. But when she returned to the United States, she publicly insisted that she witnessed no Bolshevik atrocities, repeatedly defended Lenin's regime, and lectured alongside American Socialists urging the United States to recognize and aid Soviet Russia.

As I dug deeper into records of her foreign service, I was struck by the doubts that even her closest friends, family, and colleagues expressed about Harrison's foreign adventures. Some accused her of being a Bolshevik agent. Others thought her foolish and reckless. Yet many believed she was a brave American patriot. In the shadowy world of espionage where agents and their superiors knew only as much as they needed to know, all of these assessments are possible.

One hundred years after Harrison embarked on her first mission and more than fifty years after her death, many secrets remain. One day another researcher may stumble upon a casual note written in the margin of a letter and discover yet another clue to the mystery of America's first female foreign intelligence agent. Until then, my hope is that this book sheds new light on the life of a remarkable woman.

ACKNOWLEDGMENTS

EXPLORING THE LIFE AND LEGACY of Marguerite Harrison has been a great adventure, and many guided me along the way.

First and foremost, I want to thank Alex Vinogradsky, without whose help this book would not have been possible. He translated Russian documents, provided valuable insights into Russian history, patiently listened to my incessant questions and speculations, offered suggestions, and never wavered in his support for seeing this project through.

I also want to thank my friends in Russia, including Larisa Vinogradskaya, who opened her home to me in Moscow while I was conducting research in the Central Archive of the Federal Security Bureau, and Nickolaj Golovin, who helped translate archive files.

I owe a huge debt to my friend Maureen Dezell, who spent countless hours reading this manuscript with her copy editor's eye, and David Hein, who was instrumental offering advice on how to organize this research into a coherent narrative.

I also want to thank members of the Hood College community who helped make this book possible, including the provost and Faculty Development Committee, who allowed me a sabbatical to conduct research and provided grant support to the project. Also, my thanks goes to Christie Wisniewski, who helped with the research, and my colleagues in the Hood English and Communication Arts Department, including Katherine Orloff, Donna Bertazzoni, Alan Goldenbach, and Mark Sandona, who encouraged me along the way.

Thanks are also due to Nancy Harrison, who generously shared with me memories of her grandmother and family photographs; and my former colleagues at the *Baltimore Sun*, especially Paul McCardell, Kathy Lally, and Will Englund, who offered guidance and support. I also want to acknowledge the help I received from the librarians and archivists at the National Archives in College Park, Maryland, and the Central Archive of the Federal Security Bureau in Moscow, Russia.

Finally, I am grateful to the editors of the Naval Institute Press, who had faith in this project and helped me tell the story of an amazing woman.

PROLOGUE

CAUGHT. AGAIN.

Marguerite Harrison stared at the familiar walls of her cell in Lubyanka prison. The tattered wallpaper bore witness to the agonies of the prisoners who had preceded her. Drawn on the paper were calendars marking their days of torment, defiant slogans, sketches of soldiers, and even mathematical equations. But she had seen it all before.

For the second time in two years, America's first female foreign intelligence officer sat in Russia's most notorious prison—a former insurance company building in the center of Moscow that had been converted into the headquarters of the Bolshevik secret police and cells for their political prisoners. The charge against her: espionage.

Again.

This time she had been arrested at gunpoint on November 21, 1922, on a street in the Far Eastern Republic city of Chita and whisked by train through Siberia to Moscow. She spent Christmas 1922 locked in a fourth-floor attic cell shaped like a coffin. She shared the dark room with three other women—a Russian political prisoner, a Jewish schoolteacher, and a Polish girl pretending to be an anarchist but who actually was working for the secret police and making her cellmates' lives miserable with her tantrums and propositions.

Marguerite had taken a gamble by trying to return to Russia despite having been expelled just a year earlier. In April 1920 the Bolsheviks caught her spying for the U.S. Military Intelligence Division and forced her to become a double agent in exchange for her freedom. Yet, while making regular reports to the deputy chief of Soviet secret police, Solomon Mogilevsky, she continued to sneak information to U.S. officials until Mogilevsky discovered the ruse and arrested her. That time she spent nine months in prison and was freed only after the American government agreed to give Russia food aid.

This time, however, Marguerite was not sure U.S. officials even knew where she was. The American consul in Chita knew she had been arrested and put on a train bound for Moscow, but then she was secretly taken off and held briefly in a Siberian jail. She feared the Soviets would deny any knowledge of her whereabouts when the Americans demanded her release.

As the days passed, Marguerite grew more despondent. Surely the Soviets would not want to antagonize America when it was still sending grain to starving peasants, she thought. Yet, in the brief glimpse she had of Moscow as she was being transported from the train station to Lubyanka, she could see conditions were much improved from 1921. The Russians might not be so willing to exchange her for aid this time.

Her instincts also told her there was something different about this imprisonment. She knew the secret police had been watching her for months as she traveled through Asia, but she could not fathom their intentions. During her travels she had freely conversed with Soviet military and diplomatic leaders in Japan and China and sent reports to Washington without a hint of trouble. She had walked into a trap, but she did not know who had set it.

Marguerite was giving up hope for rescue when, a few days before New Year's Day, a guard ordered her from her cell. He escorted her down stairs and through the labyrinth of winding corridors until they stopped before a familiar door. Inside the office stood her old adversary—Solomon Mogilevsky.

The Russian foreign intelligence chief had always reminded her of a black puma with his dark hair, piercing eyes, and thin mustache. He wore a black shirt, riding pants, and black boots and carried a pistol by his side. He was a formidable foe. For months in 1920 they had matched wits as he tried to uncover what she knew about foreign agents working in Moscow. That time he had won.

Mogilevsky bowed and motioned for her to take a seat in a leather armchair. "Good morning, Comrade Harrison," he said casually.

Marguerite rallied her strength to confront him. "Will you kindly tell me why I am here?" she demanded.

Coolly, Mogilevsky explained the three charges against her: the previous espionage charge, the crime of entering Soviet Russia without permission, and a new allegation—that she had been spying again.

Marguerite protested. She told him that she had inadvertently entered Russian territory when the government of the Far Eastern Republic fell to Soviet control. She adamantly denied any new espionage activities. Her purpose for touring Asia and Siberia was to gather information for magazine articles, she insisted. Then Mogilevsky calmly asked her about a conversation she'd had with an official in the U.S. State Department just weeks before she departed to the Far East. He knew the time and date of the meeting and repeated what they said almost word for word. Marguerite realized there had been a mole in the U.S. government.

She was caught.

But before she could respond, Mogilevsky pressed on. "When you agreed to work for us two years ago, you double-crossed us, but during our conversations, I became aware of the fact that you could be exceedingly useful if you could be made to work seriously. When you put yourself within our reach once more, the opportunity was too tempting."

Mogilevsky was now stationed in Tbilisi, Georgia, overseeing intelligence operations in Turkey and Persia. He had been watching her. "I have come all the way from the Caucasus to make you a most liberal offer," he said. "If you accept it, you would be set free tomorrow."

"Indeed. And what is the offer?" Marguerite asked.

"You will remain in Russia. I shall not ask you to inform on the British or Americans. Past experience has shown me that I could never depend on you to do that. Your work will be among Russians. You speak the language almost perfectly. They will trust you as a foreigner and give you information which they would not give to any Russian. You will have a comfortable apartment, all your living expenses and a salary paid in gold equivalent to two hundred and fifty dollars a month in American money."

Marguerite was incredulous. "You want me to give up all hope of ever returning to the United States. What about my son? Am I never to see him?"

Mogilevsky reassured her. "I foresaw that you might be unwilling to remain in Russia without him. He will be brought from America at our expense and he can finish his education at the University of Moscow. This is the country for youth. He will have limitless opportunities."

Marguerite's mind was racing. Could the Soviets really think she was such a valuable asset that they would risk antagonizing the U.S. government with her capture? Could Mogilevsky's intentions go beyond the desire to recruit an American spy? She thought of all their meetings in the past, their political and philosophical debates, their conversations about history and literature. Could he possibly have a romantic interest in her?

She summoned her remaining energy. "Thank you. I prefer to remain in prison. I shall never work again for any government, my own or yours. I would rather die in prison," she said firmly.

Mogilevsky reminded her that the charges she faced included high treason. "You will probably be sentenced to death, and the best you can expect is ten years in Siberia. You don't want to change your mind?"

"No," she said.

Mogilevsky shrugged and summoned the guard, who returned her to her cell.

Marguerite collapsed onto her wooden pallet, physically and emotionally exhausted. She had never felt so hopeless.

Marguerite thought of her friends and family back in Baltimore. It was the peak of the winter social season. They would be gathering for the Monday-night balls and hosting card parties for the debutantes. It did not seem so long ago that she had been among them, dressed in a French lace gown and carrying an armful of bouquets as she made her debut to society. In those days, her most pressing concern had been the color of the gown she should wear to the Hunt Club Ball and her biggest adversary had been her domineering mother, who insisted she marry a European nobleman.

She had defied her mother and married the man she loved. But when he died suddenly, she escaped the expectations that Gilded Age society placed on a woman of her position. Rather than return to her father's estate, she went into newspaper work, at first writing social announcements and then theater and music reviews for the *Baltimore Sun*. When World War I broke out, she wrote patriotic articles to support the Allies. In 1917 she had used her gift for languages to help ferret out German agents in Baltimore. But she had wanted more. She had wanted to be a foreign spy.

With fluency in four languages and knowledge of Europe, she persuaded U.S. Army commanders to hire her to spy in Germany in 1918. Her intelligence reports helped guide the decisions of President Woodrow Wilson at a time when women couldn't even vote. She had overcome skeptics who believed female spies were untrustworthy and proved that a woman could gather information without exchanging sex for secrets. Her superiors were so impressed with her work that they sent her to Russia to investigate political and economic conditions under the Bolshevik regime.

But that mission was doomed from the start. The Russians knew she was a spy before she crossed the border. A Socialist she had targeted in Switzerland had sent word to the Bolsheviks that the woman posing as an Associated Press correspondent was really an undercover spy. That time, she had played the role of a double agent in order to survive. She knew she would not be able to fool the Russians again. Even worse, American officials had grown wary of her reports and begun to suspect her motives. The first time, they had demanded her release before giving Russia much-needed aid. This time, they might not try to save her. This time, Marguerite Harrison doubted she could escape the firing squad.[1]

FOND OF ADVENTURE

MARGUERITE HURRIED to her three o'clock appointment in the Emerson Hotel at the corner of Calvert and Baltimore Streets. Dodging street cars and brushing past the pedestrians enjoying the fine fall weather that Sunday afternoon, she darted under the hotel's green awning and into the lobby. She hoped she wasn't late. This might be her last chance to become a spy.

It was almost the end of September 1918, and the Allies were a month into the Hundred Days Offensive to retake territory from the Axis powers. The headlines in that Sunday morning's *Baltimore Sun* made it clear that the Great War would soon be over. Bulgaria had surrendered, Gen. John J. Pershing was reporting victory northwest of Verdun, France, and Germany appeared near collapse. At home, Marylanders were enthusiastically responding to the call to buy war bonds to secure the final victory.

Marguerite could feel the excitement as the world stood on the brink of revolution, and she wanted to be part of it. She had written some propaganda pieces for the *Sun* and passed along to the Justice Department rumors she had picked up about suspected German agents in Baltimore. But she wanted to do more. She longed to be in Europe where she could see firsthand the events unfold. She wanted the thrill and power of knowing secrets that could change history. She was determined to become a foreign intelligence officer.

She had already tried the Office of Naval Intelligence. In her job application, she had noted her qualifications, including familiarity with Germany, Switzerland, France, and Italy, as well as her linguistic skill. "I have absolute command of French and German, am very fluent and have a good accent in Italian, and speak a little Spanish. Without any trouble I could pass as a French woman, and after a little practice, a German-Swiss," she wrote.[1] But Navy commanders turned her down, saying they did not employ female agents.

She then tried the U.S. Army's new Military Intelligence Division (MID) where she had connections. Her father-in-law, Joseph S. Ames, a physics professor at Johns Hopkins University, served on war boards in Washington and was a friend of MID director Marlborough Churchill, a distant cousin of Winston Churchill. Ames wrote to Churchill on her behalf, saying, "She is absolutely trustworthy and most anxious to do some real public service. If you use women in your foreign service, you could not find any better."[2]

Marguerite followed up with her own letter, telling Churchill that she was well suited to work in espionage. "Employment as a special foreign agent is the only work that would justify me in giving up the work I am doing now, and I believe my qualifications and training would enable me to be of real service," she told him.[3]

Churchill agreed to consider her application and dispatched Lt. Col. Walter Martin to Baltimore to find out more. When Marguerite entered the Emerson to meet Martin that afternoon, she might have recalled the advice of her governess: "Be intellectual if you must, but do not let anyone see it. It is fatal. Learn to be charming. It will take you much farther."[4] Her gaze swept over the lobby, past its marble columns and potted palms, looking for Martin. A man in civilian dress walked toward her. "Mrs. Harrison?" he inquired.

Marguerite extended a polite handshake and smiled. They sat down at a quiet table in one of the hotel's second-floor restaurants. Martin looked closely at the woman seated before him. She was almost forty, but she looked at least ten years younger. She was of average height—five feet, six inches—and about 125 pounds. Although not beautiful, she was attractive, with dark hair and blue eyes. There was something else about her—an air of culture and refinement that marked her as a member of Baltimore's upper class. From his investigations, he had learned that she was a widow with a sixteen-year-old son and was a daughter of a prominent Baltimore businessman and civic leader. She had been active in civic affairs herself, founding a school for sick children and holding a position on the state's motion picture censorship board. She now was a reporter at the *Baltimore Sun*, where she wrote music and theater reviews and war propaganda. Why would such a woman want to become a spy?

Almost immediately, Marguerite made it clear that she believed she was qualified for the work. She would not be like Mata Hari, extracting secrets from unwitting lovers. Nor would she be like the poor British nurse Edith Cavell, who was shot for helping Allied prisoners escape. Marguerite proposed to work as a different kind of female foreign intelligence officer, relying on her knowledge and skill. And unlike Hari and Cavell, she had no intention of ending up in front of a firing squad.

The Europeans had long employed women as spies. According to one estimate, from 1909 to 1919, approximately six thousand women worked in the British intelligence service in positions ranging from file clerks and translators to secret agents.[5] The U.S. War Department, however, hesitated to put women on the front lines, believing their reports on military matters could not be trusted and fearing they would fall in love with their targets. A female secretary to one of the American generals with the American Expeditionary Forces had confronted Dennis Nolan, head of the Army's Espionage Service, and demanded to know why he refused to employ women agents. "How will you justify yourself in history for not permitting American women to serve as secret agents for our army?" she asked. Nolan told her he had too many troubles without thinking about what would happen when the war ended.[6]

Marguerite was determined to prove that a woman could be a foreign agent. She told Martin that she was well past the "foolish stage" when she might act with her heart rather than her head. She didn't want to enter intelligence service on a lark. She was serious and talented, and, to prove it, she spoke to Martin in German so fluently that he was suspicious about where she had learned it.

Marguerite laughed and assured him that she was not a German agent; her family had been in the United States for eight generations. Her mother's father, Elias Livezey, was a Quaker whose ancestors had accompanied William Penn when he founded Pennsylvania. Her maternal grandmother, Elizabeth Elton Livezey, was descended from lords proprietor of New Jersey. Her father, Bernard Nadal Baker, came from a prominent family of Baltimore merchants who had earned a fortune in the glass business and then extended their wealth and influence into banking, chemical manufacturing, paint and dye making, a newspaper, and city government. During the Civil War, when Baltimore's mayor was imprisoned at Fort McHenry because of his pro-Southern leanings, her grandfather Charles J. Baker served as acting mayor.

Marguerite owed her language fluency to her ambitious mother, Elizabeth, who wanted her daughter to follow the paths of wealthy American women such as Anna Gould, Consuelo Vanderbilt, and Mary Leiter and marry into European royalty.[7] Her goal had not been a far-fetched plan. In the late nineteenth century, many European noblemen pursued wealthy American women who were interesting and well-educated and possessed hefty dowries that could shore up lagging fortunes. By the eve of World War I, nearly five hundred well-to-do American women had married into British and French royalty.[8] Elizabeth Baker had seen to it that her daughter had learned languages and traveled throughout Europe, absorbing history and culture, and meeting just the right people. And while she had intended to ready her daughter for a life hosting European salons, she had unintentionally also prepared her for work as an international spy.

But what drew Marguerite to espionage? Why leave her son and the newspaper work she enjoyed to risk her life as a spy? Many years later, in her autobiography, Marguerite wrote that entering the foreign intelligence service was the only way she could see the events unfolding in Europe, implying that she could not observe the war as a newspaper correspondent. It is true the United States did not give press credentials to women to cover the war, but many female reporters found ways around this technicality. Nellie Bly, who had quit stunt reporting to marry and run a business, returned to journalism to cover the war in Austria for the *New York Evening Journal*. Reporter Peggy Hull, who met General Pershing when he was chasing Mexican outlaw Pancho Villa in Texas, used the general's influence to gain access to a U.S. artillery training camp in France. John Reed's wife, Louise Bryant, ventured to the front lines in France to report for the Bell Syndicate. And United Press International correspondent Alice Rohe reported on the war from Italy. A determined woman reporter could witness events in Europe without resorting to espionage.[9]

Marguerite wasn't attracted to spying for the money. Her work at the *Baltimore Sun* and the patronage job her former brother-in-law had secured for her on the Maryland Board of Motion Picture Censors paid more. It wasn't for glamor. Spying was dirty business. It might be necessary during wartime, but it certainly wasn't something nice women did.[10]

Marguerite knew the risks. She had interviewed Edith Cavell's lawyer, and the newspapers had covered Mata Hari's case extensively.[11] Reflecting years later, Marguerite said that she understood the spy's dilemma: "If I succeeded, my efforts would never be publicly recognized. If I failed, I would be repudiated by my government and perhaps lose my life."[12]

The truth was, she told Martin, she wanted to be a spy because she was fearless, fond of adventure, and had an intense desire to serve her country.

Her suggestion was simple: She would travel to Europe under the pretext of writing feature stories for the *Baltimore Sun* and gather intelligence for the U.S. Army. Her passport and papers would say she was a newspaper correspondent. The *Sun*'s managing editor was the only one at the paper who needed to know about the espionage work, and he had already agreed to the plan.

Martin informed her that, if she did go abroad, she would take no part in fighting foreign spies. Her work would be simply to gather information to help the peace negotiators, and he cautioned her of the need for discretion. She eagerly assured him that she could keep secrets. How much would the government be willing to pay? she asked. While he could give no guarantees, he said she could probably expect $250 a month, plus an additional $250 for expenses. Fine, she said. She could start December 1.

Immediately after the interview, Martin wrote to Churchill, telling him of the meeting. "She impressed me most favorably," he said.[13] The next day, Churchill approved her employment.[14] The Army, which had never hired a female foreign intelligence officer, was willing to take a chance on the Baltimore socialite.

In the early days of American foreign intelligence, personalities and connections loomed large. The Military Intelligence Division sprang from the vision of a Harvard-educated lawyer, Ralph Van Deman, who in 1901 helped organize an intelligence operation in the Philippines and personally oversaw a band of covert agents. After he was reassigned to Washington, D.C., in 1915, Van Deman lobbied for the creation of separate military intelligence division. It took the captain almost two years to convince his superiors that the Army needed its own intelligence-gathering operation. Even after the United States declared war on Germany, Army general Hugh Scott took the position that if America needed information, it would simply ask the British and French.

As a sign of his willingness to creatively defy narrow-minded commanders, Van Deman appealed to a woman to help him. Secretary of War Newton D. Baker had asked Van Deman to give novelist Edith Wharton a tour of military bases. Knowing that she was friends with Newton, Van Deman took the opportunity to mention the Army's need for an intelligence unit. Wharton agreed to bring the matter up with Baker, who soon summoned Van Deman to his office to make his case. The ploy worked. On May 3, 1917, the Army War College created the Military Intelligence Section, which over the next year grew to a division overseeing the operations of domestic and foreign spies, code breakers, radio operators, map makers, and aviators. In the summer of 1918, when Van Deman was dispatched to Europe, Churchill, a former military attaché, assumed the MID command.[15]

Once Churchill agreed to employ her, Marguerite immediately made arrangements for her trip abroad. A MID representative outlined the plan: She would travel to New York and present to the English, French, Swiss, Dutch, Danish, and Italian consulates letters from the *Baltimore Sun* seeking permission to work as a foreign correspondent so that it would "appear to them that your reasons for traveling in these countries are perfectly legitimate, normal and usual." MID would send her a check for $750 to cover her first month's salary and expenses. More money would be directed later to the *Baltimore Sun*, so that it would appear that the newspaper was paying her salary. "It is needless, I am sure, to warn you of the absolute necessity of the most extraordinary care as to secrecy," the official wrote. "We have great confidence in you, and I believe your service will be of great value to our country."[16]

That autumn Baltimore was filled with excitement, uncertainty, and tragedy. As Marguerite prepared to go to Europe, Spanish influenza struck the city. The epidemic started with a few cases at the U.S. Army base at Fort Meade, Maryland, in late September and spread quickly to soldiers at Fort McHenry in Baltimore and then among the civilian contract employees working at the bases. At first health officials dismissed concerns that the flu was anything more than the usual virus that doctors had treated for years. But soon the epidemic paralyzed the city.

The stricken quickly overwhelmed Baltimore hospitals, and businesses struggled to continue operations as the flu felled their workers. The day after 30,000 students and more than 200 teachers failed to show up for classes, the city school superintendent closed the schools. On October 9 the Baltimore health commissioner ordered the closing of concert halls and theaters. Accustomed to writing two music and theater columns a week for the *Sun*, Marguerite suddenly had no assignments. All public meetings were banned, and even churches and pool halls closed. As the death toll mounted, the city council voted to help pay for the funerals of the poor and suspended the requirement for embalming. After a week, the crisis eased, and the city gradually lifted the restrictions on public meetings. In the final tally, 4,125 Baltimoreans died in the epidemic.[17]

The flu scare had just passed when events in Europe cast new doubt on her mission. On November 11, 1918, the combatant nations agreed to a cease-fire. The war was over. In Maryland, church bells tolled, factory whistles blew, and municipal bands played music in the streets from Annapolis to Hagerstown in celebration. In Baltimore, crowds gathered in the square in front of the *Sun* building to sing patriotic songs, and impromptu parades marched through the streets on what the *Baltimore Sun* proclaimed was "the greatest day in the history of the world!"[18]

For Marguerite, however, the feeling was one of intense disappointment. She believed she had missed her opportunity to become a foreign spy. Looking to the future, she could see nothing but the dreariness of writing concert and theater reviews and occasional off-beat feature stories. As if to confirm her fears, when the armistice was announced, the *Sun* dispatched her to Philadelphia to meet New York opera star Madam Ernestine Schumann-Heink, who was traveling to Baltimore to sing patriotic anthems in Sun Square. Marguerite gamely accepted the assignment and escorted the diva to Baltimore. When the singer demanded a pianist, Marguerite rushed to find one. But the crowd was so boisterous and noisy that no one could hear the music, and the singer cut the program short. Marguerite wearily accompanied Schumann-Heink to Baltimore's Penn Station to catch the train back to New York.[19]

Marguerite had given up hope of intelligence work, but the day after the armistice celebration, she received an unexpected summons to Washington. Marlborough Churchill told her he wanted to send her to Europe after all. As a former military attaché, he understood the importance of the United States maintaining a permanent intelligence service overseas. Many in America were tired of war and wanted nothing to do with foreign ventures, but Churchill was among a group of internationalists who saw the opportunity for America to become a world leader. He realized that in order for the United States to rise, it needed intelligence.

Even as the war was winding down, the number of officers and civilians working for MID was growing. The division hired its first woman, Anna Keichline, a pioneering architect from Pennsylvania, in June 1918, and dispatched her to Philadelphia to spy on African Americans suspected of disloyalty.[20] Marguerite would be the first woman sent overseas. Her mission would be to collect intelligence that would aid the Americans in the Armistice negotiations.

Sun managing editor Frank Kent agreed to help, illustrating the complicated relationship between the press and the government. Kent was a well-regarded newsman who had started at the *Sun* as a cub reporter in 1900 and distinguished himself with his political reporting. In 1914 the paper's editors summoned him from the Washington bureau to serve as managing editor of both the morning and evening newspapers, but he continued to cover political news as well. In the fall of 1918 he traveled to Europe to see firsthand the conditions as the war ended and returned with stories about tensions among the Allies—the first uncensored accounts of the war in four years. "The truth is, and everybody in Paris knows it, that in governmental and political circles they do not love us at all over there," Kent observed. His articles outraged U.S. officials, but journalists praised him for his honest reporting.[21]

Yet, at the time, standards of journalism objectivity were not well defined. Reporters were expected to write the facts, but they did not have to be impartial. The first national code of ethics was not developed until 1923 when the American Society of Newspaper Editors issued a policy advocating independence, freedom, and truth.[22] So Kent saw nothing contradictory about the newspaper criticizing American policies while giving cover to an Army spy. After all, the *Baltimore Sun* had been an ardent supporter of the war since the United States entered the conflict. One of the paper's owners, Van Lear Black, had headed the war bond publicity committee and assigned *Sun* clerks to sell bonds from the newspaper's office. By 1919 the newspaper had sold more than $4 million worth of bonds to 28,499 people.[23]

The newspaper assignment Kent devised to cover Marguerite's spy mission was innocuous enough. The *Baltimore Sun* had produced a motion picture titled *Miles of Smiles* to boost troop morale. The movie had been shot around Maryland showing the soldiers' wives, parents, girlfriends, and children waving and holding up messages to their loved ones. With its production complete, Marguerite would travel to Europe to show the movie to the homesick troops anxiously awaiting their return to Maryland. Once overseas, she would make her way to Germany, where she would write feature stories while gathering information for the Army.

Marguerite hurried to make her final arrangements for Europe. She placed her sixteen-year-old son, Tommy, in the care of her servant Rebecca, along with enough money to pay his expenses for a year. Only a few people knew her real mission. "I said good-bye light-heartedly, even to Tommy. We would not be parted for long and I thrilled at the thought I was to have a small part in carrying out America's mission to 'make the world free for democracy.'"[24]

On Tuesday, December 3, Marguerite took a train to New York and secured a visa at the French consulate. As she prepared to leave, she pulled out a sheet of *Baltimore Sun* stationery and typed a note to her MID commander, detailing her travel plans. She concluded her letter: "Hoping that I may be of real service and assuring you I feel very deeply the honor and responsibility the War Department has given me to do."[25]

FIT FOR A KING

MARGUERITE TOLD LIEUTENANT COLONEL MARTIN that she wanted to become a spy in order to serve her country. In truth, she was longing to escape from a life of comfort and routine that had grown intolerable.

Those closest to her were not surprised that she wanted to be a foreign agent. After all, she was a woman they could never quite figure out. She was intelligent and charming, but she could be stubborn and selfish. She could light up a ball-room with her poise and grace and engage strangers in conversation with ease, but she had few close friends. Her compassion stirred her to found a school for sick children, but after her husband died, she was almost never home to care for her own son.

Marguerite always seemed to operate just on the edge of scandal, and those who are inclined to believe in fate might have pointed to her birth as an omen of the turmoil to come. She was born on October 23, 1878, on the day a rare hurricane swept into the Chesapeake Bay, capsizing ships and killing more than fifty sailors and passengers. In Baltimore, the storm downed telegraph lines and tore the roofs and shutters off homes.[1] In the midst of it all, Elizabeth Livezey Baker gave birth to Marguerite, her first child and a daughter she did not want.[2]

The delicate and fretful baby seemed to be an unwelcome intrusion into Elizabeth's life until Marguerite began to speak at eight months. Then Elizabeth Baker started to take a keen interest in her precocious progeny. She did not suddenly feel the stirring pangs of motherhood; rather, she realized that her daughter could become a testament to the family's position in society, achieving what Elizabeth could not.

Elizabeth's ambition for Marguerite grew from her own frustrations and insecurities. Her wealthy Quaker family never quite fit into Baltimore society. Her father, Elias Livezey, was an ardent Unionist and vocal supporter of Abraham Lincoln, which put him at odds with the Southern sensibilities of Baltimore. With no pretensions to climb Baltimore's social ladder, Livezey settled his family on a six-acre estate that he called Elton Park in the village of Catonsville just west of the city and quietly amassed a fortune in the real estate business.[3]

Elizabeth, however, was determined to break into Baltimore's high society. Beautiful and spirited, she persuaded her parents to send her to Ingleside Seminary, a girls' boarding school in Catonsville, and she attended worship services at St. Timothy's Episcopal Church next door to her home rather than Quaker meetings. At nineteen, she secured her future by marrying Bernard Nadal Baker, another Catonsville resident and the son of a prominent Baltimore businessman. "I knew that he had a brilliant future before I knew that I cared for him," she recalled.[4]

Marguerite was born less than a year after they married, and a second daughter, Elizabeth Catherine, followed three years later. When Marguerite was young, the family lived in a home they called Olden on the Baker family estate near Catonsville. Once a small mill town, by the late nineteenth century Catonsville had become an enclave for wealthy Baltimoreans looking to escape the crowds, heat, and dirt of the city.[5] These residents built large Victorian houses with high ceilings and wraparound porches, and gave their estates names reminiscent of English country homes, such as Glen Alpine, Sunnyholme, Maple Lawn, Farmlands, and Uplands.

The Baltimore of Marguerite's day offered abundant financial opportunities to the well connected and the industrious. Drawing residents from outlying areas of Maryland and from Virginia and North Carolina, Baltimore's population grew to more than half a million people by 1900, making it the sixth-largest city in the nation. At the heart of its prosperity lay the city's port, deep enough for cargo ships to bring raw materials to the manufacturing plants and to carry to Europe wheat, tobacco, meat, glass, furniture, fertilizer, chemicals, canned foods, cattle, and clothing.[6]

Bernard Baker worked for a short time in his family's glass factory, but his true love was the sea. So in 1879 he founded a company that specialized in ferrying cargo around the Port of Baltimore. Two years later, with the financial backing of the Pennsylvania Railroad, he founded the Atlantic Transport Line, providing cargo services out of the ports in Baltimore and Philadelphia. The line developed a solid reputation for transporting livestock to Europe, and by the late 1890s it sailed some of the largest vessels in the world and was the preferred carrier for the Barnum & Bailey Circus.

The line also attracted wealthy passengers, including Mark Twain, who sailed with the company several times. Part of the reason privileged passengers preferred Atlantic Transport was that it provided service to and from London at a time when other steamship lines stopped at Liverpool or Southampton. Another reason the line attracted a wealthy clientele was that it offered only first-class tickets. So while guests might have to share a vessel with elephants, mules, or cattle, they did not have to worry about rubbing elbows with people beneath their social class during the ten days at sea.

The ships were not the speediest afloat, but the passengers were usually in no hurry. On the voyage, guests could lounge on the decks, walk the promenades, play shuffleboard, and compete in all sorts of races. For those not athletically inclined, there were poetry recitations, musical performances, and educational lectures. The food on board was superb. Passengers were called to dine by the sound of a bugle and served such delicacies as braised ox tongue, veal cutlets, fresh caviar, Yorkshire pudding, and vanilla ice cream.[7]

The cargo line made Baker one of the wealthiest men in Baltimore, proving his wife's prediction of success. He traveled frequently to New York and London to negotiate contracts for new ships and the goods they would carry. One night in June 1887, as he returned to Baltimore from Philadelphia, his train was struck by one northbound from Washington, D.C. Baker's leg was crushed so severely that doctors wanted to amputate, but he refused. Baker recovered, but his injured leg was four inches shorter, and for the rest of his life he had to wear a special shoe to compensate.[8]

The injury did not prevent Baker from living the robust life of a gentleman, however. A handsome man with a bushy handlebar mustache, he rode with the Elkridge Hunt Club, showed champion horses, enjoyed Rocky Mountain hunting expeditions and socialized at the Maryland Club, an exclusive Baltimore men's club that boasted having as its first president a nephew of Napoleon Bonaparte.[9] And although he was a busy man, Baker doted on his daughters, treating them like the real-life princesses they knew in Europe.

Marguerite's lessons to prepare her to be the wife of an aristocrat began with the family's annual summer vacations to Europe. They sailed on her father's ships, which offered the young Marguerite all sorts of adventures. The sailors and sea captains entertained her with fantastic stories, taught her to navigate by the stars, and showed her how to operate a compass. As the daughter of the ship's owner, she could roam freely, exploring the engine rooms and visiting the live-stock holds, where she petted the cattle bound for European slaughterhouses.[10]

Once they arrived in Europe, the Bakers always spent a few weeks in London, shopping for clothes and touring the museums and galleries. Elizabeth Baker dragged her daughters through the tourist sites until their legs ached, and before long Marguerite had memorized the exhibits in the National Gallery and knew the tales of torture and tragedy at the Tower of London. But because Elizabeth worried that Marguerite's health was fragile and susceptible to city heat and pollution, they didn't dwell too long in London. Instead, they spent weeks touring the English countryside, often accompanied by Elizabeth's unmarried sister, Josephine, who acted as nanny and nursemaid to the children.

When Bernard concluded his business meetings in London, he joined the family for excursions to the Continent. In time, Marguerite became fluent in French, Italian, and German, and often acted as translator on the holiday tours. On these trips, Marguerite also met some of Europe's most important artists, politicians, and business leaders, including Boy Scouts founder Sir Robert Baden-Powell, financier J. Pierpont Morgan, and *Dracula* author Bram Stoker. The Bakers knew all the shipping tycoons and counted as a friend the British actor Henry Irving. While staying with her father's business associates in Heacham, England, Marguerite often saw the Prince and Princess of Wales attending church services and riding horses in the countryside.[11]

Many years later, Marguerite would tell audiences that she had spurned a young Winston Churchill, whose American mother was a friend of Elizabeth Baker. "At the parties I went to, he was usually there," she said.

He was very serious. I didn't like him. He would take me out to supper and discuss the affairs of Europe, and I would want him to notice a pretty dress I had on, or dance instead. He was an awful dancer. He would step on my feet and I would try to avoid him. My mother would tell me that I must remember that she and his mother were such good friends that I must be nice to Winston. Over and over she would tell me as I was leaving for a party that I must be nice to Winston. When I think of the opportunities I had missed, I blush, as he is undoubtedly one of the greatest men in the world today.[12]

But while Elizabeth saw to it that her daughter was socializing with the best families in Europe, Marguerite often was lonely. Elizabeth discouraged her daughters from playing with other children for fear her girls might catch a contagious disease or, even worse, learn unbecoming behaviors. With few childhood friends, Marguerite took comfort in her doll, Eunice, which she carried everywhere. Eunice had her own clothes trunk, and Marguerite dressed her suitably for every occasion. The doll sat beside her at meals and slept with her at night. Marguerite showed Eunice the castles and museums in Europe, and she lectured to her doll as Elizabeth lectured to her.[13]

When it came time to formally educate her daughters, Elizabeth adopted the British custom of entrusting their lessons to a governess until she deemed them old enough to attend private schools. Their governess, Miss Nancy Gillett, took seriously her charge to turn the strong-willed Marguerite into a lady. She taught her French and music and a bit of literature and history. But more important were the lessons she imparted on how a lady should comport herself in society. She showed Marguerite how to pour tea, enter a room, make small talk, and entertain graciously—lessons that would become useful weapons in the arsenal of an international spy.[14]

The European vacations and the governess gave evidence to the Bakers' standing in society, but the ultimate proof came in 1889, when Bernard Baker purchased a 250-acre estate in Catonsville that was formerly the site of a racetrack and the girls' boarding school that Elizabeth had attended. There, he built Ingleside, a twenty-room Georgian mansion modeled after a house he had seen in England. This was to be Elizabeth's showplace, and she set about making it the epitome of opulence and fine taste. The house was situated at the end of a quarter-mile lane lined with English maples. At the other end of the road stood a gatehouse keeping watch over visitors. The three-story mansion was made of fieldstone decorated with accents of granite from neighboring Ellicott City and topped with a red terra cotta roof. The front side was sixty feet long and fifty feet high. A veranda surrounded the first floor, broadening out into piazzas in the front and back that were supported by eleven-foot white columns. A center hall, finished in white enamel, ran the length of the first floor. To one side were the drawing room and an adjoining library lined with chestnut panels. On the other side was the dining room, finished with old oak. An oak staircase led to the second floor, which included ten bedrooms paneled in white pine. The home, heated by a hot-air furnace, boasted both electric and gas lights and had nine bathrooms. A side building housed servant quarters, pantries, kitchens, and a laundry.[15]

Inspired by her love of the English, Elizabeth departed from the heavily stuffed furniture common in Victorian-era homes and selected instead the cleaner lines of Chippendale, Sheraton, and Duncan Phyfe pieces. A Steinway piano graced the music room, and oriental rugs covered the parquet floors. She indulged Bernard's propensity to collect antique clocks while she collected antique china. Her garden was her special pride. Again drawing inspiration from the English, she oversaw the planting of a rose garden, a perennial garden, and a kitchen garden surrounded by yew hedge.[16]

Yet before work on Ingleside was complete, Elizabeth was sickened with Graves' disease, a serious thyroid disorder that causes heart palpitations, weight loss, and anxiety. To ease her duties, Elizabeth sent twelve-year-old Marguerite to live with her parents a mile away and enrolled her in the nearby St. Timothy's School.[17]

St. Timothy's, which was affiliated with the church the Bakers attended, had formerly been the site of a boys' military school where her father had studied. The boys' school also had a more ignoble alumnus—Lincoln assassin John Wilkes Booth. The girls' school had opened in 1882 and in only eight years developed a solid reputation for preparing women for college. Founded by two Virginia sisters who were left impoverished by the Civil War, St. Timothy's operated under the motto "truth without fear." The school offered a curriculum in art, German, French, mathematics, geography, and science—all tempered with a healthy dose of discipline. Rules were strict. Running in the hallway, opening a window without permission, and walking without boots in the winter were prohibited. Communication with boys was strictly monitored; the teachers read all letters the young ladies wrote to young men. Students were expected to be prepared and engaged, and on at least one occasion a frustrated teacher threw a book at a student who did not meet expectations.[18]

By the time Marguerite arrived in 1890, the school enrollment had grown to seventy-one girls who came from throughout the mid-Atlantic area. A photograph from the time shows the girls posing before a three-story frame house and seeming as though they had just paused from play to look obediently toward the camera. A few of the girls sit on the lawn with croquet mallets while others stand holding tennis rackets at a net. In the background, girls lean out of the open windows on the first floor. All seems in perfect order. But besides the school's reputation, Elizabeth had another reason to send Marguerite to St. Timothy's: She could still control her daughter's social life. The school was next door to Elton Park, which meant Marguerite would live with her grandparents and not board with the other girls.[19]

Elizabeth's control over her daughter left Marguerite at a serious disadvantage when she enrolled in school. Her governess and trips abroad had provided her a solid foundation in languages, art, music, and history, but she was socially awkward and struggled to make friends at St. Timothy's. As a day student, Marguerite was excluded from many of the extracurricular activities. She tried playing on the football team, but she wrenched her shoulder in a game and was never allowed on the field again. Making matters worse, Marguerite had had such limited interaction with children her own age, she had no idea how to get along with her peers. With Elizabeth's prodding and ambition, Marguerite had developed a sense of intellectual superiority. And so at St. Timothy's, when students could not answer the teachers' piercing questions, Marguerite was happy to answer in their place, earning her reputation as a standoffish know-it-all.

During her five years at the Catonsville school, Marguerite struggled to make friends, although a relationship she had with a girl named Henry raised concerns among her teachers. The girls wrote love letters to each other and fantasized about committing suicide together. They hated men and vowed to never marry. Then came the day that Marguerite cheated on Henry. A local boy spotted Marguerite going to the store and bought her a box of caramels. The two corresponded for weeks, and one day he met her behind the barn at school and kissed her. Marguerite confessed her infidelity to Henry, who never forgave her.

The teenage years that Marguerite lived with her grandparents left an indelible impression. Although the Livezeys had servants, her grandmother taught Marguerite domestic chores such as sewing and cooking. Her grandfather, meanwhile, discussed religion and politics frankly in front of Marguerite. Over her grandmother's protests, Livezey railed against efforts to disenfranchise black voters and championed the single-tax system. He encouraged his granddaughter to think critically and gave her writings of Thomas Paine and the agnostic Robert Ingersoll, which spurred Marguerite's long-time religious skepticism.[20]

Marguerite was just seventeen when she graduated from St. Timothy's in 1896, and Elizabeth thought her too young to be presented to society. She decided a year at Radcliffe College would be a fine finishing touch on her daughter's education and preparation for life in society. At the time higher education for women was somewhat controversial, with critics complaining that it discouraged women from marrying and having children.[21] Elizabeth doubtless considered these concerns before deciding a bit of college would make Marguerite a more attractive mate for a man with social standing.

But the plan nearly had disastrous consequences.

The September after Marguerite's high school graduation, Elizabeth escorted her daughter to Cambridge and placed her in a boardinghouse operated by one of the city's most respected families. At Radcliffe, Marguerite studied English, French, German, Latin, history, and algebra, earning As and Bs, except in algebra, in which she received an E.[22] But Marguerite stayed just one semester. Wanting no part in her mother's plan that she marry for money and a title, Marguerite sought wild, romantic love. Within weeks, she began an affair with the landlady's eldest son, and the two became secretly engaged. Although she went to her classes, Marguerite did not put much effort into her studies, and spent most weekday afternoons with her fiancé walking the tree-lined streets of Cambridge and attending weekend football games at Harvard. They planned to keep their engagement a secret until Marguerite had completed her first year in college, but Elizabeth sensed something was amiss when she went to pick her daughter up for the Christmas holidays.

Had her mother's keen eye noticed the way Marguerite and the boy gazed at one another when they parted that winter morning in Cambridge? Had he held her hand a bit too long as they said farewell? Or perhaps something in the tone of her voice gave her away when her mother shrewdly asked whether she had met any interesting people in her first semester at Radcliffe.

However it happened, Marguerite had been caught, and Elizabeth was determined to put a stop to the affair. It did not matter that he came from an old and respectable family. Elizabeth had not climbed to the top of Baltimore society to see her daughter married to someone who lacked title and position. She had cultivated her daughter like the prized gardens at Ingleside, making sure she received a cosmopolitan education and was introduced to the finest families in Europe. No, her daughter was suited for the peerage, or at least an ambassador.

Elizabeth pulled Marguerite out of Radcliffe and brought her back to Baltimore. The boy wrote desperate love letters, which Elizabeth found and destroyed. Then she put Marguerite on a ship bound for Italy, reasoning that the romance of the Mediterranean was just the cure for her lovesick daughter.

And she was right. Marguerite soon forgot about the boy in Cambridge.

On her way to Europe, she carried on shipboard flirtations and sometime later became engaged again. Such engagements were not unusual given the time, when girls were told their first kisses should be given only to the man they would marry. To salve their consciences, popular girls became engaged several times before their society debut.[23]

In the winter of 1897 nineteen-year-old Marguerite made her debut to society at the Bachelors' Cotillon at Lehmann's Hall on North Howard Street in Baltimore. The event, which had been launched in 1870, defined who was and who was not in Baltimore society. A board of governors decided which girls would receive invitations, based on the family's wealth, status, and social engagements.[24] Girls' lives were ruined by being overlooked, but there was never a doubt that the daughter of Bernard and Elizabeth Baker would be among the sixty or so girls invited to make their debut at the ball.

While the event feted Baltimore's young ladies, most of the men who attended were the fathers and grandfathers of the debutantes. So like the other girls at the dance, Marguerite was escorted by a much older friend of her father. A debutante's popularity was gauged by the number of bouquets she received, and often the girls collected fifty or sixty from friends or relatives. Marguerite, dressed in a white lace Parisian gown, carried armfuls of flowers, and her parents walked behind with even more.

Glamour surrounded her and the other young ladies that night. The ballroom was adorned with draperies of blue and gold brocade and garlands of artificial roses. Pink shades hanging over the electric light bulbs imparted a soft glow to the room. A twenty-two-piece orchestra started the evening with a two-step and then proceeded to waltzes and the grand march, where the debutantes and their escorts paraded across the waxed dance floor.[25]

Marguerite deemed her debut a success. She secured partners for all of the balls that season, and she attracted no shortage of male admirers. On Sunday nights she entertained as many as a dozen young men at a time in the drawing room of the Bakers' downtown apartment on North Charles Street. Well-schooled by her governess and Elizabeth, Marguerite knew how to make small talk with her guests and keep them satisfied with refreshments until they were forced to leave promptly at midnight.

On Sunday mornings, she attended Baltimore's Emmanuel Episcopal Church, the house of worship for the city's most prominent residents. After services, she usually joined a parade of fashionable young women who strolled from the city's Washington Monument to Preston Street, vying to see who could attract the most men along the seven-block route. Marguerite thought it a great sport, but some society matrons frowned on her as being too wild. Marguerite once caused a scandal when, acting on a dare, she bowed to young men looking down upon the Sunday parade from a window of the Maryland Club. But as the century drew to a close, Marguerite had overcome the awkwardness that had afflicted her at St. Timothy's. She was popular, rich, and beautiful.[26]

But now that Marguerite had made her societal debut, Elizabeth took even greater care to make sure her daughter socialized with the right people in order to find a suitable mate. While Elizabeth scouted possible matches, Bernard's business deals helped introduce Marguerite to British aristocracy. When tensions in Britain's South African colony erupted, Bernard steadfastly backed the English, and in 1899 he donated one of his ships, the *Maine*, to be a British hospital ship. American women living in England, including Elizabeth's friend, Lady Randolph Churchill, raised donations to equip the vessel. Lady Churchill repaid Baker's generous donation by inviting his family to the Ascot Races, where Marguerite was presented to the Prince of Wales, the eventual King Edward VII. Some months later, Baker was forced to swallow his pride when Lady Churchill took credit for the donation of the ship and even made off with the *Maine*'s flag.[27]

Queen Victoria's daughter Princess Louise was another of the hospital ship's patrons. When the *Maine* returned to Southampton with its first load of sick and wounded soldiers, the Bakers traveled in the princess's private rail car to meet the ship. As Princess Louise greeted the wounded soldiers and handed them pipes and bags of tobacco, Marguerite walked behind carrying a basket with the gifts.[28] In August 1900 Marguerite made news back home when she and her parents attended a royal garden party at Buckingham Place and met Queen Victoria.[29]

By then Marguerite was showing promise of blossoming into the socialite her mother had groomed her to be. Besides the important connections she was making among British royalty, she was putting her talents to work for worthy causes. In October 1898 she joined two other women in issuing invitations to the final dance of the season at the Catonsville Country Club, instructing the women attending to wear calico dresses to add to the fun. A few months later, she helped raise money to benefit the Maryland General Hospital and the Society for Prevention of Cruelty to Animals by dancing in a musical. Her activities frequently drew the attention of the *Baltimore Sun* society columnist, who noted her fashion sense and horsemanship.[30]

Yet behind the glamorous headlines, a family crisis was looming. Marguerite had made up her mind to find a husband the year after her debut, and she set her eye on a tall, handsome young Baltimore banker, Thomas B. Harrison, who was six years her senior. Many girls pursued him, but Marguerite won him over by feigning indifference, sometimes treating him cruelly and breaking off dates to attend parties with other men. In the spring of 1898 they told her parents of their engagement.

Harrison came from a stellar pedigree. His father had been a businessman and his mother, the former Mary Boykin Williams, was descended from the Boykin family of South Carolina, whose members included Civil War diarist Mary Boykin Chesnut. After Tom's father died, his mother had married Joseph Ames, a prominent physics professor at Johns Hopkins University who would become president of the university and a founder of the American space program. Tom Harrison and Marguerite traveled in the same social circles. He was a fine horseman who hunted foxes with the Green Spring Valley Hunt Club. He was secretary of the Junior Cotillon, and his family had been listed for years in the *Social Register*. His mother and Elizabeth played cards together.

But Harrison was not the husband Elizabeth had in mind for her elder daughter. She may have opposed Tom because of the scandalous way his father had died. After losing a fortune in cotton speculation, Thomas Bullitt Harrison had had a nervous breakdown. Family members were about to commit him to an asylum when he went into his cousin's sitting room in a stately mansion on

Mount Vernon Place, sat down in front of a fireplace, and cut his throat from ear to ear.[31] The sensational death made front-page news from New York to South Carolina.

When Marguerite and Tom told Elizabeth of their plans to marry, she went into a fury and refused to allow the couple to announce their engagement. Instead, she whisked Marguerite to Italy, figuring the change of scenery was all that was needed to again squelch an undesirable romance.

On board ship, Elizabeth must have been heartened to see her daughter flirting with the count of Turin, a nephew of the king of Italy. When Marguerite and Elizabeth arrived in Rome they checked into the luxurious Grand Hotel. That season the hotel's guests included the king and queen of Italy, the duke of Cambridge, Count Leo Tolstoy, and two Russian dukes.[32] Given the royalty that abided within the hotel's gilded rooms, odds seemed favorable that Marguerite would receive proposals from at least a baronet.

Elizabeth's plan almost succeeded. At the hotel Marguerite caught the eye of Reshid Sadi Bey, the secretary of the Turkish Embassy. Sadi Bey, who had been educated in England, was a Young Turk, part of a political movement formed by students, civil servants, and military officers living in exile while waiting to overthrow the Turkish monarchy and establish a constitutional government.[33]

Sadi Bey captivated Marguerite, and Elizabeth encouraged her daughter to spend time with the young diplomat in hopes she would forget Harrison. In a short time Sadi Bey fell in love with Marguerite. He flattered her with compliments of her beauty, but he saw her potential to be more than a society matron. He shared with her his dreams of a modern and independent Turkey and urged her to imagine putting her intellectual abilities to work in creating a new country with him. He discussed with her the politics of the Turkish revolution and persuaded her to read drafts of the proposed constitution. He shared stories of his country's history and showed her its art. Walking among the ancient ruins and touring the Mediterranean gardens, they debated religion and philosophy. Just as Elizabeth and Marguerite were about to depart for Baltimore, Sadi Bey followed Marguerite to the Italian lakes and begged her to marry him. Confused and shaken, Marguerite gave no answer. She didn't love him, she knew, but he appealed to a part of her that she didn't even know existed. She was meant for more than simply being the wife of a man in position. Her talents went beyond being a hostess or club woman. She could be a partner in making a revolution. She could use her mind as well as her looks and personality.

For a time, she corresponded with Sadi Bey, who wrote her poetic letters and tried to entice her back to him. But in Baltimore she became more determined than ever to defy Elizabeth and marry Tom Harrison. Bernard finally accepted his daughter's wishes to wed because he wanted her to be happy. However, Elizabeth appealed to Marguerite's reason and social ambition. She offered up as a possible match the son of a Scottish marquis who would have happily married the daughter of a Baltimore shipping magnate. Marguerite took the hapless young man to the country club, got him drunk, and made a fool of him.

Elizabeth tried to lure Marguerite away from Baltimore again with the promise of an around-the-world cruise, but her daughter refused to go. Elizabeth beat on Marguerite's bedroom door and threatened to commit suicide if she did not give up her plans to marry Harrison. Finally, Marguerite could stand it no longer. She told her father that if her mother would not agree to the marriage, she and Tom would elope. At last, Elizabeth consented.[34]

The couple announced their engagement in the winter of 1900, and soon afterward Bernard made Harrison the secretary of the Atlantic Transport Line.[35] For Elizabeth the only thing left to do was give her daughter one of the most lavish weddings ever seen in Baltimore.

The ceremony took place on a beautiful sunny morning on June 5, 1901, at Emmanuel Episcopal Church with the church's rector as well as the priest from St. Timothy's officiating. William Paret, the Episcopal Bishop of Maryland, was on hand to bless the couple, who exchanged vows beneath an arch of roses. In honor of the bride's name, the church was decorated with masses of marguerite daisies. The bridesmaids, wearing gowns of yellow organdy over silk and carrying white parasols adorned with daisies, marched down the aisle as a twenty-voice choir sang "Lonherin." Marguerite, dressed in a gown of heavy ivory satin and Brussels point lace and a lace veil accented with a daisy design, followed on her father's arm.

After the ceremony, Elizabeth and Bernard hosted a breakfast in their downtown apartment where a thirty-piece orchestra played while the guests dined. English actor Henry Irving and the lord chief justice of England were among those sending congratulatory cables. The *Baltimore Sun* reported that the gifts the couple received were among the most expensive ever given at a Baltimore wedding: silver, china, rare artworks, a pearl necklace with diamond clasps from Bernard, and a one-thousand-dollar check from Elias Livezey. After the festivities, Marguerite and Thomas boarded her father's steamer, *Knight Commander*, which was decked out in festive flags, and left for a three-month European honeymoon.

With the wedding over, Elizabeth collapsed. She remained an invalid until her death fourteen years later.[36]

Three

BONDS OF MATRIMONY

MARGUERITE AND TOM spent three months in Europe on their honeymoon, and when they returned to Baltimore in September 1901 on board the Atlantic Transport Line steamship *Minnehaha*, Marguerite was pregnant with their son. Like Elizabeth, Marguerite would become a mother within the first year of her marriage. But she would be a very different kind of wife and mother.

Unlike Elizabeth, who viewed marriage as a means for social and economic advancement, Marguerite wanted romance. By marrying Tom Harrison, she not only took the bold step of going against her mother's wishes, she also reveled in the romantic idea that she had abandoned the trappings of wealth to marry a "poor man" whom she loved.

Tom Harrison actually was a member Baltimore's high society, but Marguerite saw him as a disadvantaged young man who had been forced to work at age sixteen to support his mother, "a penniless widow." He had not attended college like her father had, and he had not traveled throughout Europe as she had. They were different in many respects. She was naturally adventurous, and her education and travels inspired a keen interest in other cultures. She was a skilled linguist— she called it her only outstanding talent—and her ability to speak several languages fluently allowed her to understand and empathize with those far outside her Baltimore social circle.

Tom appeared to lack her intellectual curiosity and quest for adventure. She described him as a Southern gentleman—"gallant, chivalrous, high-minded, cultured, and charming"—and possessing a "delicious sense of humor and quick mind." Tom had a wide circle of friends, but they all seemed to have been rooted in Baltimore. She speculated that he was drawn to her simply because she was an elusive prize to be won. He loved hunting, tennis, and baseball and had the natural competitive instincts of a sportsman.

Tom could not have been more dissimilar to the Turkish diplomat who had captured her imagination a year earlier. Reshid Sadi Bey was willing to risk imprisonment and even death to create a free and modern nation. With Sadi Bey, Marguerite had debated political philosophies and studied draft constitutions of a far-off land. Now married, Marguerite was ready to surrender her interests and life of luxury for the sake of the man she loved. "I dropped everything that had interested me before my marriage—completely and without reserves," she recalled.[1]

Elizabeth had taunted her that she was too spoiled to marry a poor man, but Marguerite found her new life a "thrilling experience." She complained that her mother had not taught her anything about housekeeping, cooking, or shopping. After all, the Bakers employed a staff of servants for those domestic chores. Her grandmother Livezey had taught her some sewing and cooking, but she had never needed to do either. As a wife, Marguerite enthusiastically took on these new household tasks, imagining that she was proving all the more her sincere love for her husband. She bragged that she did her own marketing, she developed a talent for sewing, and she kept a spotless house, although she and Tom eventually hired a maid and cook.[2]

In her marriage, she encountered new family dynamics that surprised her. The Bakers and Livezeys had shunned even close relatives, but the Harrisons were a large, close-knit clan and proud of their Southern heritage. Marguerite at first thought her mother-in-law, Mary Ames, was "severe and uncompromising," but over time she grew to love her. "One of her favorite maxims was that a lady should display absolute self-control under all circumstances," Marguerite recalled. "I had always been an undisciplined, impulsive child and I admired this quality extravagantly. I began to cultivate it, schooling myself to repress outbursts of temper and to endure physical pain and to meet any and every domestic emergency with absolute calm and composure."[3] They were lessons that would be sorely tested in the coming years.

Still, for all her romanticism about making sacrifices for love, Marguerite's life changed very little in the early months of her marriage. The Harrisons spent their first fall with Marguerite's family at Ingleside.[4] That winter she and Tom

followed the familiar pattern of moving to an apartment in the city. As her preg-
nancy began to show, she adhered to the custom of staying out of the public eye
and did not attend society balls. Instead, she spent much of the time indoors sewing baby clothes and looking forward to his arrival.[5]

On March 15, 1902, she gave birth to her son, Tommy. Although women at
the time enlisted doctors rather than midwives and made use of chloroform to
ease the pain of childbirth, Marguerite experienced a difficult delivery. Almost
immediately after their son was born, she and Tom decided against more children, joining an increasing number of young couples who limited the size of
their families.

In her memoir, she described her young family as a happy threesome. In the
first couple years of their marriage, the Harrisons migrated with the seasons. In
the winter they lived in Baltimore; in the summer they rented a cottage in Green
Spring Valley north of the city or stayed with Marguerite's parents at Ingleside.
After a few years they settled in a handsome four-story brick row house at 1206
North Charles Street that Bernard had purchased in 1902. The house, with seventeen rooms plus a kitchen and laundry, was located a few blocks north of
the fashionable Mount Vernon neighborhood and the Peabody Conservatory of
Music.[6] To help run the home, the Harrisons employed two domestic workers
that Marguerite described as "old-fashioned colored folk who regarded themselves as members of the family."[7]

Their fortunes fluctuated, but Tom and Marguerite lived as people always
accustomed to having money. When they had it, they spent it. When they didn't,
they were frugal. They always expected some new business opportunity to turn
up, and at first it always did. They also didn't worry much about money because
status in Baltimore was only partially connected to wealth. Profession and family
were more important than dollars in the bank. So the Harrisons continued to
live a comfortable life in the society spotlight.

The winter after their son's birth, Marguerite and Tom returned to society
events. Tom was the secretary of the Junior Cotillon and in that role led off the
evening dances.[8] The *Baltimore Sun*'s society reporters noted the comings and
goings of the Harrisons: their attendance at the Pimlico horse races, their renting
a cottage for the summer in the Baltimore countryside, their hosting a dance at
the summer retreat, and their visit to see Elizabeth at a Rhode Island resort.[9] In

1906 they were the center of attention when they showed up at Pimlico race-track in an automobile shared with Chicago retail magnate Stanley Field and his wife.[10] Another time they joined a moonlight picnic with members of the hunt club.[11] Frequently, Marguerite's impeccable fashion sense was noted in newspaper articles about the events she attended.

With her marriage to Tom Harrison, Marguerite also discovered a love of the outdoors. Tom was an accomplished hunter, equestrian, and athlete. While at St. Timothy's School sports had been prized for building spirit and good-natured rivalry, Elizabeth had forbidden Marguerite from playing. With Tom, Marguerite joined the nation's new obsession with physical fitness, taking up lawn tennis at the Catonsville Country Club and shooting at the Green Spring Valley Hunt Club. Within a year of marrying Tom, she had learned to shoot a 16-gauge shotgun well enough to win a trap-shooting contest.[12]

Fully embracing her new role as her husband's companion, she accompanied Tom on duck-hunting expeditions. Early in 1903 Tom arranged to lease hunting rights on seven thousand acres near Camden, South Carolina. Joining him in the venture were several prominent Baltimoreans, including Bernard Baker. Harrison bragged that the land was so rich in game, members might bag three or four deer a day.[13] He also bought hunting rights at the San Domingo Club, a duck-hunting retreat on the upper Chesapeake Bay that had been a favorite game spot of President Grover Cleveland. Tom and Marguerite, with young Tommy along, spent their weekends there during the winter hunting season. On those trips, a black hunting guide, Vernon, accompanied them to a cottage where his wife cooked their meals. In her memoir Marguerite paints a vivid picture of a typical outing. They rose well before dawn, leaving Tommy asleep in bed, and followed Vernon on the morning hunt with their Chesapeake Bay retriever. They boarded a rowboat, and Vernon took them three miles to a duck blind where they waited in the frigid cove for the birds to take flight.

She recalled the moment when a flock appeared over the horizon: "Here they come, Mardie," Tom whispered excitedly. Tom quickly dispatched three birds with a pump gun. Marguerite wounded one with a shotgun, and their retriever fetched the quarry. After several hours of hunting, they returned to the cottage, washed in a basin of cold water and feasted on ducks that Vernon's wife prepared.[14]

Tom and Marguerite were enjoying the life of young aristocrats, but their fortunes were tied to Bernard Baker's shipping enterprise. In 1902 their lives were shaken when a series of missteps cost Baker the company he had spent decades building. The loss was especially bitter because it happened just as Marguerite's father had hoped to expand his shipping business.

Baker had long been a staunch advocate of a robust American merchant marine. The number of American ships carrying cargo had plummeted after the Civil War, in part because of damage inflicted on U.S. ships during the conflict and because of changes in building methods and government regulations. So while U.S. farms and businesses were producing more goods than ever, fewer American ships were carrying the cargo to overseas markets. Americans instead had ceded much of their transport to British and German shipping interests.[15]

In 1901 Baker planned to rebuild the U.S. Merchant Marine and at the same time increase his fortune. His idea was to join forces with financier J. Pierpont Morgan in a vast shipping conglomerate that would control the Atlantic sea lanes. The negotiations dragged on for months. Morgan purchased Britain's Leyland Line, but progress acquiring other lines stalled. Baker spent much of his time in London working on the deal, only briefly returning in June for Marguerite's wedding. Eventually the agreement to join Morgan's International Mercantile Marine was reached: Baker would sell his Atlantic Transport Line to the shipping conglomerate in the expectation that Morgan would put him at the helm of the combined company. In anticipation of the deal, Baker ordered ten new ships for his fleet, almost doubling the tonnage of Atlantic Transport Line.[16] Success of the plan, however, depended upon securing a U.S. government subsidy to help pay for the construction and operation of the new vessels.

Despite assurances from politicians in Washington that the legislation would pass, the Ship Subsidy Bill failed. Baker, overleveraged, was forced to sell the Atlantic Transport Line to Morgan for less than he intended. Adding insult to injury, Morgan named one of Baker's rivals, Clement Griscom, the politically astute president of the American Line, as head of the new conglomerate. Although Baker held a position on the board of directors of the International Mercantile Marine, he had little say in its operations. At the end of 1902 he stepped down as president of the Atlantic Transport Line. About one-third of the company's 225 employees lost their jobs in the merger, including Tom Harrison, who was the company secretary.[17]

Marguerite blamed herself for contributing to her father's failure. She imagined that her mother could have helped Bernard navigate the complicated business negotiations and the politics of the Ship Subsidy Bill, but Elizabeth's health had declined rapidly after Marguerite had defied her wishes and married Tom. In July 1901 Elizabeth suffered a serious fall, and over the next several years she was injured in two car accidents. She no longer accompanied Bernard on overseas trips and his annual visit to the Carlsbad spa in Bohemia. Instead, she opted to vacation at health resorts in New York, Pennsylvania, or Rhode Island.[18]

The loss of the shipping company was a huge blow to the Bakers and Harrisons, and for the next several years they struggled with new financial ventures. Tom and Bernard invested in a glass manufacturing plant near Annapolis, Maryland, but it failed after just a few months.[19] They were elected officers of Universal Seal and Stopper, but in February 1904 the bottle sealant company was lost in the Great Baltimore Fire that destroyed more than 1,500 buildings across seventy city blocks.[20]

Gradually, Tom and Bernard began to recover from the loss of the shipping company and pursue other business and philanthropic projects. In 1904 Tom secured a partner to create a real estate firm, Harrison & House, which they parlayed into a stock brokerage firm and purchased a coveted seat on the Baltimore Stock Exchange.[21] Bernard, meanwhile, was chosen to head a major bank, the Baltimore Trust and Guarantee Company, and took on a greater role in the affairs of the city. For months he worked on a plan to extend streetcar lines throughout the suburbs and served on a commission to promote Baltimore's industry.[22] One of his most ambitious projects was a plan to build a subway system that would rival New York's. He even offered to pay one million dollars for the subway franchise, but city leaders later scuttled the plan.[23]

A true gentleman of the Progressive Era, Baker devoted considerable energy to various charitable projects. Like many of his generation, he believed that business and government had an obligation to help those in need and he worked for an astounding variety of causes. When Maryland created the first state chapter of the American Red Cross, Baker served on its executive board.[24] Despite his love of big-game hunting in the Rocky Mountains, he was a leader in the Society for the Prevention of Cruelty to Animals (SPCA).[25] A devoted patron of the arts, he worked to establish an art museum in Baltimore.[26] He helped organize a horse show that for a time was a premier social event, and he was vice president of a bird protection society.[27] Between business deals, Baker experimented with new farming techniques at Ingleside, and when the United States entered World War I, he donated land on his estate for food production.[28] He championed improvements in public education. Inspired by reformer Milton Fairchild, he headed the Moral Education Board that advocated a school curriculum to instill values—honesty, trustworthiness, and thrift.[29] An early proponent of national parks, in 1909 he led the National Conservation Congress to preserve America's natural resources, calling conservation "a new national patriotism."[30] At one point he was rumored to be in the running for U.S. secretary of the interior. The appointment didn't materialize, although evidence of his diplomatic skills showed in his success in bringing together in September 1910 the Progressive former president Theodore Roosevelt and his business-centered rival, President William Howard Taft, to the Conservation Congress gathering in St. Paul, Minnesota.

While few could match Baker's extraordinary varied business and philanthropic interests, activism was a hallmark of the Progressive Age. "Certain things were expected of one in Baltimore," Marguerite wrote. "We were Episcopalians, Catholics or Presbyterians because everybody belonged to some church or other. We belonged to the Monday germans or to this club or that because all the other people in our position were members. For the same reason most of the young married women in Baltimore 'took up' some charity, did church work or taught Sunday school. That was all part and parcel of our well-ordered way of living."[31]

Everyone seemed to champion a cause. Workers unionized for better wages and conditions. Settlement houses such as Jane Addams' Hull House in Chicago aided immigrants. Groups organized to reform government, expand health care, and tackle juvenile delinquency. Women's clubs, which began in the 1860s, grew in power. Some were social groups focused mainly on the pleasure and entertainment of their members, but others tackled municipal corruption, economics, and international relations. Extending their sphere of influence from the home to society, women's groups started kindergartens, built playgrounds, and established parks and libraries. The women's movement coalesced in 1890 with the creation of the General Federation of Women's Clubs, and by 1896 about 100,000 women were club members.[32]

The Baker and Harrison women lent their time and talents to many charitable endeavors. Despite Elizabeth's poor health, she supported the arts and maintained her memberships in the Women's Branch of the SPCA and the Arundell Club, which worked for good governance.[33] She also devoted much of her time to helping poor children. Politicians and philanthropists who urged reform of schools, orphanages, and hospitals often touted the curative powers of fresh air and sunshine.[34] Elizabeth shared this belief and donated buildings on the Ingleside estate to Hollywood Home, a facility that gave disadvantaged Baltimore children the chance to escape the dirt and crowds of the city and spend a few weeks each summer in the countryside.[35]

Meanwhile, Bernard's mother had for years patronized a Baltimore orphanage with an unfortunate name, Home of the Friendless. It was one of the first charities for which Marguerite volunteered, and she was elected its treasurer, although she said she did not like the work because the institution was run like a prison, with strict rules and mandatory uniforms.[36] She also supported the SPCA and hospital charities, applying an artistic flair to philanthropic projects, such as helping bring a vaudeville show to the University of Maryland Hospital to raise money for telephones in the wards.[37]

But by far her most influential contribution was the establishment of a children's hospital school that became one of the most innovative institutions of its kind in the country. Marguerite was inspired to pursue the project after taking her son to a leading Baltimore orthopedic surgeon, Dr. William S. Baer, for treatment of a minor ailment. On one visit the doctor told her about an indigent boy suffering from the crippling effects of tuberculosis. Baer lamented that the boy would not be able to attend school while undergoing a lengthy convalescence.

"Why couldn't we start such an institution?" Marguerite asked. And she set about making it a reality. The founding of the hospital school was testament to Marguerite's vision, determination, and connections. She persuaded two friends to contribute five hundred dollars each to help its launch. Dr. Baer borrowed hospital beds from another facility, and a friend absconded with furniture from his mother's country estate to help furnish the rooms. The school, initially called the Ingleside Convalescent Home, opened in summer 1905 in a large, stone house Bernard owned in Catonsville. Marguerite recruited her sister, Elizabeth, and aunt Josephine Livezey to serve on the board of directors. She and Baer enlisted nursing students to volunteer to care for the children. The first year, the institution was open for just two months and cared for sixteen children who had been discharged from hospital care but were too sick to return home. The next year, the facility cared for forty children and was open for three months.[38]

The young patients suffered from a variety of ailments: orthopedic deformities and diseases such as meningitis, typhoid fever, polio, and tuberculosis. A newspaper account described the devotion the children showed toward Marguerite when she visited them. "The children who were strong enough to rise ran up to the carriage and cried out joyfully: 'How do, Mrs. Harrison.' The others came hobbling along on crutches and the weak, pale little girl who was recovering from typhoid lay in her carriage and only smiled a welcome."[39]

In 1909 the facility was incorporated and renamed the Children's Hospital School. As its reputation grew, it admitted not only indigent children but patients whose parents could pay for their care.[40] By 1910 Marguerite viewed her work not simply as volunteerism but as an occupation. In that year's national census she listed her work as a treasurer of a charitable trust.[41]

Marguerite invented all kinds of schemes to raise money for the school. Early on, supporters contributed fifty dollars to endow each bed. The school arranged to place barrels in local businesses to collect coins. In 1912 Marguerite organized a charity baseball game pitting city clergy against physicians. Probably her most ambitious fund-raising effort was a "society circus" that featured prominent Baltimoreans in the roles of circus performers.[42]

By 1911 Children's Hospital School had outgrown its facilities in Catonsville and relocated to new quarters on seventeen acres on Baltimore's Greenspring Avenue. The hospital school expanded to more than one hundred beds and provided vocational training as well as medical care.[43]

Because of her role founding Children's Hospital School, Marguerite Harrison emerged as a prominent figure in city reform movements. In 1911 she joined her mother-in-law at the inaugural meeting of the Women's Civic League of Baltimore and was named to its board of directors. The women outlined their goals:

- Better street cleaning, so that health conditions will be improved and the atmosphere freed of dust
- Better street paving
- Improved conditions in the public schools
- Improved conditions in alleys and small streets
- Encouragement and assistance for public movements such as the Playground Association and organizations which have similar purposes[44]

But the group balked at endorsing women's suffrage, saying it would take no position on the issue in order to attract a diverse group of women.[45] The tactic was wise, considering how controversial women's voting rights were in Maryland. The state's leading politicians refused to support women's franchise, fearing the vote of black women and arguing that women should not be involved in the dirty business of politics.[46] Many women agreed. The Maryland Woman Suffrage Association, which advocated equal voting rights, had fewer than two hundred members in 1904.[47]

Marguerite was ambivalent about women's suffrage. She recalled that the movement "left me cold" and added, "I believed theoretically that women were entitled to vote, but I was not prepared to lift a finger to bring about the franchise."[48] Her willingness to advocate for women's rights and identify with feminist causes was still years away. As an upper-middle-class, married, white woman, she didn't need to vote in order to exercise power and influence. As with others in her social position, she enjoyed the advantages of sisterhood—bonds built in girls' schools and women's clubs. From these institutions the women developed close relationships and exercised real power in their families and in society. Over time, the woman's realm broadened to include issues related to children, health care, and the poor. Many upper-class women, however, saw no reason to entangle themselves in politics.[49]

The success of the Children's Hospital School was the one bright spot in a difficult period in Marguerite's life. Her father left the Baltimore Trust and Guarantee after three rather unsuccessful years. While still popular and politically well connected, Bernard was beset with controversies. The former stockholders of Atlantic Transport Line brought an unsuccessful lawsuit against him, discord broke out within the ranks of the SPCA, and a neighbor at Ingleside even accused him of abusing his dog.[50]

Baker still was hoping to find a way to return to shipping. In 1910 he led dozens of other Baltimore businessmen who put up a thousand dollars each to create the Baltimore Shipping League to lobby for renewal of U.S. shipping interests.[51] One of the most important developments of international shipping at this time was the construction of the Panama Canal, which shortened the shipping route from the East Coast to the West Coast by nearly eight thousand miles. The United States took over the project from the French in 1904 and spent the next ten years digging the channel. As construction proceeded, Baker visited Panama several times at the behest of President Taft in order to recommend transportation policies. After a trip in 1909 he urged the president to support independent American steamship companies through mail contracts that would subsidize their operations.[52]

By late 1910 Baker was ready to take action to regain his position in transnational shipping. After numerous meetings with President Taft and the postmaster general, Baker announced plans to create a steamship company to carry U.S. mail through the Panama Canal. His plan depended upon the United States agreeing to provide mail contracts and favorable routing arrangements on the government-owned Panama Railroad.[53] Early in 1911 it appeared his plan was about to come to fruition as Congress took up a bill that would have required ships carrying American mail through the canal to be built by U.S. shipyards. To bid for the mail contract, Baker created the Atlantic Pacific Transport Company, and he planned to build fifteen steamships that would serve ports on the Atlantic and Pacific coasts.[54] But Baker's plan ran into trouble from some unexpected places. The Ship Subsidy Bill drew sharp opposition from Democrats in Congress, including Maryland senator Isidor Rayner, who called the measure "undemocratic and un-American."[55] Although Baker himself was usually supportive of Democratic platforms and his son-in-law, Albert Ritchie Jr., was a rising star in the state Democratic Party, the leaders of the party saw the bill as needless corporate charity.

The debate in Congress over how to revive the U.S. Merchant Marine continued throughout 1911, but Baker remained optimistic a ship subsidy bill would pass. In September 1911 he incorporated the Atlantic Pacific Transport Company. Joining him in the venture were several former officials of the Atlantic Transport Line, including his son-in-law, Tom.[56] Baker immediately embarked on a cross-country trip to raise the $15 million of capital he needed to run the company and build new ships. At first Baker had reason to be optimistic as he met with prospective investors. "From Seattle to Charleston, I found people enthusiastic in their promises of support," he said.[57] But Baker failed to raise enough capital to meet a November 25 deadline to submit a bid for the mail contract. A week later he complained that the railroads and banks were blocking creation of the shipping company out of fear they would lose business.

Baker alleged the railroads were threatening shipyards that agreed to build vessels for the independent shipping company.[58] His complaints spurred a congressional investigation, and he was called to testify numerous times.[59] Ultimately Baker could not gain enough support for his vision of an independent steamship line providing service through the canal. Without the government subsidy, he was unable to attract enough investors to bid on the country's mail routes. A last-ditch effort to find financing in Germany failed as war broke out in Europe.[60] About the same time J. P. Morgan's grand shipping conglomerate collapsed as well, which Baker attributed to gross mismanagement.[61]

Marguerite helplessly watched her father's business struggles. His failure to launch the Atlantic Pacific Transport Company was also a blow to her husband, who was to be an officer in the new company, even though he did not share her family's enthusiasm for the sea. With that being the case, Marguerite had hoped that her father would pass the business on to her son.[62]

Amid Baker's efforts to persuade Congress to support subsidies for a merchant marine, more trouble befell the family. On February 13, 1915, Elizabeth Baker died unexpectedly at Ingleside. She had been in poor health for many years, but her death was still a shock.[63]

Marguerite said she felt no keen sorrow over her mother's passing; they had long been estranged and her death was just one of a number of difficulties she faced at this time. The outbreak of World War I in Europe was sending ripple effects throughout the United States. Although Baltimore generally profited by sending goods to Europe, the uncertainty of the war played havoc with the stock market. In the summer of 1914 Tom's brokerage business was dealt a blow when the New York Stock Exchange closed for four months. Marguerite was vacationing with Tommy at a New Jersey beach when her husband called with the news. They lived off Tom's commission, so the closing of the stock exchange meant the family had little income. For the first time Marguerite seemed genuinely worried about money.

Her anxieties were compounded when she learned that Tom had become involved in business speculations and had borrowed large sums from his sister. In her memoir Marguerite doesn't specify what the business ventures were, but the financial troubles coincided with the failure to raise capital for the Atlantic Pacific Transport Company.

A close reading of newspaper accounts indicates Marguerite and Tom might have been drifting apart. Early in their marriage, the society pages covered their activities together: hunting trips, horse races, opera performances, and dances. But as the years passed, the couple increasingly enjoyed separate activities. Tom played tennis and baseball while Marguerite devoted her time to the Children's Hospital School. She took vacations with her parents or sister and without Tom. In 1908 she joined her sister for several weeks in the Poconos.[64] In 1911 she and Tommy spent the summer with her father in Europe, traveling to London to see the coronation of King George V and then to the spa at Carlsbad.[65]

The outbreak of World War I in Europe further illuminated the differences between the couple. Marguerite's foreign travels had made her attuned to the events, and she again started to follow the news from abroad with interest. She was annoyed that Tom seemed indifferent to the war, and when he did take notice it was to offer his wholehearted support of the Allies. Marguerite, however, was conflicted. She was suspicious of the virulent anti-German propaganda and despaired of the attacks on Austria, a country she loved.

Baltimore, with a large immigrant population, was a fractured city. Poles, Lithuanians, Russians, and Germans organized to send aid to their homelands. German influence had always been strong in the city. According to one estimate, more than one-quarter of the white population of Baltimore was of German descent. The Maryland General Assembly required every law to be published in German, and the Germans had their own schools, societies, and newspapers. With the outbreak of war, many German Americans stood solidly behind the Kaiser, including the "Sage of Baltimore," *Sun* columnist H. L. Mencken.[66]

In October 1914 German and Austrian women living in the city rallied to support soldiers in their homelands. They raised one thousand dollars' worth of supplies for war hospitals and organized sewing circles to make uniforms and bandages.[67] Despite Tom's pro-Allied views, Marguerite joined the German and Austrian women in their work. "I thought of all the gentle, kindly Germans I had known, peace loving, sentimental, and rather commonplace," she later wrote. "They were intensely patriotic it was true and I could imagine them fighting wholeheartedly for what they believed to be the future of the Fatherland, but I believed that many of them must have at first opposed the military camorra that forced the issue of war on Germany. As for my beloved Austrians, my heart bled for them. I could never regard them as enemies."[68]

Despite her worries over the unfolding conflict abroad, she had more pressing concerns at home. Money was tight and that winter the Harrisons were forced to rent their townhouse to one of Marguerite's former teachers. But the rental income was still not enough to pay their bills, so Marguerite made the daring decision to help the family by going to work. Although attitudes toward women working shifted significantly at the beginning of the twentieth century—female participation in the labor force grew from 16.5 percent in 1890 to 20.2 percent in 1920—it still was unusual for a married woman of Marguerite's standing to work outside the home. The prevailing view was that married women should not take the jobs that rightfully belonged to men. As a result, only 10 percent of married women were gainfully employed in 1910, a number that dropped to 9 percent in 1920.[69]

Yet Marguerite nevertheless decided to go into partnership with a female friend and open a shop they called the Flower House Studio, offering goods ranging from home accessories to Vogue sewing patterns, and jams and pickles. Marguerite had inherited her mother's aesthetic sense, and she painted lamp shades and furniture and scoured antique stores looking for items to resell. Marguerite and her partner knew little about running a business and had no idea about the complexities of keeping inventory and calculating overhead and depreciation. When it came time to apportion the profits, they divided the income according to who needed it more.[70]

Marguerite's worries grew as she noticed troubling signs in Tom's behavior. He had grown lethargic in his business and quick-tempered, even abusive, toward her. In late 1914 he began to complain of frequent headaches that grew worse in the passing weeks. Initially doctors believed he was suffering from sinus trouble. But then a Johns Hopkins Hospital neurologist made a devastating diagnosis: Tom was suffering from a brain tumor.

Neuroscience was still in its infancy in 1915, and while Johns Hopkins Hospital boasted some of the most talented surgeons in the country, doctors could not completely remove brain tumors. At best, they could try to extend patients' lives by partially removing the growths.[71] Over the next six weeks Tom underwent nine surgeries as doctors tried to find and remove the tumor. The first few procedures left him blind and paralyzed, but Marguerite approved more operations in a desperate attempt to save his life.

Throughout the ordeal Marguerite tried to remain cheerful even though she sensed Tom would never recover. She and Tommy, now thirteen, stayed with her in-laws, and she continued to work at the Flower House Studio until the last ten days, when she did not leave the hospital. Tom rarely was conscious in the final weeks, but at one point he had a brief moment of lucidity. Marguerite asked him if he wanted her to stay while he was given an anesthetic. "'I want you with me always,' he answered, and those were the last intelligible words he spoke," she later recalled.[72]

Tom Harrison died at Johns Hopkins Hospital on June 30, 1915, after being in a coma for nearly two weeks. He was forty-two years old.

Marguerite's comfortable, well-ordered world was thrown into disarray. She was no longer the daughter of a renowned Baltimore shipping magnate and the wife of a successful stockbroker. Her mother was gone, her father was struggling to regain his fortune, and she was a thirty-six-year-old widow with a teenage son. According to the custom of the day, she should have gone to live at Ingleside with her father. Baker certainly would have welcomed her and his only grandchild.

But Marguerite Harrison had other plans.

OUT ON A LIMB

AS A CHILD, Marguerite Harrison thrilled at climbing the tall spruce trees at her family's Olden estate in Catonsville and swaying on the high branches while her mother pleaded for her to get down. Only when she was good and ready did Marguerite scamper to the ground, her hands and smock sticky with sap.[1] In choosing to live alone with her son after her husband's death, Marguerite again was refusing to do what was safe and secure. Staying in her home offered freedom to live as she pleased, but she faced an uncertain financial future. In addition to losing her husband's income, she had inherited his debts, mainly to his sister, that Marguerite felt obligated to pay.[2]

Heeding her mother-in-law's advice to always remain calm no matter the circumstances, Marguerite returned home after Tom's funeral, pulled up the blinds, opened the windows, and decorated the house with flowers. She explained in her memoir that she put on a brave face because he did not want her son to fear death. She had not let Tommy see his father's body, and she would not allow him to think of his father as dead. She told him that his father had only taken another form and that he would always be with him.[3]

Yet Marguerite herself doubted whether anything existed beyond the darkness of death. By the late 1800s science had superseded religion in guiding Americans' views of life.[4] Darwinism theorized how creatures came into being and their place on the Earth. Although Marguerite was too romantic to embrace a completely logical view of the world, she nevertheless saw fallacies in the faiths of her friends and family.

The Bakers had been stern Methodists, forbidding activities such as dancing and card playing. To Marguerite, the God of the Bakers was harsh and judgmental. The Livezeys were Quakers, encouraging self-reflection. Their God seemed detached and impersonal. Her parents' Episcopalian God felt too formal and elusive. Her nanny, a devout Roman Catholic, had surreptitiously taken Marguerite to Mass, and she had loved the Latin chants and smell of incense. Nevertheless, Marguerite's doubts about God grew as she became older. Her grandfather Livezey had encouraged her to think critically and question even the existence of a Supreme Being. Marguerite continued to attend Episcopal church services and say prayers by rote, but her faith waivered. She at turns was an atheist, an agnostic, and a spiritualist. In ensuing years, she believed in reincarnation, imagining she had lived in Russia or the Middle East in a previous life. Eventually she wrote, "I still instinctively believed in God, but I gave up trying to find him."[5]

In the summer of 1915 she put aside her doubts about an afterlife and focused her attention on her temporal needs. She did not make enough money at the Flower House Studio to support herself and her son, so she decided to take in boarders. She recalled that her friends were shocked when she told them she planned to run a boardinghouse, yet she felt no shame.

Her cook, Lizzie, and maid, Rebecca, were indispensable to running the establishment, which offered lodgers breakfast and dinner. Lizzie, whom Marguerite described as "so fat she could not climb the stairs to get to her bedroom," knew how to make palatable food within a budget. Rebecca, meanwhile, whom Marguerite called "shrewd, intelligent, kindly and absolutely devoted," took care of selecting the tenants, who usually were young professional women or students. Most of the boarders came with references, but Marguerite recalled one case in which she rented a room to an unknown young man whom Rebecca disliked. He turned out to be a drug addict who rarely paid his rent. Marguerite lacked the heart to turn him out, but Rebecca did not. One day, Marguerite came home and discovered that Rebecca had packed his bag, called him a cab, and "sent him off without ceremony."[6]

The rent Marguerite collected from the boarders was adequate to cover food and lodging for herself and Tommy, but it did not meet all the family's expenses, much less allow her to repay the debt to Tom's sister. Tommy attended Gilman, one of the most prestigious boys' preparatory schools in the city, and tuition was $420 a year.[7] Later Marguerite said that she took work outside the home because she did not want Tommy to have to leave the school. However, her explanation is not convincing. Despite her father's business setbacks, he was still a wealthy man and adored Tommy, his only grandchild. He certainly would have paid the Gilman tuition.

It seems more likely that by fall 1915, Marguerite, now thirty-seven, was adrift, grieving for her husband, and looking for a new purpose in life. She continued working each day at the Flower House Studio and spent evenings making lamp shades and other items to sell, but the business no longer interested her.

Given her age and experience, Marguerite's career choices were limited. Teaching and nursing were the most common professions for women in that day. But despite her work with the Children's Hospital School, Marguerite had no training in either field. Changes in industry were opening new clerical jobs, such as telephone operators, bookkeepers, typists, and stenographers. But Marguerite was notoriously inept at math and did not know how to use the new office machines. Sales work in the burgeoning department stores offered another career opportunity, but she found similar work in the home décor shop uninspiring. Then she had the idea: "Suddenly it occurred to me I would like to have a job on a newspaper."[8]

In many ways, this profession made perfect sense. Women who needed money had long tried their hands at writing, including Louisa May Alcott, Sarah Josepha Hale, and even Lady Randolph Churchill, who turned to publishing a literary journal after her husband died. Another reason the news business might have attracted Marguerite was its familiarity. Since she was a child, newspapers had chronicled her family's activities, mostly giving favorable coverage to the Harrisons and Bakers. She had gained insight into how reporters work from the numerous stories they had written about her founding of Children's Hospital School. Moreover, her education and social standing gave her confidence that she could interview sources and write articles.

In late 1915, when she contemplated her options, Baltimore was home to four major newspapers: the *Baltimore Sun*; its sister paper, the *Evening Sun*; the *American*; and the *News*. Marguerite chose to apply to the Sunpapers because Van Lear Black, part owner of the papers, was a longtime friend, and his wife was a member Children's Hospital School auxiliary board.

With a letter of recommendation from Black in hand, Marguerite walked through the double copper doors of the imposing Sun building at Charles and Baltimore streets, climbed the marble staircase to the second-floor newsroom, and announced she was looking for a job.

She had never seen anything like the scene before her. The *Sun*'s large newsroom was furnished with rows of oak desks, and the air was thick with tobacco smoke and the sharp odor of printer's ink. Reporters, their coats off and shirt-sleeves rolled up, loudly banged out stories on typewriters, and yelled "Copy!" when finished. "I found it positively exhilarating," she later wrote. "I knew I would like being a newspaperwoman." The *Sun*'s managing editor, Frank Kent, looked skeptically at the well-dressed woman who stood before him. Later she recalled, "I was almost tongue-tied before the little man with keen, steely blue eyes and a whimsical mouth, who looked me up and down quizzically as if he found me insignificant and rather amusing."[9]

By this time women in newsrooms were not rare. For nearly thirty years, the *Sun* had employed women, starting with May Garrettson Evans, who was hired in 1888 to write about theater, concerts, religion, and fashion. Evans' mother used to chaperone her daughter on assignments until the intrepid reporter took to carrying a stiletto the staff gave her to defend herself on the dangerous streets of Baltimore.[10] Another woman, Gertrude B. Knipp, arrived later and covered a myriad of local stories. She recalled that she worked for a month without pay until the accounting office noticed her and paid her ten dollars a week.[11]

Although the editors at the Sunpapers may not have held women in particularly high esteem, female reporters had made significant strides throughout the country, distinguishing themselves with daredevil stunts, investigative reports, and war correspondences. At the turn of the twentieth century 2,193 women were employed in journalism, and by 1920 that number had grown to 7,105.[12] By the time Marguerite Harrison decided to pursue journalism, Ida Tarbell had written a famous exposé on the Standard Oil Company, Ida B. Wells had campaigned against lynching, Nellie Bly had exposed horrors in a New York insane asylum and traveled around the world in seventy-two days, and Dorothy Dix was penning a personal advice column that would eventually engage millions of readers.

Nevertheless, Marguerite stood before the managing editor of the *Baltimore Sun* nervously awaiting his answer. Frank Richardson Kent, at thirty-eight, was only a year older than Marguerite, but he was a newspaper veteran.

Later, Marguerite recalled the interview:

"So you want a job do you?" he asked, pressing the tips of his fingers together in front of him and looking down at them as if he had just discovered them.

"Yes," I answered faintly.

"What kind of job?"

"I don't know—writing of course," I added hastily.

"Hmm—ever written before?"

"No, but I think I could."

"Hmm—you know almost everybody in Baltimore, don't you?"

"I suppose so."

"Very well—I'll make you assistant society editor."[13]

Although Kent's passion was political reporting, he recognized the importance of attracting female readers and, in turn, the advertisers who wanted to reach them. Society pages had become a staple of daily newspapers since Joseph Pulitzer introduced them in the *New York World* in the 1880s.[14] The *Baltimore Sun*'s society columns went by various names, including "Brief Items about Baltimoreans and Their Friends," "Society Gossip," and "Events in the Polite World." For the most part, they were short listings of the comings and goings of Baltimore's high society: who was visiting whom, who was hosting a dinner or card party, who was vacationing at the resorts, and who was wearing what to the balls. Society matrons read the pages with great interest, and they competed to prove that their parties were worthy of newspaper coverage.

The day after her meeting with Kent, Marguerite reported to work as the assistant society editor, a position that paid sixteen dollars a week. She was assigned a desk with her own telephone next to the society editor, Mary McCarty, to whom she took an instant liking. McCarty was about the same age and patiently took the novice reporter under her tutelage. She handed her a slip of paper with names scribbled on it and told her to write an announcement for the society page. "You turn up the lid of your desk to get at the typewriter," she explained.

Marguerite was taken aback. She did not know how to type. It had never occurred to her that journalists needed this skill even though typewriters had been standard equipment in offices for decades.[15] McCarty was surprised at Marguerite's ineptitude, but then she laughed. "Bluff it out and don't let anybody know it," she advised. She showed her how to put the paper in the carriage and peck out the letters on the keyboard. Painstakingly, Marguerite typed her first news item. "It took me nearly an hour," she recalled. "The next item was easier and it was not long before I developed a considerable degree of speed if not accuracy."[16]

At first Marguerite found the transition from society matron to society reporter uncomfortable. She had to call her friends for details about their parties, weddings, and vacations. Her editors expected her to ferret out stories about engagements and out-of-town guests before the columnists at rival papers got the scoop. With the start of debutante season, she and Mary McCarty had to call each young lady to find out what she planned to wear to the balls. They collected articles for the Sunday paper and gathered photographs of Baltimore's social leaders, always keeping an eye on the competition. Gradually Marguerite caught on and soon developed a news instinct and a flair for writing.

After writing for the *Baltimore Sun*'s society pages for a year, in late 1916 her editors offered Marguerite the job of music critic. She vividly recalled the thrill of covering her first assignment, which she remembered as the opening performance of the Metropolitan Opera Company's spring tour. "I went in fear and trembling," she wrote. "I had never done anything of the kind and I was terribly nervous. I dashed to the *Sun* office with my notes after the opera was over. I pounded away at my typewriter with trembling fingers until the paper was almost ready to go to press." Her editor scanned the copy quickly and then asked for her initials. "I could scarcely believe my ears or the evidence of my own eyes as I saw him scribble 'M.E.H.' at the foot of my copy."[17]

Marguerite's memory of her first music review does not appear to be accurate, however. Rather than a story about the opera, her initials first appeared on a column about the opening concert of the Baltimore String Quartet in December 1916. In her review, she confidently compared the performance she witnessed with concerts given at the time of Mozart and Haydn.[18]

In March 1917 Marguerite began a music column titled "Through Our Own Opera Glasses," and in September she also became the *Sun*'s theater critic and started another column, "Overheard in the Wings." She was so busy with the new assignments that she stopped writing society news. In addition to writing articles and reviews several times a week and two columns on Saturdays, she traveled frequently to New York to cover the openings of new plays and gather theater gossip. She recalled meeting some of the biggest stars of the day, including Otis Skinner, Henry Miller, and Lionel and Ethel Barrymore.[19]

Besides her newspaper work, Marguerite held a political patronage position on the Maryland Board of Motion Picture Censors. Her brother-in-law, Attorney General Albert C. Ritchie Jr., saw to it that she received an appointment to the three-member panel, which paid $2,500 a year.[20] Marguerite said she took the position because she needed the money, not because she wanted to protect the public from motion pictures. "Personally I do not believe in censorship of any kind," she wrote. "Raw indecency and obscenity should be eliminated by police interference; an arbitrary control of public manners and morals by a small group of individuals savors too much of paternalism in government to suit me." Marguerite reasoned that, if anything, she could help defend free speech from the excesses of ignorant religious bigots: "Having heard that other censorship boards had insisted on secretly marrying poor lovely Camille and Hester Prynne before they would permit *Camille* or the *Scarlet Letter* to be shown in their states, I cherished the hope I might preserve them from such a fate."[21]

Efforts to censor movies began almost as soon as the first flickering films were projected from peep-show machines, and censorship intensified in the early twentieth century as Protestant churches became alarmed over the new entertainment. In 1907 Chicago was the first city to enact a censorship ordinance, giving the police superintendent the power to license motion pictures. A few years later, states began establishing movie censorship boards, starting with Pennsylvania in 1911 and then Ohio in 1913, Kansas in 1914, and Maryland in 1916.[22] When an interstate film conglomerate, Mutual Film Corporation, tried to argue that movies were protected free speech, the U.S. Supreme Court unanimously ruled that motion pictures could be censored because "they may be used for evil."[23]

During the Maryland board's first year, from June 1, 1916, until May 31, 1917, it examined more than 11,000 reels of film covering 4,769 subjects. The board approved the vast majority, rejecting or eliminating only 468 films. But the board drew criticism from all quarters, with some charging it was a waste of money. And while some bristled that the panel was censoring free speech, others attacked the board for being too lenient.[24] In July leading Baltimore residents signed a petition to the governor, complaining that the board had approved movies that should have been withheld because they were not suitable for children. The board members responded aggressively, arguing that banning all movies not appropriate for children would not be fair to adults. In responding to one particular critic, the board members pointedly asserted it was their judgment, not hers, that would decide what movies were shown. "We wish to make it perfectly clear to you and to anyone else who may be interested, that we do not propose to be coerced, or bullied, or frightened by threats of any kind into approving or rejecting any films against our judgment," board members said in a statement.[25]

Although claiming not to be prudish, Marguerite could be unbending when she perceived that a theater was operating outside the law. Early in her tenure she discovered a movie poster plastered outside a West Baltimore Street theater that she considered too "raw" and so ordered the manager to take it down until the censorship board could consider it. When the manager refused, she took the matter to Attorney General Ritchie. Not surprisingly, he found that his sister-in-law was within her rights to order the poster removed. In documenting the incident, the *Baltimore Sun* noted: "When Mrs. M. E. Harrison, secretary of the Board of Motion Picture Censors, goes after what she considers to be an immoral moving picture film or poster, she does not let a little thing like the haughty attitude on the part of the manager of the show and his refusal to submit to the board's authority to stand in her way."[26]

Her relationship with Albert Ritchie went beyond that of having an important ally in the government. In her memoir Marguerite wrote fondly about her brother-in-law, whom she described as "like a brother." But according to Marguerite's granddaughter Nancy Harrison, her grandmother carried on a love affair with Ritchie that permanently ruptured her relationship with her sister.[27] Historian Elizabeth Olds, who interviewed Tommy Harrison before his death in 1993, said the sisters became estranged after "Marguerite became an unwilling rival of her sister in a serious affair of the heart."[28]

Described by one Maryland historian as a "Gibson man" with good looks and Southern charm, Ritchie was born in Richmond, Virginia, in 1876 and grew up in Baltimore.[29] His mother was the descendant of a Virginia governor and the Cabell family, which had close ties to Thomas Jefferson. Ritchie graduated from Johns Hopkins University and received his law degree from the University of Maryland.

He was Baltimore's assistant city solicitor when he married Elizabeth Baker on May 18, 1907. In contrast to Marguerite's lavish wedding at Emmanuel Episcopal Church six years earlier, Elizabeth and Ritchie wed in the drawing room at Ingleside in a ceremony attended only by close friends and family. The *Sun* nevertheless called the marriage "one of the most notable weddings of the season and one of great interest to society" because the bride was the daughter of a prominent Baltimore businessman and Ritchie was the son of former city judge and a rising star in state Democratic politics.[30] But their marriage was not happy. After less than three years together, they separated and Ritchie moved back home with his mother.

If Marguerite and Albert Ritchie did have an affair, it likely would have occurred after Tom's death in June 1915. That would also account for the strange timing of the divorce. Although the Ritchies separated in 1910, Elizabeth did not file for divorce until 1916. In her court petition, Elizabeth accused Ritchie of abandonment, saying he had left her to live with his mother when the lease expired on a house they were renting. But why did she wait six years to file for divorce? Was she hoping for a reconciliation? Or could Elizabeth have discovered that her sister was having an affair with her estranged husband? In his response to the divorce petition, Ritchie did not deny the abandonment charge but explained that "irreconcilable differences in their respective views of life, and the mutual obligations to each other of husband and wife, have always existed between them, and prevented the possibility of a happy conjugal existence."[31]

Marguerite made no mention of a break with her sister in her memoir. Instead she described a life-long separation that was due to their different personalities and temperaments:

My sister was born when I was nearly three years old and she was an adorable baby—fat and rosy, placid and even-tempered. When she was tiny I played with her as if she were one of my dolls, but as she grew older and developed a will of her own she refused to be treated as a plaything. I could not coax her into sharing my madcap adventures, she began to resent the fact that my mother made a great deal more fuss over me than she did over her—we played together only because we had no other companions.

She said that after she went to live with her grandparents at Elton Park, she rarely saw her sister.

I cannot recall a single episode in which she had any part. We were always strangers. I have no remembrance of any affection or any dislike for her, or even of what she looked like. She is a blurred outline in the dim recesses of memory. Probably neither of us was to blame for this state of affairs. When I dally with the doctrine of reincarnation, which has always had a tremendous fascination for me, I imagine we must have lived our previous lives in different periods and among peoples alien in blood and civilization. She was never part of my life.[32]

But Marguerite's account is belied by evidence that shows the sisters working together for charitable causes and socializing for many years after they were grown. Elizabeth was Marguerite's maid of honor at her wedding in 1901, and when Marguerite founded the Children's Hospital School in 1905, she recruited her sister to the auxiliary board, a position she held for several years. In 1908 the *Sun* reported that Marguerite and her sister vacationed for several weeks together in the Poconos Mountains.[33]

The break in the sisters' relationship appears to coincide with the failure of the Ritchies' marriage, although word of the couple's separation was slow to get out. As late as 1912 the *Sun*'s society column reported that both Albert and Elizabeth were to spend the summer with the Bakers at Ingleside, but court papers showed that by that time the couple had been estranged for two years.[34]

Given the stigma of divorce in that day and Albert Ritchie's aspiring political ambitious, it is not surprising that the couple kept their separation quiet. In 1910 Maryland political leaders were starting to take notice of the handsome young lawyer, and he gained widespread attention after he was appointed assistant general counsel to the Public Service Commission and embarked on a crusade to bring cheaper electricity and gas rates to Baltimore. In selecting Ritchie to fight against the utility company, Public Service Commission chairman Philip D. Laird said, "We are going to put Ritchie on the job. He is as clean as a hound's tooth—smart, bright, a hard worker, and absolutely beyond the reach of any improper influence."[35]

In 1912, when Ritchie won lower utility rates for the community, he became a public hero. The *Baltimore Sun* called him the "people's champion" and described Ritchie as "young, virile, alert." The story recounted Ritchie's family lineage, education, and early legal work. As for his marriage, the article noted: "He was married to Miss Elizabeth Catherine Baker, daughter of Bernard N. Baker, in May 1907." The piece concluded: "Personally he is attractive. A big, handsome man, genial, game and fond of a joke, the whole of his makeup is the sort men like. And one of his chief qualities is that very, very, very rare virtue—intellectual honesty."[36]

Just three months later, when Ritchie decided to leave his position with the Public Service Commission because of the low salary, he again was the subject of a large profile story. The article, topped with a banner headline: "Albert C. Ritchie: 'The People's Advocate,'" was accompanied by a photograph showing a handsome young man with deep-set eyes gazing intently away from the camera. The article's description of Ritchie makes it easy to see why women would be attracted to him: "Seen at his desk in the Calvert Building, surrounded by evidence of a heavy legal business, his hair shows gray around the temples. He is stocky, strongly built, square jawed, and has gray eyes that can smile or flash as occasion requires and back of them there is a touch of cynicism at times." The article recounts his physical prowess on the squash court and in the gym, noting, "Mr. Ritchie is an example of youth climbing the ladder by all the rules of the copy book regarding early rising and industry." Again, the newspaper made a brief mention of his marriage to Elizabeth.

Given his success in lowering utility rates and attracting favorable news coverage, it was not surprising that Ritchie, running on the Democratic ticket, was elected attorney general in 1915, defeating his Republic opponent by more than 25,000 votes.[37] Not until the next June, however, when Elizabeth filed for divorce, did the *Sun* report the dissolution of the marriage. Despite the *Sun's* support of Ritchie, the paper recounted dispassionately the allegations of abandonment outlined in the divorce complaint. The paper did note, however, "The friends of himself and Mrs. Ritchie say that their tastes and views of life are so dissimilar that they have been unable to live together happily, although they have genuine respect for each other."[38]

If Elizabeth was as placid as Marguerite described, she indeed may have been an unsuitable wife for the dynamic young politician. Yet Elizabeth Baker and Albert Ritchie had known each other for at least ten years before they wed, so it is surprising that they discovered they were incompatible after just a few years of marriage. Nancy Harrison says the family legend gives the reason for the divorce as sexual incompatibility. Family members painted Elizabeth as cold and frigid compared with the passionate Marguerite.[39]

Regardless of whether their relationship was a sexual one, Ritchie was one of Marguerite's closest confidants at a time when her once wide circle of friends and family was shrinking. In summer 1916 her father set Baltimore tongues to wagging by marrying a much younger woman. His bride, Rosalie Barry, had been one of Marguerite's childhood friends and a bridesmaid in her wedding. Although the announcement in the newspaper expressed surprise that Bernard Baker would marry a woman so much younger, Marguerite supported his choice. "I was glad to think that he might find some things he had missed in life and some compensation for the disappointments he had suffered in his business career."[40]

For a time Marguerite found escape from her loneliness and grief by working, often fourteen hours a day. She screened films in the morning with the censorship board and went to the newsroom in the afternoon. She covered concerts and plays at night. What little socializing she did was squeezed between work assignments. She usually had lunch with Mary McCarty or her father and rarely went home for dinner. She saw her teenage son in the mornings before he went to school and on Sunday afternoons. She spent Sunday evenings with Albert Ritchie and his mother. "I rarely saw anyone else," she recalled.[41]

Her routine was disrupted on April 6, 1917, when the United States declared war on Germany. She had been ambivalent about the war when it began, but she cheered when the news of the American war declaration came over the wires in the *Sun*'s newsroom.[42] She had become a firm supporter of the Allied effort and was caught up in the war fever sweeping Baltimore. Domestic controversies such as women's suffrage and Prohibition were put aside as Marylanders rallied to support the war. Thousands flocked to work in Baltimore's steel mills and shipyards, and, as men went off to war, women took up the slack, working in offices and factories. Food shortages prompted observances such as "Sugarless Mondays," "Meatless Tuesdays," and "Wheatless Wednesdays." The Women's Civic League turned playgrounds and vacant lots into "liberty gardens," and Bernard Baker handed over the Ingleside estate for food production.

With its declaration of war, Congress passed the Sedition Act, which made almost any statement that might be considered critical of the war or might offer any sympathy to the Germans treasonous. One woman received a ten-year prison sentence for advising women not to bear children who could be sent to war.[43] Industry and government alike demanded patriotism. The Maryland General Assembly passed a compulsory work law. The Chesapeake & Potomac telephone company required its employees to take a loyalty pledge. Suspicion fell on Baltimore's large German population, forcing German newspapers to suspend operations or publish in English. Baltimore's German Street was renamed Redwood

Street in honor of the state's first war casualty. And as Maryland's war casualties mounted, some demanded that Baltimoreans of German descent swear allegiance to the United States.[44]

Rising anti-German sentiment even crept into the concert halls. In late 1917 Pittsburgh barred noted Austrian violinist Fritz Kreisler from performing at Carnegie Music Hall, and his appearance in Baltimore weeks later aroused anger, with one *Sun* letter writer arguing, "Let all patriotic Baltimoreans remember that he is an enemy alien."[45]

Marguerite covered the Kreisler concert at the Lyric Theatre and gave differing accounts about what happened. In her memoir she wrote that the violinist was booed and left the stage in tears. She said she rushed backstage to comfort him, saying, "Don't let a few ignorant people hurt you. Your art is all that matters to most of us, Herr Kreisler."[46] But in her *Baltimore Sun* review of the concert, Marguerite observed that the audience greeted Kreisler warmly: "Contrary to the expectations of many persons and perhaps to the disappointment of some, the violin recital by Fritz Kreisler at the Lyric last evening was attended by no untoward incident." She added, "The great violinist received a perfect ovation at the close of the concert and the audience had to be literally invited out by having all the lights turned down."[47] Nevertheless, three days after his Baltimore performance, Kreisler asked to be released from his contract because of threats made against him.[48]

About this time Marguerite began to work diligently to suppress pro-German propaganda in the movies that came before the Maryland Board of Motion Pictures Censors. The most controversial movie the board rejected during her tenure was Herbert Brenon's *War Brides*, which was based on a successful play of the same name. Starring Alla Nazimova, the film depicted a young pregnant woman whose husband was killed in battle. When an unnamed king shows up at her village, she kills herself in front of him rather than bear a child who will be sent to war.[49] The censorship board initially approved the film, but when the United States declared war on Germany on April 6, 1917, it withdrew the film's license. The film distributors responded by filing a lawsuit in Baltimore City Court.

Testifying at the hearing, Marguerite asserted: "I consider the film to be distinctly injurious to the morale of the country at this time. In showing the scenes that it does, of women in agonies over the war, and showing the casualty list, I think it shows scenes that are calculated to react indirectly on the fighting forces themselves." When the lawyers representing the film's owners asked whether she thought there was anything obscene about the movie, she answered affirmatively. "I do," she said. "I think the purpose of the picture is to encourage pacifism." Again Attorney General Ritchie was involved in the controversy, representing the censorship board in giving closing arguments. The judge ultimately sided with the board in banning the movie.[50]

As the weeks passed, Marguerite promoted the war in articles she wrote for the *Sun* with the approval of the government's Committee on Public Information. President Woodrow Wilson had appointed former muckraker George Creel to head the committee a week after the United States entered the war. At the time many Americans opposed getting involved in what they considered a European conflict, and they well remembered Wilson's campaign slogan, "He Kept Us Out of War." Given the lack of enthusiasm for the war, the so-called Creel Committee had work to do.

Initially set up to disseminate information about the war, the committee became a controversial conveyer of propaganda. Capitalizing on war fever, Creel parlayed a small staff working from a library in the Navy building near the White House into an organization that employed 395 staffers and thousands of volunteers. The Creel Committee rallied the war effort through posters, films, cartoons, billboards, and songs; distributed government speeches; developed lesson plans for the schools; and issued ten press releases a day to fill the nation's newspapers. One of its most original ideas was the "Four Minute Men" program. Meant to recall the Minutemen who defended the country during the Revolutionary War, this squadron of volunteers delivered pro-war speeches—supposedly no more than four minutes long—in public places such as movie theaters and concert halls.[51]

Part of this work also enlisted sympathetic journalists. The *Sun* dispatched a reporter to follow Maryland troops in Europe and sent journalists around Baltimore and Washington to write about the home front. Frank Kent suggested that Marguerite look for stories that would stir patriotism and bolster military enlistment. "I responded enthusiastically," she recalled. "I racked my brains to find suggestions for stories that would be entertaining and at the same time serve as useful propaganda."[52]

Marguerite's first byline appeared on a four-part series about the work of the Red Cross. In the series, which began on June 14, 1917, under the headline

"Red Cross, Greatest of Agents of Mercy," she wrote: "The American Red Cross organization is destined to play a truly great part in the war upon which the United States has entered." She also provided an account of her visit to the Red Cross headquarters in Washington, D.C., where desks overflowed into the corridors and workers were so dedicated that they paid no attention to the time of day.[53] In July she wrote a series for the *Evening Sun* describing the ways wives of government leaders in Washington were supporting the war effort.[54] In a similar vein, she scored the first newspaper interview with Herbert Hoover's wife, Lou Henry Hoover, who detailed her efforts to conserve food and fuel in support of the war.[55]

Marguerite's love of danger and adventure is evident in an article she wrote about the Army's aviation camp on Long Island, New York. In this vivid account, she described riding to the hangar on an Army motorcycle, changing her hat for a helmet and goggles, and swapping her sweater for a leather coat.

"It must be glorious to soar through the air with such absolute mastery of your machine and nothing to worry about," Marguerite told the pilot breathlessly.

"No, nothing except the undertaker," the pilot replied grimly.

Marguerite's response: "I'm getting in."

The pilot strapped Marguerite into the front seat, and he took the rear. The noise of the engine and wind was deafening as the plane lifted off the ground. Marguerite was enthralled. "I could easily understand the spirit that goes to make men meet death joyously in the air," she gushed.

They soared for forty-five minutes, and then, as they headed back toward the hangar, the propeller blades stopped turning. The engine coughed and became silent. Marguerite's reaction: "Well here goes for a real thrill."

The pilot managed to land the disabled plane in a field. "Engine trouble," he said tersely.

A mechanic on a motorcycle quickly brought tools and repaired the motor on the spot. Marguerite climbed back into her seat and the plane made a "beautiful landing" at the hangar. "In my experience there had been nothing terrifying," she said. She only regretted that her white shoes and stockings were splattered with grease.[56]

In spring 1918, as more women poured into the labor market, Marguerite set out to determine what kinds of jobs women could obtain—a quest that took her to factories, offices, and department stores. Her writing shows ease and confidence as she recounted the hiring managers she met and the work and wages they offered her. In applying for sales positions, she wrote that she always ended up being referred to the stores' millinery departments. "It may have been because of the season, but I suspect it was psychological and related to a suppressed desire deep down in my conscious for a new spring hat," she wrote.[57]

One of Marguerite's most ambitious assignments, in May 1918, hearkened to the old days of stunt-girl reporting. Marguerite donned khaki overalls and worked for a week in the Bethlehem Steel shipbuilding yard. The result was a nine-part series that began: "I have had the most wonderful, the most unforgettable experience of my whole life. For a week I have been a shipbuilder—the first woman to take part in the great program of the Emergency Fleet Corporation. I have helped to build the ships that are to transport men, food and ammunition 3,000 miles overseas to win the greatest war in history. With every rivet I felt I was helping drive another nail in the Kaiser's coffin."[58]

Marguerite felt genuine excitement working in the plant. She described in detail her first day on the job, rising at five-thirty on a Monday morning and taking the train from her home in downtown Baltimore to the yard at Sparrows Point. Dressed in overalls and a cap like those worn by women workers of the Baltimore & Ohio Railroad, she entered the yard, hands in her pockets, hoping the workers wouldn't notice she was a woman. Of course, once she was assigned to the first work crew, the secret was revealed, and men gathered to watch. The plant superintendent, anxious to promote the company, assigned her to various tasks, from pounding rivets to cutting metal, and Marguerite accepted each challenge with aplomb. She wielded a pneumatic hammer, drove white-hot rivets, and descended into the bellies of ships. One afternoon she watched proudly as a ship she had helped build was launched into the Patapsco River.

In addition to detailing her experiences working at the yard, Marguerite also offered her opinion of what should be done to improve the work of the plant, including hiring women to alleviate the labor shortage, providing more housing to the workers, and giving laborers better training. She also hinted that she gave the superintendent some unsolicited information on the plant workers. She related an exchange in which she asked the employment manager how he screened out pro-German workers who might be bent on sabotage. The manager replied that the workers were monitored. "Later on, when I told the general manager, Mr. Anderson, of some remarks I had overheard in a certain shop, I found that he was well aware of the feeling that existed there," she wrote.[59]

In the summer of 1918 Marguerite's editors took note of her linguistic talents and assigned her to write a series about the attitudes of Baltimore's immigrants to the war. Interviewing Bohemians, Germans, Lithuanians, Greeks, Serbs, Poles, Russians, and Italians, Marguerite reported on a strong sense of patriotism among the groups. Large portions of the articles included the names of immigrants who had enlisted to fight for the Allies and recorded ethnic communities' support for the Red Cross and Liberty Bonds. Of particular interest were Baltimore's Germans, and Marguerite wrote three articles on their patriotism.[60]

Her articles documenting their support of the war stood in contrast to the suspicions that arose about Americans of German descent. By early 1917 the agents in the U.S. Department of Justice had compiled a list of German Americans in Baltimore who were suspected of being "strongly in sympathy with the Teuton cause."[61] With the war under way, Americans saw German spies everywhere. A New York grand jury indicted a German consul based in Baltimore on charges of providing a passport to a confessed spy.[62] Sabotage was blamed on a fire that destroyed $80,000 worth of merchandise, including German submarine equipment, at Baltimore's Locust Point.[63] In one proven case a Baltimore shipping executive of German heritage ran a sabotage ring from his offices at the corner of Charles and German streets, funneling thousands of dollars to agents who planted bombs on ships and trains throughout the United States.[64]

While genuine instances of espionage occurred, some suspected spy cases sprang from the public's irrational fears inflamed by Creel's propaganda. In one instance both tragic and comic, the government ordered the deportation of a Baltimore man after he argued publicly with his wife. During the fight, she screamed that he was a German spy. Someone overheard heard her and reported the incident to police, who arrested both of them. "After denouncing her husband, Mrs. Sadie Xanders regretted her action and clung to him when they were arraigned," the newspaper reported.[65]

Given the threats, both real and imagined, Chicago businessman Albert Briggs organized a group of superpatriotic volunteers to help the U.S. Department of Justice uncover spies and saboteurs. Within weeks after the declaration of war, the American Protective League had established branches in one hundred cities around the country and eventually would recruit 350,000 members offering to spy on their neighbors and coworkers. American Protective League members targeted not only suspected German operatives but also Socialists, Communists, labor organizers, and war protestors.[66] The organization operated with the blessing of the Justice Department and eventually came under the supervision of the U.S. Military Intelligence Division, which employed the citizen spies to help locate deserters and draft dodgers.[67]

In the spring of 1917 Marguerite began to report to the government tips about suspected German spies in Baltimore. No record indicates she was a member of the American Protective League, but the organization's Baltimore branch was headed by Tilghman Pitts, whom Marguerite knew socially, both having spent summers at the Baltimore County resort Chattolanee.[68] She never revealed her role in hunting German spies, but several sources indicate that this work was the beginning of her espionage career. Col. Ralph Van Deman, the driving force behind the creation of the U.S. Military Intelligence Division, wrote that Marguerite was "quite helpful in many ways in the United States."[69] The Russians knew this as well. In the interrogation report from her first Russian imprisonment, the list of her espionage work begins with a single line: "On May 13, 1917, she volunteered to fight German spies in Baltimore."[70]

On the day listed, Baltimore was preparing for the arrival of French war hero Marshal Joseph Joffre, who was on a tour of the United States to raise support for the war. Baltimore officials had tried for weeks to attract Joffre to the city and finally succeeded in getting him to make a brief appearance as he traveled from Philadelphia to Washington on May 14, 1917. Marguerite recalled that the *Sun* assigned her to interview Joffre and to act as his interpreter that day. "'Papa' Joffre took to me with pathetic eagerness," she wrote. "He did not speak a word of English and he was so tired of listening to speeches and bowing his acknowledgments that he found an immense relief in being able to relax and talk about something besides the war. He kept me beside him for most of the day and I did not leave him until he took the afternoon train for Washington."[71]

Did Marguerite learn of German agents while writing about the immigrant communities or working in the shipyard? Or did she hear rumors of trouble preceding the Joffre visit? The details of Marguerite's domestic spying are unknown, but the work must have provided the impetus for her decision to become a foreign agent. Clearly, Marguerite was thrilled to take an active role in the war effort. She was writing exciting stories, stymying subversive movies, and hunting German spies in Baltimore. But as months passed, she sensed that she was missing out on momentous events overseas that were transforming the world. Each day she devoured the news from abroad and weighed the rumors that Germany might be near collapse.

Marguerite had undergone a complete change from her days with Tom, when she cared nothing about the world outside her home. The woman who had been content to sew baby clothes and stock her pantry had vanished. "The years I had spent with Tom seemed like a dream, a happy interlude," she wrote.[72]

Now, she had awakened.

Marguerite Harrison, who had been raised to navigate the social milieu of Europe as easily as the country clubs of Baltimore, rediscovered her sense of adventure. The woman who for a brief moment thought that she could help create a revolution in Turkey imagined again that she could play an influential role in world events. Newspaper work had been a diversion. Foreign espionage promised danger, thrills, and the chance to shape history. This was a career to set her free.

IN THE WEB

WITH EXCITEMENT AND ANTICIPATION for the mission that lay ahead, Marguerite sailed from New York on December 5, 1918, on board the French ocean liner *Espagne*. Marguerite loved the sea and even many years later, when air transportation became the norm for long-distance travel, she continued to book passage on ocean liners and cargo ships.[1] Sailing summoned fond memories of the voyages she made on her father's ships when she was a child. But, sailing to France, Marguerite knew that the Europe of her childhood had vanished. More than 16 million soldiers and civilians had lost their lives in the war. Old empires had died, and new countries were being born from the carnage. Even before her ship landed, Marguerite was reminded that this was no holiday excursion when the *Espagne* struck an underwater mine as it entered the Gulf of Gascony. The ship listed but managed to stay afloat, creeping slowly toward its port.

After docking in Bordeaux, Marguerite boarded a train to Paris. Along the way she caught her first glimpse of the war's aftermath when she passed a prisoner of war camp. The sight of the men dressed in drab gray uniforms and huddled behind the barbed-wire fence troubled her. "There was something repulsive to all human instincts in the sight of men herded together like animals in a pen, but my heart hardened as I thought thousands of our Allies had been thus herded and humiliated in Germany," she recalled.[2]

She found that Paris, the City of Light, had become a city of women, children, and old men. Houses were unpainted; sandbags still were piled in front of hotels and offices. Here and there were signs of the German aerial bombardments: craters in the street, the black skeletons of burned buildings. American and British soldiers swaggered down Champs-Élysées. As she began to reacquaint herself with the city, she noticed the war had had a profound psychological impact on those around her. "Few of the men I met were absolutely normal," she recalled. "To begin with, most of them were desperately homesick, and lonely. Some were disillusioned, some heartsick and demoralized by the horrors they had seen."[3]

Passing the Luxor Obelisk where the guillotine once executed enemies of the French Revolution, Marguerite made her way to No. 4 Place de la Concorde and the office of Col. Ralph Van Deman. A thin, bookish-looking man with wire-framed glasses, Van Deman's appearance belied his role in creating an intelligence branch employing an army of military and civilian spies. Her Washington superiors had told her that she would not be involved in tracking down foreign spies and saboteurs, but Van Deman was in charge of counterintelligence for the Paris Peace Conference, and he had other plans.

Marguerite and Van Deman later gave starkly different accounts about the objectives of her mission to Germany. She wrote that her orders were to show the *Sun's* morale-boosting movie, *Miles of Smiles*, to Maryland troops in France and then travel to Germany posing as a reporter to gather information on the economic and political conditions in Berlin and the attitudes of the people. Van Deman, who wrote his recollection more than fifty years later with the aid of a diary in which he had recorded names and dates of meetings, recalled that Marguerite was assigned to Paris to keep an eye on the approximately one hundred newspaper correspondents assigned to cover the peace conference. A few weeks after she arrived, Van Deman learned that American Communist Robert Minor was distributing propaganda leaflets to U.S. troops. "Marguerite Harrison came into the office and I read the report to her. She offered to go to Germany herself and persuade Minor to come out with her in order that we might apprehend him in either British or American territory. For this purpose, she was authorized to go to Germany which she did and during the period she spent in Berlin she also witnessed and reported on the Communist uprising there."[4]

Whatever her original mission to Germany, Marguerite did not leave right away. She spent several weeks in Paris and was there on Christmas Eve when she received shocking news from home: Her father had died suddenly in California. She was devastated. While she had felt no grief at the passing of her mother in 1915, the loss of her father was a blow. She adored him and recalled that he was the one person who had seemed to accept her ambitions—even her decision to become a spy.

When she learned of her father's death, Marguerite reacted as she had when her husband died: she threw herself into work. "I did not shed a tear. I could not feel. I dared not think," she wrote. An old friend from Baltimore, a general in the American Expeditionary Forces who was staying at her hotel, understood she needed to keep busy. He took her to the Johns Hopkins Base Hospital at Neufchâteau where she helped hang Christmas decorations in the ward and distribute gifts to patients, most of whom were German prisoners. "When I went back to Paris the next morning, I put everything out of my mind except my work," she recalled.[5] She wrote several articles for the *Baltimore Sun*, including one on the Christmas celebrations at the hospital, an interview with an unrepentant Prussian officer, and a profile of deposed Russian president Georgy Lvov, who was in Paris soliciting support to fight the Bolsheviks.[6]

Two weeks later, Marguerite finally completed arrangements to visit the Maryland troops stationed in small towns around northern France. She had imagined she would be showing *Miles of Smiles* in recreation halls and was surprised to find the accommodations were much rougher. Often the men assembled to watch the film in dilapidated huts with earth floors that turned to mud in the unrelenting winter rains. Sometimes there was no shelter at all, and she was forced to show the movie outdoors. Electricity was unreliable, and once the men had to hook the projector to the engine of a downed German plane. The men asked Marguerite to stop and start the movie over and over again so they could see the grainy images of their wives, girlfriends, children, and pets.

Marguerite wrote about these experiences for the *Baltimore Sun*. With censorship ended, she could describe the abominable conditions the Maryland troops suffered while they waited to return home. "The pictures are needed more than anything else at this time because the men are desperately homesick," she wrote.[7]

Before long, she understood why the American troops were so unhappy. "The streets were a sea of mud," she wrote.

> The roads, the streets, the bypaths and often the floors were covered with it. . . . The men at Seigneulles had no "Y"[MCA] director, no books, magazines or papers, no amusement facilities. It was dark at four o'clock, mess was served to the men standing in line in the darkness and usually in the rain, for it rains six days out of seven in Northern France during the winter months. Some of the companies had sheds where the

men could stand and eat, but most of the doughboys had to take their meals in the open or carry them back to their billets.[8]

Although the troops offered Marguerite the best accommodations available, she endured hardships as well. In one house, she took a look at the filthy bed sheets and opted to sleep outside in her travel rug.

It was almost mid-January 1919 when she gave the last showing of *Miles of Smiles* and handed the film to Col. Milton A. Reckord, head of the 115th Infantry Regiment, so he could continue showing the movie to his men. She now was ready for her assignment in Berlin. In October her superiors at the Military Intelligence Division had instructed her to keep quiet about her travels, and she carried no credentials or passes to enter Germany. Nevertheless, her destination was not a secret. In a letter Reckord wrote to his wife that was published in the *Baltimore Sun* in late February, the officer noted that Marguerite was "on her way to Germany."[9]

Reporting on German spies in Baltimore had posed minimal risk, but heading into Berlin, Marguerite faced real dangers. In the months following the armistice, Germany had devolved into political and economic chaos. While remnants of the German government attempted to negotiate a peace deal with the Allies, Communist-backed Spartacists were organizing mass worker demonstrations in preparation for seizing control. Food shortages and unemployment grew. Thousands were dying of disease and starvation. By early January the protests were growing larger and more violent. Marguerite took a slow-moving train filled with soldiers and German workers to Frankfurt, where she heard rumors that fighting had broken out in the capital. She pressed on to Berlin.

The exact day of her arrival is uncertain. She recalled reaching the city shortly after the assassination of Spartacist leader Karl Liebknecht and before government troops shot to death another Spartacist leader, Rosa Luxemburg. However, Liebknecht and Luxemburg were both arrested and executed on the same day— January 15, 1919—as government troops pretended to transport them to prison. In one car, the soldiers drove Liebknecht to a dark street, shot him to death, and dumped his body at a mortuary, saying they found it by the road. Luxemburg, traveling in another car, was killed by a gunshot to the head. Her body was dumped in the Landwehr Canal and washed up four months later.[10]

The executions temporarily quashed the Spartacist uprising, but when Marguerite reached Berlin the factions were still fighting in the street, so it seems likely she arrived before the deaths of the Spartacist leaders, probably around January 10. On the night she arrived at the Anhalter Bahnhof station, she was unable to find a cab, possibly due to the transportation labor strike gripping the city. Instead, she hailed a horse-drawn carriage driven by an ancient-looking German and ordered him to take her to the only lodging she knew, the grand Hotel Bristol, where she had stayed as a child. The driver protested, saying only the military could pass through that section of the city at night. She flashed her press pass and he relented, muttering something about shooting in the streets.

As they headed down Budapester Strasse toward the hotel, she heard the crackle of gunfire. The driver asked whether he should continue. "Certainly!" she answered. The patrol on the Brandenburg Gate inspected her pass and waved her through, although they must have been astonished to see a lone American woman riding through the dangerous streets at night. She and her driver had traveled just a few more blocks when they encountered a gun battle between government troops and Spartacist insurgents. "Bullets bounced on the pavement and ricocheted from the walls of the building around us," she later recalled. As the driver whipped his horse into a gallop, Marguerite clutched her suitcase in front of her as a shield. In a minute they were at the hotel. The driver dumped her bags on the curb and sped away. The hotel night porter unlocked the door and pulled her inside to safety. Marguerite took the harrowing incident in stride. "I had an excellent supper and was soon fast asleep in a room facing an inner court," which was, needless to say, quieter than the rooms facing the fighting on the street.[11]

Espionage, like newspaper reporting, was a profession Marguerite was learning on the job. But now a mistake could cost lives. While her superiors had great faith in her abilities, Marguerite apparently had no training whatsoever. This was partly because of the rush to assemble the Military Intelligence Division when the United States entered the war. At first applicants who were already in the Army took a screening test for an espionage assignment and then spent two weeks studying at the War College in Washington, D.C. Intelligence officers assigned to the American Expeditionary Forces in Europe received eight to twelve weeks of training in France before being assigned to their units. Code breakers, airmen, and signalmen received additional training at schools devoted to their specialties.[12]

But the civilian spies were another matter. In Marguerite's case, she was hired based upon the reference of her father-in-law and an interview in a Baltimore hotel lobby. She possibly received some brief training at Chaumont, France, in December before she headed out to show *Miles of Smiles*, but there is no record that she ever was given any instructions beyond the guidance provided by her supervisors. She was not trained in handling sensitive communications or in responding to enemy interrogations. Her husband had taught her how to handle a shotgun, but she carried no weapon, only a typewriter. Nevertheless, with the same confidence she had pecked out her first society announcement, she set about gathering information in Berlin.

About a week after she arrived, Germans went to the polls to select the Weimar National Assembly that was to write the country's new constitution. For the first time, Marguerite witnessed women voting, although the sight did not allay her concerns about women's suffrage. When she asked her maid for whom she intended to vote, the woman responded: "That is just what I'm asking myself. I have three fellows, each belongs to a different party and I promised each one that I would vote for his. Now, I like Franz best, but I cannot remember whether he is a Deutsch National or an Independent Socialist." Marguerite noted that many German women nevertheless were ready to play a part in creating a new country, including the thirty-seven women elected to the first assembly.[13]

Marguerite's newspaper credentials gave her access to government officials and allowed her to pass through military checkpoints. In many respects, she approached the work of espionage as she did journalism. One of her main missions was to ascertain the political and economic conditions in the capital as well as the morale of its citizens. To gather the information, she talked to shopkeepers, chambermaids, soldiers, prostitutes, and bankers. She toured factories and gathered data on unemployment and food supplies.

Marguerite also worked to identify potential enemies. She collected the names of Americans living in Berlin and tried to determine their attitudes to the war. She reported that a Detroit businessman who was in Berlin attempting to purchase sugar beet seeds "makes no secret of his pro-German feelings." She said she heard a Baltimore man who was married to a German woman defend the sinking of the *Lusitania*.[14] Of course, Marguerite herself had once seen the shipping catastrophe as one of the unfortunate consequences of war. Now, however, she saw such a view as suspicious.

Marguerite made friends with the "irreconcilables" who wanted to reestablish the monarchy. Among this group were Gen. Hans von Below, who had commanded troops against the Allies at Argonne in 1918, and his American wife, the former Philadelphia society matron Nina Bryce Turnbull. Not surprisingly, Frau von Below and Marguerite knew many of the same people in America, and Marguerite was happy to share with her the latest gossip. She became a regular guest in the von Below home, and they put her in touch with others who wanted to cultivate a fear of Bolshevism as an excuse to regain power. Marguerite told her superiors that she did not know how real the Communist concerns were, but her reports on the irreconcilables helped thwart their plans to take control.[15]

It is impossible to know the extent to which Marguerite worked with other U.S. agents while she was in Berlin. When the war ended, the Military Intelligence Division employed 282 officers, 29 sergeants, and "nearly 1,000 civilians," most of whom were working in the United States.[16] Marguerite noted that the intelligence officers attached to the military mission in Germany were occupied with repatriation of prisoners of war, and so it fell to civilian agents to ascertain conditions in the streets and determine the strength of the warring factions. Sometimes her military leaders identified suspects she should monitor, including one woman thought to be a German agent trying to sway Allied opinion toward Germany. "I sat in her apartment night after night, emptying my wine into a jardinière behind me, laughing and joking and always on the alert to prevent her from drawing out her guests," Marguerite wrote.[17]

One account by New York *Sun* correspondent Thomas Johnson a decade after the war and reportedly based on interviews with unnamed intelligence officers, including Marguerite, describes the American spy network as a complicated labyrinth designed so "the left hand knoweth not what the right hand doeth." Johnson, who had covered the war, described forty teams of three to six agents working throughout Europe. They were selected based on their intelligence, self-control, and knowledge of the people and language in the territory where they operated. With the war ended, the teams in Germany focused on watching for factions that could overthrow the fragile Republic and reestablish the monarchy or align with the Bolsheviks.[18]

Johnson described Marguerite as the mysterious "Agent Q" or "Number 8," an agent so valued that her reports went directly to President Woodrow Wilson. While not naming her, the description of the agent as "a member of a well-known southern family, cultured, intellectual, attractive" who became a spy after her husband's death, was clearly Marguerite. "She was indefatigable. Here was what she had sought, occupation so engrossing, so exacting she had no time to grieve," Johnson recounted.[19]

Berlin in 1919 was a city of contrasts. During the cold, gray winter, the city's massive stone buildings loomed menacingly over the city. The armistice had unleashed powerful and competing forces that previously had been subdued during the fight against the Allies. Now, as President Wilson joined British prime minister David Lloyd George and French prime minister Georges Clemenceau in dividing the spoils of war, Germany devolved into political and social infighting. Food was strictly rationed and the poor were starving, forced to subsist on soup made from potato skins and bread made of sawdust. At the same time, wealthy Berliners dined on delicacies such as venison, oysters, and steak. A quarter million city residents were without work, but wives and daughters of war profiteers ordered gowns designed by a former French prisoner of war. Provocateurs from Turkey, Russia, Ireland, and India sought sympathy among the disaffected Germans.

But despite the hardships and political intrigues, life in some respects went on as normal. At the Kaiser Wilhelm Institute for Physics, professor Albert Einstein was looking forward to a solar eclipse on March 29 that would prove his general theory of relativity.[20] An aspiring concert violinist named Marlene Dietrich had recently graduated from high school and was trying to find work as a chorus girl. Music halls and cabarets were filled to overflowing as many Germans tried to forget their troubles with revelry and drunken orgies. Marguerite, raised in respectable Baltimore society, was appalled. "Love-making was brazen, the fun was coarse beyond description. It revealed to me a side of the German character I had never known, and I found it repulsive," she wrote.[21]

Marguerite wrote volumes of reports and discreetly left them in a hotel lobby for her supervisor, who relayed them to France where peace negotiations were under way. The pages, typed single space, were crammed with economic data, quotes from the people she interviewed, and her own observations. Upon learning that the Allies intended to punish Germany for its transgressions, she warned against punitive sanctions that could fuel radical elements within society.

True to her word, Marguerite refused to use sex to pry secrets from unsuspecting targets. "So far as possible, I made myself absolutely sexless and impersonal, partly as a measure of self-protection in an atmosphere fraught with dangers of this description and partly because I had a contempt for such tactics," she wrote. "I often used to smile when I compared my own life with that of the beautiful and baleful spies of popular fiction and the movies, who stole secret documents from drunken diplomats and officers after champagne suppers or cajoled their lovers into revealing state secrets."[22]

Time and again she recalled using "humor and a little tact" to escape from men who pursued her. One night, as she walked back to her hotel, a Prussian accosted her on the street, asking to walk her home.

"With pleasure," she answered.

He did not notice her American accent and did not inquire where she lived. He walked her through the Brandenburg Gate and down the street to her hotel, where Germans were not admitted.

"Here is where I live," she told him. "I was really rather nervous about that lonely walk through the Tiergarten and I want to thank you for your chivalry in succoring an alien enemy."[23]

On another occasion, a passenger on an overnight train pestered her and suggested they share a room when they reached Danzig. Marguerite had already made reservations at a hotel requisitioned by the Allied Military Commission, but she did not tell her amorous companion. Instead, when they arrived at the station, she asked him to carry her luggage—a suitcase, typewriter, bedding roll, and a hat box—to her hotel. The man excitedly agreed until they reached the hotel and the clerk barred him from entry. The stymied lover made the "air blue with his remarks," she recalled.[24]

Yet not all of her adventures were so amusing. Marguerite witnessed horrific street violence during her months in Berlin. In March Spartacists made one final stand, and again worker strikes were met with gunfire from government soldiers. On one occasion Marguerite was interviewing a shopkeeper on Dirksenstrasse when troops searching for insurgents fired into the crowd without warning. The violence lasted just a few minutes, but several were killed, including "a young girl whose head had literally been blown to pieces."[25]

Marguerite went back to the scene the next day after hearing that sailors had joined the Spartacists in the fight. She watched intently as insurgents tried to storm the police headquarters and saw snipers shooting from the roofs. A few feet away, a girl was killed by a stray bullet. "I was trembling with horror but a woman who stood next to me seemed quite unmoved," Marguerite wrote. "'Dreadful isn't it,' she said in much the tone she might have used if she had seen a dog run over. Then she went into a delicatessen shop and bought some sausage for supper!"[26]

Throughout the spring, Marguerite mailed articles to the *Baltimore Sun*, but because of the slow postal system, the pieces were not published until a month after she wrote them. She wanted her accounts to be informative and entertaining, yet she had to be careful not to divulge sensitive information. In the first article she described how rich Germans were hoarding and profiteering from American food aid. In the next she wrote a first-person account about what it was like to live on the official food ration. Much of the information she later retold in her autobiography, including how her maid, Johanna, had arranged for her to have lunch with her sister, a young mother of three, struggling to feed her family with a meager food allotment.[27]

In a second series Marguerite focused on political conditions as Germany attempted to form a new government in Weimar. She covered the first meeting of the National Assembly and noted the lingering nationalism in the provisional government.[28] Several of her articles hinted at anti-Bolshevik bias that her editors played up in headlines and introductions. She wrote an entire article based solely upon an anonymous man who described difficult conditions in Communist Bavaria. In the story's introduction the *Sun* editors noted the piece showed the "rottenness of Bolshevik pretensions."[29]

Her most riveting reports detailed the street battles she witnessed and call to mind Edward R. Murrow's radio dispatches in London a generation later. She wrote: "Today in the heart of Berlin, there is a devastated region almost as large as Verdun—a district where the inhabitants are spending days and nights of terror, sleeping in cellars, living from hand to mouth without water, light or heat, while their own countrymen are killing each other in the streets." Touring the wreckage, she stopped to talk to a young woman leaning against a light post. The woman told Marguerite that she had been unable to get milk for her four-month-old boy. "I am standing here because I cannot endure it in the house a minute longer," the woman said. "My baby has cried almost all the time since the day before yesterday, and now he is so weak he just whimpers."[30]

The carnage Marguerite witnessed began to take its toll on her. She had expected to be in Europe for just a few weeks, but as peace negotiations dragged on, her time in Berlin stretched into months. She was tired and lonely. "I longed for a woman friend—a real companion—someone with whom I could work as I had worked with Mary McCarty in Baltimore," she wrote. One day, she expressed this desire to George Young, a correspondent for the *London Daily News* who suggested that she get in touch with a British newspaperwoman, Stan Harding. "You are doing the same sort of work," he told her, although it is not clear what work he meant.[31]

Constance (Stan) Grace Lesslie Harding was born July 12, 1884, in Toronto, Canada, into a prosperous and religiously conservative merchant family.[32] Chafing at the restrictions placed upon her, Harding left home at age twenty and roamed throughout Europe and Asia, gravitating toward Socialist colonies and making a living as an artist. She spent a number of years in Italy, where she met and married a German surgeon, Karl Krayl.[33] One diarist called Harding a "courageous Englishwoman" who walked throughout Italy carrying a revolver for protection.[34] Marriage changed Harding little. She and Krayl maintained separate apartments, and Harding continued both her art career and her wanderings.[35] She had an apparently brief but intense affair with the artist Stephen Haweis, whose wife, poet Mina Loy, immortalized Harding in her poem "Lion's Jaw," describing the character Mrs. Krar Standing Hail as a self-righteous hypocrite.[36] Harding eventually turned to writing and in the fall of 1918 traveled to Berlin, where the struggles of the working class solidified her support of socialism.

Marguerite called on Harding, who was then thirty-four years old and living in a tiny room of a "cheap lodging house" that Marguerite described as "poorly furnished, under heated, and dreary beyond description." She said she took an instant liking to the British woman. "She was a frail-looking woman, with delicate features, hair close-clipped like a man's and the most engaging smile," she recalled.[37]

Harding told Marguerite she had been working for a London newspaper but had been abruptly fired, leaving her without means to support herself. Marguerite said she took pity on her, gave her food from the American Military Mission, and visited her every day.[38]

Over time, she learned that Harding was seeking to divorce her husband and had resumed using her maiden name. Harding also told her that she had a brother who was a British diplomat stationed in China. According to Marguerite, Harding visited her brother and gave information to British intelligence officers about what she had seen when she traveled up the Yangtze River. Marguerite said that during the last year of the war, Harding had entered the intelligence service and was sent to Germany to gather information before the armistice. She intended to work undercover as a journalist until the peace treaty was signed, then return to England and pursue a career in interior decorating.

Marguerite was captivated by Harding: "She appeared to me quite the most gallant and romantic woman I had ever met. I admired her courage and her sportsmanship, her keen mind and her independence of thought, although I did not share her apparent sympathy for the extreme radicals in Germany."[39] Soon Marguerite proposed that they share her room at the Adlon Hotel. Harding accepted the offer, and, Marguerite wrote, "it was not long before we became inseparable."

Harding's account of their relationship is vastly different, and she adamantly denied ever spying for the British service. Harding was a Socialist and counted among her friends Left-leaning radicals in Berlin. She alleged that Marguerite proposed that they share a hotel room so she could spy on her.[40] Because part of Marguerite's mission was indeed to monitor suspected Bolsheviks, Harding's accusation cannot be discounted. Marguerite's American connections had put her in touch with the monarchists, but she needed entre into the Leftist circles. Harding might well have provided that access.

But in April Harding discovered that Marguerite was working for the Military Intelligence Division. Marguerite had traveled to Prussia to gather information on the Polish and German communities because Allied negotiators, who were drawing country borders, needed to know the people's loyalties in the area. After making a reconnaissance, Marguerite rushed back to Berlin. In a hurry to reach Coblenz to give her report to Gen. Dennis Nolan, the head of intelligence for the American Expeditionary Forces, she tore up notes and threw the scraps in the wastebasket of her hotel room. It was a costly mistake.

When she returned to Berlin three days later, she found Stan Harding sitting complacently at her desk. She told Marguerite that she had found the pieces of paper in the trash and read them. Harding understood that these were not notes for a newspaper story, and she suggested that they work together. Realizing she had been compromised, Marguerite relayed the news to her supervisor, who agreed to pay Harding for tips. Despite what might be seen as blackmail, Marguerite could not bring herself to dislike Harding. "When I left Germany, I honestly regretted having to say good-bye to her," she wrote. "I hoped to see her again someday, when we had settled down into a humdrum, peaceful existence."[41] But they had learned too much about each other to ever be friends again.

The Versailles peace accords, signed on June 28, 1919, bitterly disappointed Marguerite. She perceived that the harsh terms imposed on Germany would sow seeds of discontent that would grow into uncontrolled nationalism and anti-Semitism. The victors had abandoned Wilson's Fourteen Points, his plan for a just peace, and instead insisted on punishing Germany for its aggression. Marguerite lamented what she believed was the nonsensical creation of new countries and the forced reparations that would burden Germany for generations. She understood that the country's humiliation would foster the rise of extremists who would blame Jews for the country's troubles. Before she left Berlin, she saw a crowd storm a Jewish-owned business and beat a clerk senseless, and she knew this was just the beginning. "The gradual disillusionment with regard to the peace was slowly changing the average German from a sane, well-disciplined, sentimental, unimaginative person into a bitter, neurotic and excitable creature, easily swayed by this movement or that," she wrote.[42] Yet America was turning its attention away from Germany to a new threat: Bolshevism.

Workers in the United States were joining labor unions and demanding better conditions. A few politicians were campaigning on Socialist platforms. U.S. military commanders worried that the homesick troops were becoming susceptible to Communist propaganda. Their alarm grew when they discovered subversive pamphlets circulating among American soldiers stationed in Germany. The Army wanted Marguerite's help in catching those responsible.

When suspicion fell on journalist Robert Minor, authorities arrested him in Paris. The details of Marguerite's role in his arrest are not entirely clear. Van Deman wrote that Marguerite was dispatched to Germany in January 1919 to catch Minor. Marguerite, however, provided a different version of her involvement. According to her memoir, which largely agrees with the official account she provided to her superiors at the Military Intelligence Division, she was preparing to return to the United States in July 1919 when Nolan asked her to return to Germany to secure evidence against Minor. Authorities had arrested him but lacked proof to prosecute him. Marguerite knew Minor, having met him several times and listened to him talk candidly about his Communist sympathies. She agreed to go to Dusseldorf posing as a Socialist and gather the evidence. She interviewed local Communists who verified that Minor was a party member and located the printer who had produced Minor's pamphlets. Armed with this information, she returned to Coblenz.[43] In her memoir Marguerite wrote that she hated carrying out the mission because it forced her to pose as a Socialist. Although she had collected Army intelligence while writing for the *Baltimore Sun*, for her, it had been a point of pride that she had avoided outright lying about work. "I was rather sick at heart over the role I had been forced to play," she said.[44]

Minor never went to trial, however. He was the son of a prominent Texas judge and well regarded among American Socialists, including muckraking journalist Lincoln Steffens, who confronted Van Deman over Minor's arrest. Intelligence officials wanted him prosecuted, but the uproar over his incarceration forced the United States to release him. Minor returned to America where he later worked as a journalist, cartoonist, and an active member of the Communist Party of America, running several times for Congress on the Worker's Party ticket.[45]

In her memoir Marguerite expressed relief that Minor was released. "I have always been devoutly thankful that I and not Bob Minor was the one who suffered most from the consequences of his arrest," she wrote. Hinting that her later imprisonment was related to her role in the Minor investigation, she added, "I paid dearly for my part in the affair." With the Minor incident concluded and the peace treaty signed, Marguerite looked forward to returning home. She was exhausted and disheartened. "I felt that I had accomplished nothing constructive," she wrote.[46]

But even before she left Germany, commanders in the Military Intelligence Division were planning her next assignment. Col. Edward Davis, who ran a successful spy ring from The Hague, wanted her to work from Berlin as the chief agent in charge of contiguous countries. "By moving about in that fashion, she can take care of the outside of the spider web while other people nearer Berlin can take care of the center of the web," he wrote to Churchill. Davis had heard that Van Deman wanted to send Marguerite to Japan, but the colonel thought that foolish. "'White folks' can't get very far in Japan," he argued.[47] Another idea was to dispatch Marguerite to Mexico, but Davis thought that would be a waste of a good agent. "It seems to me that whenever it comes to a choice as to missions for capable agents, Germany ought to be their field in preference to Mexico," he wrote.[48]

The matter was still not settled when Marguerite returned to Baltimore. She was happy to be back home with her family and friends. Tommy had turned seventeen while she was away, although in her memoir she wrote of the joy of being with "my little son." She returned to the *Baltimore Sun* and renewed her friendship with Mary McCarty. Because of her Berlin news stories, the city treated Marguerite as celebrity, and women's clubs asked her to speak about her experiences.

Her father's estate was not yet settled, but she had enough money. Her servants had kept the boarding house running smoothly while she was away, and her home was full of lodgers. Her editors at the *Baltimore Sun* were delighted to have her back and immediately assigned her to write about her adventures in Europe. The newspaper promoted her stories as accounts from the "first American woman to enter Germany since the declaration of war in 1914 and one of the few Americans who succeeded in getting to Berlin since the armistice."[49] Her articles included accounts of a Baltimore woman married to a German, of rising anti-Semitism in Poland, and of German efforts to retake parts of its lost territory. Although still writing theater and music reviews, Marguerite also received plum feature assignments. The *Sun* sent her to New York to cover the arrival of Belgian cardinal Désiré-Félicien-François-Joseph Mercier, and Marguerite snagged an exclusive interview with the church leader because no other journalist covering the event spoke French.[50]

But after just a few weeks at home, Marguerite grew restless. Theater reviews and society gossip no longer interested her. Events that she would have thought important a year ago now seemed boring. "What interest could I take in a State Democratic Convention after having seen the adoption of the Weimar Constitution? What thrill was there in a front page murder to anyone who had seen wholesale murder in the streets of Berlin?" she wrote. Even Albert Ritchie's campaign for governor that fall held little interest. During her months away, she had grown distant from her friends and family, and even her son. "I was still unable, as I had been ever since my husband's death, to lead an existence that was entirely personal," she wrote. "I still felt afraid to form close ties. I did not even want to love my little son too much and I dared not risk being made to suffer again by an unexpected blow, such as I had experienced at the time of my husband's death."[51]

Not only had Marguerite changed, but so had the United States. Americans no longer cared about promoting democracy around the world. Instead, debates raged over Prohibition and immigration. The American Protective League turned from finding German spies to pursuing anarchists and Bolsheviks. Millions joined the resurgent Ku Klux Klan, including several thousand in Maryland. Marguerite was disgusted by the hypocrisy she saw. Profiteers bragged about winning the war, but returning soldiers could not find work. Wilson, whom she had admired immensely, returned from the peace conference defeated. The great vision for an international organization to settle disputes and promote peace around the world withered when the U.S. Congress refused to join the League of Nations. Marguerite, the international adventurer, could not endure it.[52]

Soon after she returned to Baltimore, she met with Marlborough Churchill to discuss her next assignment. He was pleased with her work in Germany, and she was eager to return to the field, but she wanted more money. Marlborough initially wrote to Davis to tell him that he had decided to send Marguerite back to Germany, provided they could agree on her salary. Davis was so thrilled that he drafted a telegram agreeing to pay her $400 a month for six months. Yet a month later the plans inexplicably changed. Churchill settled on paying her $150 a month, plus $250 a month to cover her expenses for six months. Marguerite was given a cipher book and assigned a code name: "B."

She also had a new mission. Instead of sending her to Berlin, Churchill was dispatching her to Russia.[53]

AGENT B

AMERICA'S RUSSIAN SPY NETWORK was in a shambles in the autumn of 1919. The head of its Moscow cell, Xenophon Kalamatiano, was in prison after being caught the year before in a plot to overthrow the Bolshevik government. The chief of the Petrograd ring, Vice Consul Robert W. Imbrie, had fled to Finland after the Bolshevik Revolution, but several of his accomplices had been captured over the summer trying to aid the White Army as it prepared to storm Petrograd.

Almost two years had passed since the Bolsheviks had seized power, and yet the United States still had no coherent Russia policy. On the one hand, President Wilson advocated the right of countries to choose their own forms of government. Yet he and many of his advisers detested Communism and secretly aided anti-Bolshevik efforts to oust Vladimir Lenin.[1]

America desperately needed intelligence to guide its decisions. So Marlborough Churchill sent Marguerite, one of his best agents, to Russia to obtain it.

The challenge was enormous. Unlike the German assignment, this time Marguerite did not know the language and could not pass as a local resident. Her mission in Russia depended entirely on her being able to convince the Reds that she was merely a journalist who wanted to tell American readers about the grand Bolshevik experiment. But the Russians were alert to this ruse. Several British agents had posed as newspaper correspondents, and Kalamatiano had claimed to run an information service gathering economic data—until Cheka police found a list of ciphers, agents, and military positions hidden in his cane.[2]

Marguerite, nevertheless, was eager for the assignment. Russia had captured her imagination since 1900, when she saw the country's exhibit at the World

Exposition in Paris. Mimicking a ride on the Trans-Siberian Railroad, the display introduced passengers to the golden-domed churches of St. Petersburg, the Kremlin fortress of Moscow, the snow-capped Ural Mountains, the steppes of Siberia, the pine forests surrounding Lake Baikal, and the Pacific Coast city of Vladivostok. She begged her parents to take her to Russia, but the Bakers thought it was too far and obtaining the compulsory passport too much bother.[3]

The overthrow of Czar Nicholas II in March 1917 reignited Marguerite's interest in Russia. She supported the revolution, but then she heard stories from Baltimoreans who visited the country that the Alexander Kerensky provisional government was losing control. A new movement, based on the teachings of Karl Marx and led by Vladimir Lenin and Leon Trotsky, was gathering support, they said. Then, in November 1917, the Bolsheviks seized power. Marguerite devoured John Reed's accounts of the revolution and his most famous work, *Ten Days That Shook the World*. As she contemplated the upheavals brought about by World War I and the unsatisfactory settlement of the Treaty of Versailles, Marguerite grew increasingly curious about Bolshevism. Imperialism and militarism had failed, and growing unrest in America made her wonder if democracy might be doomed as well. Could Russia have found the answer to governing? "I foresaw that my generation would live through an era of change and experiment. Bolshevism was one of these experiments, and I wanted to see it in operation," she recalled.[4]

Reliable information on Russia was scarce. Its vastness and complexity had always made it a difficult country for journalists to cover. After the fall of the czar and the eruption of civil war, the mysteries of the country deepened. Few reporters made it inside, but the ones who did included some intrepid women. *New York Mail* reporter Rheta Childe Dorr attached herself to a regiment of female soldiers in Petrograd and witnessed clashes between government soldiers and the Bolsheviks until she left in September 1917.[5] Peggy Hull, who had covered U.S. troops in France, accompanied the American Expeditionary Forces to Siberia in 1918. But as the Bolsheviks solidified their control, they carefully screened foreign journalists. They expelled Associated Press correspondents in late 1918 and refused entry to journalists from "bourgeois" newspapers, thus making it difficult for Western readers to get impartial news of the country.[6]

The American government was in the dark as well, even as the Wilson administration debated whether to recognize the Bolshevik government. The president had dispatched nine thousand American troops to Siberia to aid Czechoslovakian prisoners stranded when Russia withdrew from World War I. But as the White Army assembled in Siberia to make a final stand against the Bolsheviks, the United States was pressed to decide whether to remain neutral or join the fight. The situation was so confusing that the Military Intelligence Division (MID) supplied the American Expeditionary Forces with handbooks on Russia that included blank pages for the officers to record their own observations. No one bothered to collect the books.[7]

Marguerite's mission to Russia was complicated by uncertainties plaguing MID. With the war ended, U.S. leaders questioned the need for a military organization charged with espionage. Army troops no longer faced the threat of subversive German propaganda, and many opposed giving the military the authority to spy on Americans at home. After weighing these concerns, Secretary of War Newton Baker decided the Army would no longer play a role in domestic spying, ceding the job to U.S. Attorney General Mitchell Palmer. MID was left with a narrow mission of code breaking and foreign espionage, and even the latter was phased out by 1921. MID's ranks dropped from 1,159 military and civilian employees in 1918 to just 234 in 1920, most of whom were investigating graft and fraud cases.[8]

With its reduced resources, MID turned its attention to the threat of Bolshevism and rising labor unrest that was made worse by the failure of the United States to ease the transformation from a wartime to peacetime economy. Food prices skyrocketed and wages fell. The Army released millions of young men with just sixty dollars in their pockets. As veterans struggled to find jobs, thousands of factory workers went on strike to maintain the salaries and benefits they had won during the war. Labor violence erupted, and federal troops were sent to restore peace in West Virginia and Boston, Massachusetts. With the rising tensions, the War Department drafted plans to deploy U.S. soldiers in the event of insurrection.[9]

Even though the war was over, the Sedition Act and similar measures remained in effect. One law, passed in 1918, specified that aliens who advocated anarchy or the violent overthrow of the government could be deported. Some U.S. officials advocated a "ship or shoot policy" toward suspicious immigrants. Mobs attacked Socialists during May Day parades, and the American Protective League turned from hunting German saboteurs to searching for suspected anarchists, Socialists, and Communists. In Chicago a sailor argued with a man who refused to stand for the national anthem. After the man brandished a gun and ran, the soldier shot him in the back, critically wounding him. The crowd applauded.[10] Even Nellie Bly, back from Austria where she had fled to escape debt collectors, professed that the United States "was nearest and dearest to her heart" and offered to spy for MID to save the country from Bolshevism. Marlborough Churchill told his men that her proposition "should not be taken seriously."[11]

Yet the press and public demanded that the government take action in spring 1919 after anarchists planted bombs aimed at government officials and business leaders, including John D. Rockefeller. At first, Attorney General Palmer, a level-headed Quaker and Wilsonian Progressive with presidential ambitions, remained calm. He had recognized the excesses of the American Protective League and insisted that the government regain control over domestic surveillance. Early in his tenure, he had secured presidential pardons for about half of those imprisoned for violating the Espionage Act.

But on June 2, 1919, anarchists struck again. Bombs killed a New York security guard, blew up a Philadelphia church, and destroyed the home of a Boston judge. That night Palmer heard a noise outside his home in Washington, D.C., and stepped outside to investigate. Suddenly, an explosion shook his house. The gruesome remains of the bomber were scattered in Palmer's yard, along with pamphlets calling for the proletariat to overthrow the government. Palmer was unhurt, but his patience had run out. With the aid of a large congressional appropriation, he launched a campaign to rid the country of radicals. One of his first steps was to create an intelligence agency within the U.S. Department of Justice's Bureau of Investigation devoted exclusively to fighting domestic terrorism. He selected as its head a young and organized file clerk, J. Edgar Hoover.[12]

Churchill, too, was concerned about Bolshevism's threat. Although MID no longer was authorized to spy in America, he shared the division's intelligence files with agents from the Justice Department, and sometimes MID questioned suspects. Both agencies stepped up their work against Bolsheviks and anarchists in late 1919. Justice Department agents rounded up immigrants suspected of subversive activities, and in early December loaded 249 detainees, including anarchists Emma Goldman and Alexander Berkman, on a ship to Finland.

Meanwhile, Churchill directed his reduced forces against Bolshevism overseas. He wanted Marguerite to travel to Russia to gather intelligence about the enemy and try to determine what had become of imprisoned Americans, including U.S. agents. As he had before, *Baltimore Sun* managing editor Kent furnished Marguerite with credentials that allowed her to pose as a correspondent. She also secured assignments from the *New York Evening Post* and Underwood News Photo Service, which provided an excuse for Marguerite to carry a camera. Additionally, Churchill arranged for her to meet Robert M. Collins, the Associated Press's London bureau chief, who would give her letters affirming she was a wire-service correspondent.

Marguerite later claimed they all were naïve in failing to recognize the danger of her assignment. "None of us, not even General Churchill, imagined that any worse fate could befall me than expulsion as an undesirable alien," she wrote. "My functions were to be purely those of an observer. I was not to meddle in Russia's internal politics, I was simply to study conditions and report them fairly and impartially. It never occurred to us that technically I would be considered guilty of espionage if I were found out."[13]

But such claims in face of the reality are incredible. She and Churchill knew very well the risks. At least thirty Americans were being detained in Russia and several American intelligence officers had been sentenced to death at the time they planned her mission.

Yet despite the danger, Marguerite decided to take Tommy with her to Europe and enroll him in a Swiss boarding school while she journeyed on to Russia. "I felt that a year at school abroad would help him with his languages and give him a cosmopolitan outlook," she explained. "Besides I wanted to have him near me. We had been separated for nine months and I did not want to leave him in the United States."[14]

Ever since Tom's death, Marguerite had struggled to balance the responsibilities of being a single mother with her insatiable desire for work and adventure. "Whenever I found myself loving Tommy too much I repressed the feeling remorselessly," she recalled.[15] Work consoled her and validated her in a way motherhood could not, a fact she recognized and often lamented. Repeatedly, she told herself she was an unfit mother and resolved to spend more time with her son, only to again accept another assignment away from him. Taking Tommy to Switzerland for a time eased her conscience. They could enjoy the voyage together and maybe visit Italy when she returned from Russia, she told herself. She did not perceive the selfishness of her actions.

While Marguerite had been in Germany, Tommy had become a stand-out athlete like his father. He was captain of the Gilman football team, and the school's 1919 yearbook praised his "fighting play and spirit." He also served on Gilman's War Activities Board, ran on the relay team, played on the soccer squad and was a member of the school's Christian association.[16] Tommy's daughter, Nancy Harrison, says her father resented Marguerite for taking him out of school his senior year. He had hoped to go to Princeton, but he never graduated from high school. "She was very selfish," Nancy Harrison said of her grandmother.[17]

Oblivious to her son's sacrifices, she proceeded with plans to enter Russia. The United States did not have diplomatic relations with the country, so she applied to Russia's unofficial representative in New York, Ludwig Martens, who arranged commercial agreements between the two nations. Martens, however, refused her request for a visa. The Soviets were admitting only journalists who worked for Socialist newspapers, he told her. His decision eliminated the option of official travel through the Baltics. Undeterred, Marguerite decided to attempt entry into Russia from Poland, even though the two countries were at war. She believed that if somehow she could enter Russia, she could persuade the Bolsheviks to let her to stay.

Her new assignment began in October 1919, even before she and Tommy departed America. While making travel arrangements in New York, she met several suspected Bolsheviks. If she had reluctantly posed as a Socialist in Germany, she appeared now to have no qualms about pretending to be sympathetic to Communism in order to win suspects' trust. She continued the ruse during the voyage to London on board the White Star Line's RMS *Adriatic*. En route, she encountered Julius F. Hecker, a Russian American YMCA worker who lived in Lausanne, Switzerland. He told her that he had been in the United States for two months giving lectures and "introducing Soviet propaganda." He said he had been especially successful in distributing pamphlets at theological institutions, including Union Theological Seminary in New York. Marguerite sought to win his trust by pretending she also was a Bolshevik and asking him for tips on how she could distribute propaganda when she returned to the United States. She even asked Hecker to help look after Tommy while he was in Lausanne.[18]

In London she moved quickly to establish connections with the Associated Press. It is not clear why Marguerite needed the AP credentials given that she already had verification from the *Baltimore Sun* and the *New York Evening Post* that she was a legitimate journalist. Nevertheless, bureau chief Collins agreed to write a letter documenting that he would pay her fifty dollars a week if she succeeded in getting news from Russia. He ended his letter: "Wishing you all success, and an interesting and valuable experience."[19]

From London she and Tommy proceeded to Switzerland. Marguerite had arranged for Tommy to study in Lausanne at Lavilla School, which billed itself as "a school for gentlemen's sons."[20] The situation in Switzerland was bleak. Most of the boarding schools had closed during the war and the tourists had fled. Large hotels and ski resorts were shuttered, and the souvenir shops had vanished. Of the people who remained, many were refugees, government officials, and spies.

In Berne she gave American military attaché Col. W. F. Godson the information she had gleaned from her meetings in New York and with Hecker on the *Adriatic*. Godson likely ordered Marguerite to meet Hecker again in Lausanne to gather more evidence against him. In any case, the State Department, acting on the information she provided, detained Hecker in Switzerland, revoked his passport, and sent him back to the United States for questioning.

Mata Hari's French handler, Georges Ladoux, once warned his spy that espionage was "a game involving luck and betting against the odds."[21] Marguerite did not yet know it, but when she filed the report on Hecker, she had drawn a losing card.

That realization was still several months away. In the meantime, Marguerite sent news dispatches to Baltimore, solidifying her cover as a foreign correspondent. From England she wrote an article for the Baltimore *Evening Sun* about Lady Nancy Astor's successful campaign for her husband's seat in the House of Commons. She wrote three stories from Switzerland: an account from an anonymous banker predicting France would rebound more quickly from the war than other countries; an interview with exiled Greek king, Constantine; and a piece on a German prince expecting to visit New York.[22]

In less than a week, she departed Switzerland on the diplomatic train. She told herself her son was happy in his new school and refused to believe otherwise. She also would not contemplate the possible dangers that lay ahead. "When I said good-bye to Tommy, I told him cheerily that I might be back in time for the Easter holidays." She would not see him again for almost two years.[23]

As she traveled to Poland, Marguerite continued to lay a trail of newspaper stories. When her trained stopped in Vienna for two hours, she disembarked and interviewed an unidentified girl standing on a street corner and a businessman at a café. From that lean reporting, she wrote an article about starvation in Vienna that the *Sun* published on its front page. And in case anyone doubted Marguerite's itinerary, she noted in the article she was on her way to Warsaw.[24]

Marguerite was thrilled to enter Poland, a country that had been reborn in the aftermath of war from parts of Russia, Austria, and Germany, but her first impression of Warsaw was "cold, dirt, patriotism." She recalled, "Everything was a dirty gray—snow, streets, houses and sky, and all objects, animate and inanimate alike, looked as if they needed a good scrubbing." Russians had occupied Warsaw for decades, but now the people reveled in their new independence. The Russian double-headed eagles carved on buildings and monuments had been decapitated, and pedestals that once bore statues of Russian czars and generals were bare.[25]

Marguerite had not expected to stay in Poland for long. But when she contacted the military attaché in Warsaw, she received word from Churchill that she should delay her entry into Russia. The Soviets were cracking down on suspected interlopers, and he felt it best for her to wait until the situation quieted down.

She used the interruption to study Russian, add to her compilation of stories, and figure out how she would cross the border once Churchill gave permission to proceed. Two days after arriving in Warsaw, she wrote about Baltimoreans working in the city, including an engineer who was assisting the Polish government with housing refugees and a woman Marguerite described as a cousin who was working with the Young Women's Christian Association overseeing twenty Polish American girls volunteering in hospitals and nurseries.[26] In another piece, published a day later, she wrote about a Polish count who was the son-in-law of former Maryland governor Edwin Warfield. The nobleman described Bolshevik atrocities in Poland, including the murders of his father and uncles.[27]

Conditions were harsh in Poland that winter. Five years of war had left Warsaw in shambles. Poland, which had emerged from the remnants of three empires, struggled to gain a foothold in the new European order. But Lenin calculated that Poland provided the best means to expand the Communist experiment to the west. Border skirmishes gave way to full-fledged war of ideologies. The winter of 1919–20 was unseasonably cold, and many Warsaw houses lacked fuel. Basic items such as food, clothing, and blankets were scarce, and prices were exorbitant for what little there was. In the poorer sections of the city Marguerite often saw funeral processions behind the tiny coffins of children who had died of hunger and disease.

Refugees from the east flooded into Warsaw, making it difficult to find lodging. Marguerite paid a bribe to obtain an unheated "small, dark, dingy and dirty" room in the Hotel Bristol. Despite the primitive conditions, the hotel afforded her the opportunity to meet foreigners and Polish leaders, including the former prime minister and his wife who were staying there.[28]

She remained in Poland six weeks, writing articles for the *Baltimore Sun* and compiling reports for MID, even though collecting intelligence risked exposing her to an extensive network of Bolshevik spies. She observed several sessions of the Polish diet, the country's assembly, where factions argued and tried in vain to find a way to address the economic problems. She monitored Russian propaganda flowing into the country and interviewed numerous government officials, including Chief of State Józef Piłsudski, the commander of the Polish army, whose single-minded focus was to secure Polish freedom from Bolshevik control. In Warsaw, as in Berlin, political intrigues spawned campaigns of information and misinformation. In one MID report Marguerite conveyed the views of an unnamed "Russophile" who favored immediate peace with Russia and provided statistics on the misery of unemployment, disease, and hunger.[29]

As Marguerite awaited orders to proceed to Russia, Colonel Godson in Berne complained of staff reductions and asked Churchill to send her back to work with him in Switzerland. Although she had only been in Switzerland a week, she had provided valuable information on Hecker and John De Kay, a meatpacking magnate whom MID suspected of Communist sympathies. "If the prohibition against the intended trip is to be in force for any length of time I earnestly request the person referred to be directed to return here for the purpose of continuing the already excellent work begun," Godson wrote, adding "Switzerland is to be found a center of intrigue, which menaces the United States as well as France and Italy."[30]

Churchill responded six weeks later, noting "the agent referred to was sent to Europe on a special mission and for a special purpose." He said that if the agent "visits Switzerland in the future, you are at liberty to make a further recommendation and if possible your request will be approved." Surprisingly, Churchill wrote that the delay in sending Harrison into Russia was only "a week or so," but Marguerite was still in Poland when he replied.[31]

In late December Marguerite sent a cryptic letter to MID that began, "Dear Friend, I have been in Warsaw nearly four weeks and have at last perfected my plan for going further." Yet the message did not elaborate on the plan and for unknown reasons she remained another month in Poland.[32]

Meanwhile, the winter holidays were approaching, and Marguerite socialized frequently with Americans from the aid missions working in Warsaw. At a Red Cross dance shortly before Christmas, a nurse introduced Marguerite to a young aviator in a Polish officer's uniform. "This is Captain Cooper," the nurse said. "He wants to meet you because you are fellow Southerners."[33]

Merian C. Cooper had grown up in Jacksonville, Florida, and served as a pilot with the U.S. Army Air Service in France. He was only twenty-six, but already had experienced a life's share of adventures. He had won acceptance to the U.S. Naval Academy but was expelled during his senior year for misconduct. He had worked briefly for several Midwestern newspapers and then served with General Pershing pursuing Pancho Villa in Mexico. During World War I, he flew bombers over France until the Germans shot down his plane and took him prisoner. With the war's end, he ventured to Poland to help with food aid. But that work was too tame for the adventurer. He went to Paris, recruited other former American pilots, and formed a bombing squadron to help Poland fight Russia.

Although Marguerite was fifteen years older than Cooper, the two hit it off immediately. They had mutual acquaintances and, even more important, a love for danger and excitement. The day after they met Cooper returned to his squadron, but they later would share many adventures. "Curious the tricks that Fate has up her sleeve when we least suspect them!" Marguerite wrote.[34]

For the second time in two years, she spent Christmas away from her family. She celebrated with her cousin and other women with the YWCA in a cottage on the outskirts of Warsaw. Along with Polish officers and American men from the aid societies, they feasted on goose, sang carols around a Christmas tree lighted with candles, and danced late into the evening. But on her way back to her hotel, she saw a group of children caroling in the street, and she suddenly thought of Tommy, who was spending his first Christmas away from home. She felt a pang of loneliness, but her mood brightened when, ten days later, she received a letter from her son saying he enjoyed the holiday skiing and bobsledding with his friends. With her conscience eased, she set about fulfilling her mission.[35]

INTO RUSSIA

MARGUERITE WAS BECOMING hardened to misery. Shortly after Christmas, she ventured to Bialystok, one hundred miles north of Warsaw. Germans had plundered the town when they evacuated, leaving the residents, who were mainly Jews, with few provisions. Near the town she saw a prison where the inmates were wracked by hunger and disease. Corpses lay in bunks until they could be collected in wheelbarrows. She had never seen so much suffering. "The sight of so much human misery made be physically ill," she wrote. Yet, a few hours later, she thought no more about the unfortunate prisoners. "I recovered my equanimity sufficiently to don my one party frock for the New Year's dinner," she wrote. "It was a relief to sit at table surrounded by a lot of wholesome-looking, clear-eyed young Americans, who talked about their home folks, laughed, sang and told stories."[1]

Yet while Marguerite shared fond memories of home, agents from the U.S. Justice and Labor departments were making final preparations for actions that would strike at the heart of America's freedoms. On January 2 government agents descended on the meeting halls, pool parlors, clubs, and restaurants in thirty-three cities around the country. They rounded up suspected radicals and confiscated books, photos, and papers, sometimes without warrants. More than four thousand were arrested and jailed that day. Some would be held for weeks in abominable conditions without formal charges. Eight hundred men were held incommunicado for ten days in Detroit, confined to a space with one toilet and a single water fountain. In Boston crowds jeered and taunted four hundred detainees who were paraded through the streets. In Hartford, Connecticut, authorities took the additional precaution of arresting those who visited the captured.[2]

America was wrestling with its identity. The rights to speak and assemble freely clashed with beliefs in patriotism and free enterprise.

In many ways Marguerite embodied the nation's struggle. For a year she had posed as a journalist pretending to write objective, truthful accounts of life in postwar Europe while gathering intelligence on suspected Socialists and Communists. As she was finding personal liberation through her adventures as a foreign agent, she was helping to arrest those whose views challenged American orthodoxy. These incongruities between her work and her ideals would never be completely resolved. The tensions, in fact, were about to get worse.

Near the end of January Marguerite was finally ready to enter Russia. Although she had been studying Russian since before she left the United States, she was not proficient enough to attempt travel without a translator. Fortuitously, she met a Russian Jew who had lived for a time in Chicago. The woman, Dr. Anna Karlin, had returned to Russia to work as a physician in the Red Army, but she was captured by the Poles. Claiming American citizenship, Karlin was allowed to go to Warsaw, but she was unable to obtain a U.S. passport to return to America. Karlin was stranded without a country when Marguerite saw her in the waiting room of the American consulate. Marguerite described the doctor as "a funny little soul, fat and dumpy, with a ruddy complexion, blue eyes that seemed to express perpetual astonishment and a head covered with tight reddish curls." Marguerite asked her to accompany her to Russia as her interpreter. "She was so simple and straightforward that she never suspected me of being anything but a newspaper correspondent," Marguerite wrote. Withholding the truth protected them both. The doctor would not divulge Marguerite's true mission, and, if Marguerite were caught, Karlin might be spared.[3]

Marguerite decided to cross the border near Minsk, a city on the front line where Poles and Bolsheviks had established an uneasy peace to allow for the exchange of war prisoners. Contraband flourished in the region, and Marguerite hoped she would be able to persuade military authorities to allow her to accompany traders into Russia. When she and Karlin left Warsaw on a cold January morning, only a few people knew her about plan. Her baggage consisted of her typewriter, an Army bedding role, several pairs of shoes, felt boots, towels, a collapsible rubber washbasin, and a half dozen cartons of cigarettes. She packed toiletries and chocolate in a bag slung over her shoulder and carried one suitcase packed with underwear, blouses, a tailored suit, a felt hat, and a dinner dress. She wore a fur coat that fell to her heels and a fur cap and fur-lined gloves.

In Minsk ravages of the war were everywhere. Shops were empty; streets and sidewalks were rutted. Her dilapidated hotel room had no hot water and no towels. The door had no knob or lock, so she propped a chair against it at night. She continued to mail articles back to the *Baltimore Sun*. While the stories did not appear until a month later and were not printed in the order she wrote them, they nevertheless clearly laid out her travels as she edged closer to the Russian border. In Vilna she interviewed an instructor of the Polish Women's Voluntary Legion, a fighting force that helped battle the Bolsheviks. Marguerite called the woman a modern Joan of Arc and lauded her heroism, which included capturing a machine gun with a bayonet charge when she was seven months pregnant.[4] She wrote about Polish prisoners who had been exchanged at the border, noting with surprise that some were wearing furs and jewels and had been treated well by their Bolshevik captors. And her last article from Poland, written just days before she crossed the border, described in detail the number and position of Polish soldiers camped in Barysaw awaiting the spring offensive.[5]

Because of her knowledge of the troops, Marguerite had trouble persuading Polish military leaders to let her cross the border. The general in charge of the sector refused to provide her safe conduct through the lines, telling her the risk of being shot was too great. Even if she somehow survived, she knew too much about the size and position of his troops, he said.

Marguerite believed that attempting to enter Russia at another location along the battle lines would be even more dangerous, so she left Karlin in Minsk and traveled to Vilna to appeal to the commander of all the forces on the Russian front to let her through the lines. On that overnight trip, Marguerite awoke in her hotel room to the sound of someone trying to open the lock on her door. She switched on the light and the door opened. Standing at the threshold was a drunk Polish officer she had met earlier that day. Marguerite showed no fear. "What do you want?" she asked him sternly.

"Come to tell you all about the dance," the soldier mumbled.

Marguerite softened her tone. "Go back to your room and go to sleep. You can tell me about it in the morning."

The drunk lurched toward her. She jumped out of bed and pretended to reach for her dressing gown. Instead, she turned suddenly and grabbed him by the shoulders and pushed him out the door with all her strength. He fell with a thud. She closed the door and locked it securely. In a few minutes, she heard someone dragging the man away.[6]

When she returned to Minsk the next day, she discovered that Karlin had found contrabanders willing to take the two to Barysaw. There Marguerite showed a commander the permit she had received from the general in Vilna. A Polish officer escorted Marguerite and Karlin to a log dugout camouflaged with evergreens. Inside, a surly intelligence officer advised them to turn back. He related stories of Bolshevik atrocities and predicted she would be shot if she continued. Marguerite insisted on going forward. At last he relented and led the two women through a maze of barbed wire until they emerged from the woods on the edge of no man's land. In front of them stood a few houses where the officer told Marguerite she would be able to find a sleigh to take them to the next village. In a short while a bearded peasant brought them a broken-down sleigh pulled by an emaciated horse. The women felt so sorry for the horse that they piled their bags into the sleigh and trudged on foot through the snow to the village. The peasant left them at a school where a teacher welcomed them inside. Then they could only wait for the Red Army patrol.[7]

On February 7, 1920, Lt. Col. E. E. Farman, the military attaché in Warsaw, sent a coded message to Marlborough Churchill. "From the information we received today we are informed that 'B' crossed the Polish frontier for Russia on February 6, 1920."[8] Marguerite actually crossed the border a few days later, but the inaccuracy indicates how far she was from help, should she need it. She was on her own except for her interpreter, who gamely went along with the adventure like Sancho Panza following Don Quixote.

After about an hour waiting at the school, the Red soldiers arrived. In halting Russian, Marguerite explained that she was a foreign correspondent who wanted to tell American readers the truth about the Soviet government and that she wished to go to Moscow. The young commissar in charge of the patrol was taken aback by the two women. He telephoned his superior and received orders to send Marguerite to the next town about ten miles away. The commander at the company headquarters was suspicious, but Marguerite's confidence grew. She doubted that the soldiers would shoot her because she provided an interesting distraction from their lonely and dull life on the frontier.

Her instincts proved correct. The soldiers and peasants she met were pleased to tell her about their lives, share their meals, show their schools and hospitals, and teach her stories and songs. The soldiers continued to refer her up the chain of command, and so she made her way slowly toward Moscow. From the company headquarters, she moved to the regimental headquarters and then to the brigade headquarters at Krupki, where she and Karlin stayed for nearly a week. Despite their suspicions, the commanders continued to answer her questions and show her their facilities, including a school where Red Army soldiers learned to read by memorizing phrases of Communist propaganda such as *"Mui ne rabui—mui radi"*—"We are not slaves, we are glad."

Eventually the women received permission to continue to the division head-quarters at Vitebsk, where officials telegrammed Moscow. Marguerite and Karlin lumbered along in a box car for three days, eating blini and canned meats and getting out to stroll through villages when the train stopped. Upon reaching Vitebsk they received permission to continue on to Moscow, and, at last, on February 21, they arrived at Alexandrovsky Station northwest of the city.

Disembarking from the train, Marguerite considered her options. It was impossible for her take up residence in Moscow unnoticed. The Bolsheviks had nationalized the restaurants and hotels, so she could not rent a room or even order a meal without credentials. Her only choice was to telephone the Foreign Office and announce her arrival.[9]

In a half-hour a small, stooped man appeared in the station waiting room. Immediately, he approached Marguerite and in excellent English asked her, "Will you be good enough to tell me how you got to Moscow?"

Marguerite explained that she was a newspaper correspondent who had come from Poland with help from the Red Army. He was obviously displeased. "Do you know that you have done a dangerous and absolutely illegal thing in coming to Moscow without permission?" he told her.

She pointed out that she had not entered the country surreptitiously and that the army officials could have stopped her.

"I realize that," he answered. "You are not entirely to blame. Those who were responsible for your entry into the country will be held to account. But I warned you that you have rendered yourself liable to immediate deportation—if not something worse."

He led them to a small room, closed the door, and demanded to see their papers. Marguerite pulled out her newspaper credentials and the letters of intro-duction she carried. The representative from the Foreign Office told her that the Bolshevik leaders had already refused petitions from the Associated Press and the *New York Evening Post*. Her entry was a flagrant violation of their decision.[10]

The Bolsheviks had good reason to keep out the foreign press. They were fighting to retain their hold on power in face of opposition from monarchist, Socialist, and other Communist parties. The nationalization of industries and a blockade imposed by Western countries had created havoc in the economy, so food and fuel were scarce. A few months before Marguerite arrived in Moscow, Russian poet Marina Tsvetaeva poignantly described how people would remember the year 1919: "not a fleck of flour, not a speck of salt (clinker and clutter enough and to spare!), not a speck, not a mote, not a shred of soap!" Tsvetaeva's husband, a White Army officer, was in exile. Unable to feed her daughters, she placed them in an orphanage where the younger child, not yet three, died of hunger in February 1920, the month Marguerite arrived.[11]

Francis McCullagh, a British intelligence officer who arrived in Moscow just a couple of weeks after Marguerite, described a hellish scene of decay and deprivation that he called "the desolation of a ruined civilization." Upon approaching the city, his train passed lines of abandoned engines and wagons. At suburban stations, he saw gangs of poorly clothed men and women setting out to collect food in the countryside. When he reached Moscow, two of McCullagh's companions ventured out to have a look. One returned to the train saying he had taken two sleighs and that the horses of both collapsed and were unable to rise. The second came back, exclaiming, "My God! My God! This is no place for a man to live in."[12]

Then McCullagh went to look for himself. "How can I convey a just idea of what present-day Moscow looks like to an Englishman who has never been there?" he wrote. "It is a town of mystery and misery; of secret executions and a lawless Government; of freedom to wave red flags and preach free love, and use language which would ensure one's instant arrest even in Hyde Park, but at the same time an irony—a tyranny which will not allow a word to be said against itself. It is an inconceivable topsy-turvydom."[13]

However, Marguerite wrote that her first impression of Moscow was not of suffering but of a city on the move, with vast numbers of people trampling through the snow-covered streets and sidewalks carrying bundles of provisions. She noted long lines outside the government food stores, but she otherwise painted a colorful scene: Men wearing long caftans and brightly colored sashes drove sleighs through the snow. Banners and colorful posters adorned boarded shops. "Sleigh bells jingled, the winter sun shone bright and the city had an almost festive appearance for it was the second anniversary of the founding of the Red army and all Moscow was in gala attire," she wrote.[14]

The representative of the Foreign Office escorted her to a one-story government guesthouse about two miles from the Kremlin where she and Karlin would stay until officials could decide their fate. The residence at No. 10 Malyy Kharitonyevskiy Pereulok had once belonged to a rich German merchant and retained remnants of its former grander. Marguerite's room was furnished with velvet curtains, an Oriental rug, a brass bed, and a large couch. She ate her meals in an oak-paneled dining room along with other residents, who included a correspondent from the *Chicago Daily News*, a Norwegian businessman, a Korean representative to Russia, and workers of the Foreign Office. Their "host" was an official from the All-Russian Extraordinary Commission, the Cheka.[15]

Marguerite had heard of the ruthlessness of the Cheka, which ran an extensive spy network on behalf of a party that demanded absolute obedience. Founded in December 1917 to combat anti-Bolshevik strikes and sabotage, Cheka had grown to a powerful force by the time she arrived. Conservative estimates put the number of national and local Cheka members at 37,000 by January 1, 1919.[16] In the months preceding her arrival the Cheka had killed more than 10,000 dissidents in the first phase of the Red Terror aimed at quelling opposition. Yet Marguerite saw no signs of violence. "So far my impressions of Soviet Russia had been favorable rather than otherwise. I had seen no evidence of the Terror. A large part of the economic ruin throughout the country was, I felt, attributable fully as much to the World War, the civil war and the Entente blockade as to the Red Terror." In her view, oppression—even mass executions—was a logical extension of revolution. It was "regrettable but inevitable."[17]

The day after she reached Moscow, the Foreign Office informed her she would be allowed to stay in the city for two weeks. She radioed the Associated Press to report her arrival and arranged to interview the head of the Foreign Office, Georgy Chicherin, the next day.

Once a wealthy landowner who had lived in exile in Europe, Chicherin had returned to Russia in 1918. A quirky revolutionary, he worked only at night, and so Marguerite's appointment was set for midnight. She still waited almost two hours before she was escorted into the office of a delicate-looking man wearing a woolen muffler around his neck. He spoke almost perfect English, and he asked her how she had slipped into the country. After she described her journey, their conversation turned to politics, the war with Poland and the internal affairs of the United States. Chicherin told her he was pleased the United States had outlawed alcohol because he believed that would hasten the progress of the workers' revolution.

Over the next several days, she continued to interview Bolshevik officials, including Felix Dzerzhinsky, the dreaded head of the Cheka. At the secret police headquarters in Lubyanka Square, she was ushered down a long corridor to a room lined with bookcases. After waiting for a few minutes, she was amazed when a clerk opened one of the bookcases that led to a secret passage and into a room occupied by a small man with thinning hair and a pointed beard—Dzerzhinsky.[18]

The commissar had been born into a wealthy Polish family but had been imprisoned for eleven years under Czar Nicholas II for his revolutionary activities. Dzerzhinsky once had aspired to the priesthood, but he had transferred his religious zeal to establishing a Communist state. With an unremitting hatred of the upper class and absolute conviction in his cause, he threw himself into his tasks overseeing the secret police. He worked, ate, and slept in his office, sometimes fainting from exhaustion. He refused to eat any food other than what was served to his men, and by the time Marguerite met him, he showed ravages of tuberculosis and was coughing blood. His personal sacrifices earned him the named "Iron Felix," but he could be unexpectedly emotional, even remorseful. On New Year's Eve 1918 he reportedly got so drunk at a party that he begged Lenin and others to shoot him because he had killed so many people that he didn't deserve to live.[19]

When Marguerite arrived the first wave of the Red Terror was over, and on Dzerzhinsky's recommendation Lenin had signed a decree temporarily abolishing the death penalty, except in districts where there were military operations. Despite his fanaticism, or perhaps because of it, Dzerzhinsky demanded that his officers be above reproach. The ideal Chekist, he said, was to possess "a cool head, a warm heart, and clean hands."[20] Nevertheless, throughout the months of terror, Chekists subjected victims to horrific and ingenious tortures, including scalping, impaling, and stoning. In Odessa, Chekists strapped victims to planks and pushed them slowly into blazing furnaces. In Kremenchug, peasants were buried alive.[21] Even the decree to outlaw the death penalty did not deter the violence. Just as the newspapers were preparing to announce the order, Chekists in Moscow and Petrograd pulled suspects from the prisons, drove them outside the cities, and shot them.[22]

Marguerite was prepared to ask Dzerzhinsky many questions, but he began to speak immediately, explaining the history and work of Cheka and defending its mass executions as necessary for the cause of revolution. Most of those killed, he told her, had been bandits, speculators, and spies. He gave no explanation for the thousands of arrests made every week, and Marguerite thought it best not to ask.

Over the weeks, Marguerite studied Russia's progress toward establishing Communism. Every worker received cards for food, clothing, and other necessities, but she learned there were not enough cards to go around, so a black market flourished. She realized that her lodging and meals were far better than those of most Russians. Despite the food shortage, the Bolsheviks made sure the foreign guests had enough to eat. Marguerite's meals included soup with meat and occasionally stewed fruit. She was given sugar or bonbons with her tea and twenty-five cigarettes every other day. She ate off fine linen, and the table service in the guesthouse was silver. "We lived like real bourgeois," she recalled.[23]

The Foreign Office arranged for her to tour schools, hospitals, nurseries, dining halls, and theaters but kept close watch, monitoring all her interactions with locals and requiring her to submit her stories to a government censor. Marguerite wired dispatches to the Associated Press and continued to mail articles to the *Baltimore Sun.* In the first two articles, she described her journey to Russia and her reception in Moscow. She was less than candid when she wrote that she was surprised to learn that the authorities were not admitting journalists from bourgeois newspapers. Of course, she knew that before she entered Russia, having failed to obtain Russian news credentials from Martens in New York.[24]

Soon after she interviewed Dzerzhinsky, Marguerite heard from the Foreign Office that she would be allowed to remain in Russia another month. She was thrilled. She had started to feel herself at ease in the country, and her Russian had improved immensely. She loved the people, whom she found sentimental and generous. She tremendously admired their willingness to endure hardship for the cause they believed in. "I had always been a champion of 'Causes,'" she wrote.[25]

She never imagined that the Bolsheviks suspected her of being an American spy. She had not communicated with MID, having committed to memory the information she intended to report to Churchill in person once she left Russia. But the Cheka's spies were everywhere, and she later realized they were "playing with me like a cat with a mouse."[26]

Marguerite had been in Moscow a few weeks when a frail-looking man in a sheepskin coat knocked on her door. He was Francis McCullagh, a British intelligence officer who had been left behind at Omsk when British troops retreated from Siberia. After a harrowing, three-week journey, he had arrived in Moscow without documents and was trying to persuade authorities that he was a British journalist. The Foreign Office had moved him into the guesthouse, but he doubted the Reds believed his story.

Thinking quickly, Marguerite invented a scheme to help him. She telegraphed the Associated Press to report that the "well-known correspondent of the Manchester *Guardian*" had arrived in Moscow from Siberia. The ruse worked, and McCullagh took up reporting in the capital, often working alongside Marguerite.[27]

McCullagh later described the control that the Bolsheviks exerted over the foreign correspondents. Reporters were given visas to stay only for three weeks. If they did not write positive news about the Russian government or wrote nothing at all, they were expelled. Every aspect of their lives was monitored. They lived in a guesthouse along with officials from the Foreign Office. They were not allowed visitors without permission. The Bolsheviks arranged all their interviews and accompanied them when they attended meetings, toured institutions, and even went to the theater. Chicherin personally screened every story and wire dispatch before allowing reporters to send their items through the mail or radio. Even if reporters could somehow escape the censor, they knew they would be expelled immediately if they violated the rules.[28] But most insidious of all, Bolsheviks controlled journalists by sowing seeds of distrust in their work. A garbled message or a fake story could cast a journalist as a Bolshevik and thus a persona non grata in his or her own nation.[29]

Under these conditions Marguerite continued to gather information for articles and for the MID reports she would write later. In early March she attended the opening session of the Moscow Soviet and for the first time saw Vladimir Lenin. "When he appeared on stage, my first feeling was one of disappointment. He was a short, thick-set, unimposing-looking little man. . . . After his first words, however, I became absorbed in his speech. His tremendous sincerity, utter self-confidence and the forcefulness of his personality fascinated me."[30]

Marguerite moved increasingly closer to the circles of Bolshevik power. She met Angelica Balabanova, the secretary of the Third International, the organization of Communists from around the world. Balabanova, who shared with

Marguerite a history of a wealthy family and a domineering mother, gave her a ticket to the annual meeting of the Communist Party and introduced her to the eccentric Alexandra Kollontai, one of the most powerful women in Soviet Russia. Dressed in a green velvet gown and matching slippers, Kollontai espoused to Marguerite her views on free love and child rearing, including the belief that children should be the property of the state.

Given how closely the Bolsheviks monitored journalists, Marguerite should have been suspicious that they gave her access to information not afforded to other Western reporters. Chicherin even allowed her to bypass the Foreign Office and read reports sent directly to the Russian news agency Rossiyskoye telegrafnoye agentstvo, or ROSTA. Each night Marguerite went to the wire service's central office and copied dispatches about peasant uprisings, meetings, and strikes— news that even Russian newspapers were not allowed to publish.[31]

With this information she began to formulate her assessment of Russia that she planned to relay to Churchill, views that the Bolsheviks themselves would probably approve: The Reds were securely in power; Allied attempts at intervention were merely strengthening the Bolsheviks' hand; the people in Russia were not ready for representative government; and the fantastic stories about the Red Terror were unfounded. "If only I can make them understand at home that the only way to combat Communism is to let all the world see and follow the experiment in Russia," she thought.[32]

In late March Marguerite and McCullagh managed to get inside the secure walls of the Kremlin to attend an exhibition, where they saw maps detailing ROSTA's propaganda work around the world. They later gave different accounts of the incident, and McCullagh, who published his version while Marguerite was in prison, did not mention that she was with him at all. Both said they bluffed their way past a Kremlin guard using a pass from a previous interview. Each described leaving the show and seeing Trotsky crossing a courtyard. McCullagh wrote that the two exchanged pleasantries. Marguerite said she rushed up to the second most powerful man in Russia and asked, "Citizen Commissar, may I speak to you for a moment?"

She said Trotsky turned, surprised at being stopped by a foreign woman. She hurriedly explained that she spoke Russian poorly but would like to speak to him in French, English, or German. He chose the first and she proceeded to ask him questions about the workers' army. He then asked her questions about

America and her impressions of Soviet Russia. After a few moments, he said goodbye. Marguerite held out her hand, and Trotsky kissed it. "Au revoir, and a pleasant visit, Madame," he said.[33]

A few days after the encounter Marguerite grew suspicious about the freedom she had been given to interview officials and see uncensored reports at the ROSTA agency. The Foreign Office notified her that she, Karlin, and McCullagh would have to move from the guesthouse to the Savoy Hotel, which was known to house those under suspicion. She had no choice but to comply. Then one night, as she feared, a soldier stopped her as she walked from work at the Foreign Office.

"Your name?" he demanded.

"Garrison," she replied, because the Russian alphabet has no letter for H. "Margherita Bernardova."

"You're arrested," he announced, handing her the order.[34]

The soldier led her to the Cheka headquarters, a large building on Lubyanka Square that had once housed a life insurance company. The sign above the doorway still read: "It is prudent to insure your life." Marguerite was searched, photographed, and fingerprinted and then taken upstairs to a floor that once had been a dormitory for the insurance company workers. She was placed in a small room furnished only with a table and a bed made from wooden planks. The room's one window had been whitewashed, and a large waste can in the corner served as the toilet.

Marguerite later said she did not panic because she did not believe the Cheka had any real evidence against her. So she threw her fur coat over the board bed and slept until she was awakened by someone who turned on the light and stared at her through a peephole in the door.

The next morning she was handed a broom to clean out her cell. Then a woman entered, tossed a small piece of black bread on a wooden bowl, and left. She was followed by a soldier who brought in a kettle of weak tea. Hours passed and she grew restless.[35]

Unbeknownst to her, McCullagh and Karlin had also been arrested. Marguerite later vaguely described the experience of waiting for her interrogation, but McCullagh provided a vivid account of what the suspense was like. For the most part, his room was silent, "broken only by terrifying sounds, with which they surrounded me, and also the disquieting sights they sometimes permitted me to see," he wrote. "I could not help but reflect on the cruelty of treating delicate women in this way. And delicate women were so treated. Mrs. Harrison of the American Associated Press had been arrested in the Savoy the same day as myself, and, as I afterwards learned, was at that very moment being subjected to the same terrible regime in another part of the building."[36]

Finally, in the afternoon, a guard appeared at her cell and ordered her to follow him. He escorted her through a maze of corridors to another part of the building where she was admitted to a large room furnished with leather arm-chairs, a large desk, bookshelves, and walls covered in diagrams resembling genealogical charts that showed alleged foreign spy networks in Russia. A short man who looked like a peasant slumped in a chair smoking a cigarette. At the desk sat a slender man dressed in black, who Marguerite thought resembled a puma—Solomon Mogilevsky. And lying on a sofa in front of the fireplace was a tall, thin man, Vyacheslav Rudolfovich Menzhinsky, one of Dzerzhinsky's chief lieutenants. The presence of Menzhinsky and Mogilevsky, two of the most power-ful members of Cheka, indicated the Bolsheviks did not view this interrogation as a routine matter.

Mogilevsky spoke first, addressing her in impeccable French. "We have been watching you for some time, Citizeness Harrison," he said. "We are fully aware of the nature of your mission."

Marguerite didn't flinch. "What do you mean?" she asked.

"We know perfectly well that you are here as a representative of the Ameri-can Secret Service. You acted in a similar capacity in Germany last year. We have reports from both America and Germany to prove this."

Mogilevsky proceeded to describe her movements in detail. She was amazed but kept her composure. "Where is your proof?" she demanded.

Mogilevsky opened a briefcase and pulled out a document—the report she had written on Julius Hecker's Bolshevik activities that she had given to the American attaché in Switzerland.[37] After the State Department arrested Hecker and sent him back to the United States for questioning, he soon realized who was responsible for reporting his activities. Two weeks before Marguerite's arrest, Hecker's wife had appealed to the embassy in Berne for her husband's release. Apparently, Hecker's friends in Russia tipped authorities to Marguerite's mis-sion, and a mole in the Military Intelligence Division had supplied the report as proof.[38]

Marguerite knew it was useless to deny the accusation in face of the evidence. "Very well," she said. "I acknowledge it. I am an agent of the United States government. But that is my only crime. If you have followed my activities as closely as you seem to have done, you know that I am merely an observer, that I have never obtained any information by illegal means, that the only illegal thing I have done has been to enter Russia without the permission of your authorities. I suppose you will have me deported."

Mogilevsky smiled. "No, my dear lady, you know too much for that."

Suddenly, the access she had been given to Bolshevik leaders and uncensored news from the provinces made sense. She had been trapped.

"We shall not deport you," Mogilevsky continued. "Your fate will depend entirely on your own attitude. Do you realize that we could order you to be shot as a Polish spy?"

"That is preposterous," Marguerite responded. "You know perfectly well that I have never served any other government than my own."

"Yes, we do," Mogilevsky said. "But nevertheless you might technically be found guilty of espionage on behalf of Poland. However, we are not going to take any extreme steps just now."

Mogilevsky wanted information on foreigners, in particular Francis McCullagh. Repeatedly he asked Marguerite what she knew of his activities, but she was careful not to reveal his true identity. At last Mogilevsky gave up that line of questioning. He rang a bell and an attendant brought in tea and cigarettes. The conversation drifted to general topics. All three Chekists were exceedingly intelligent, Marguerite realized. Menzhinsky spoke ten languages, and Mogilevsky was a lawyer with a fondness for French literature.

Marguerite wondered what more they could want with her. Finally, Mogilevsky spoke. "We are prepared to give you your liberty, Citizeness Harrison, but under certain conditions."

She asked what they were.

"First you will make no attempt to leave Moscow, and I must tell you that your stay is likely to be indefinite. Secondly, you will report to me once a week, and oftener if it is desirable. You will give me information about the foreign visitors in your guesthouse where you will continue to live as usual. Your freedom will depend on how useful you are to us, of this I must warn you."

Marguerite quickly sized up the situation. To refuse his ultimatum meant going to prison and being unable to give MID the information she had collected. Agreeing to his terms would allow her to gain even more insight into the operations of the Cheka's spy network. She could play along, give the Bolsheviks harmless tidbits, and still pass information to MID as opportunities arose. Churchill had hired her for six months, but she knew that her stay in Russia would be much longer.

She later recalled the moment melodramatically: "Like a drowning person who sees all his past life in a second, I saw the image of Tommy waiting in vain for me in Switzerland. I thought of my friends, my secure peaceful life in Baltimore. In that moment I renounced everything that hitherto made up my existence. It was finished—and I felt as if I had already died and been born into a new nightmare world. I looked Mogilevsky full in the eyes. 'I accept your proposition,' I answered calmly—so calmly I wondered at myself."[39]

DOUBLE TROUBLE

MARGUERITE ONCE DESCRIBED herself as a chameleon. She could be a flirtatious debutante, a devoted housewife, a music and drama critic, a foreign correspondent, and an American secret agent. But spying for Cheka demanded an adaptability far beyond that of her previous roles. Her freedom, perhaps even her life, depended on giving Mogilevsky information he wanted while not betraying her American mission. Accomplishing this in Bolshevik Russia meant sorting through layers of lies, gossips, and intrigues.

She moved back to the Kharitonyesky guesthouse, where no one was who he or she appeared. Foreign agents pretended to be Communists, and Russian agents pretended to be ordinary cooks and maids. The guesthouse's "host," Ivan Axionov, was a poet, interpreter, and scholar of Elizabethan literature. He was also a known Red agent. But what about the delegate from the Korean Socialist Party? Or the Norwegian businessman? Or the Japanese journalist? Or *Chicago Daily News* correspondent Michael Farbman? Who should be suspected, and who could be trusted?

Western intelligence agencies had been trying to decipher the mysteries of Russia for decades. The British deployed scores of agents posing as journalists and businessmen. *Daily News* correspondent Arthur Ransome carried on an affair with Trotsky's secretary, who gave him access to the inner workings of the Bolshevik Party. Agent Sidney Reilly adopted two aliases—a successful Greek businessman and a Middle Eastern entrepreneur—allowing him to gather economic and military intelligence in Russia until he was caught and shot in 1925.[1] Griffin Barry, a correspondent for the *London Daily Herald*, pretended to be a Bolshevik, but he also had worked for the U.S. State Department. McCullagh described him as "a dangerous communist agitator."[2]

The collapse of the Kalamatiano and Imbrie spy networks had seriously impeded America's ability to gather information, but an unknown number of agents still fed information to the U.S. State Department and Military Intelligence Division (MID). In addition to paid agents such as Marguerite, American agencies received informal reports from journalists, businessmen, and aid workers. When Mogilevsky questioned Marguerite about American spies, she answered—probably truthfully—that there were others, but their identities were kept secret from each other.[3] It is likely the arrangement was similar to what had existed in the Kalamatiano cell, with each agent knowing only two or three others.

Yet even with the most trusted agents, doubts lingered in the minds of their superiors as to whether they had been co-opted by the enemy. One of the Cheka's favorite tactics was to discredit American and British journalists by censoring their works so severely that their news reports became Bolshevik propaganda. Ransome's favorable articles on Russia made British intelligence operatives suspect that he might be a double agent, and both the Americans and the Bolsheviks distrusted Griffin Barry.

Amid all these uncertainties and with knowledge there was a leak in America's spy network, Marguerite still tried to fulfill her mission. One of her assignments was to find out what had become of the Americans who were implicated in the anti-Bolshevik plots. Kalamatiano's fate was especially precarious. He had been sentenced to death but for two years languished in prison. Nothing was known of Imbrie's assistant, Zinaida McKenzie Kennedy, captured by Cheka during the summer of 1919. As many as two dozen other Americans were held for suspected espionage. Marguerite managed to locate several of them with the help of foreign aid organizations. In mid-April, she slipped out a report that a dentist named Lambrie, a former consulate worker named Hipman, and "Kalmachenko" (probably Kalamatiano) were in prison. Another of her tasks was to track down Bolshevik agents who might try to enter the United States and foment discontent. In that regard she reported that a man named Koely (probably Royal Keeley) had been working for the Russian government and was returning to the United States. She warned he possibly could be a spy.[4] She was suspicious of several other businessmen and journalists, but discerning a true Communist from someone pretending to be one was not easy.

In a spy system in which operatives received information on a "need to know" basis, rumors swirled. Lt. Col. E. E. Farman, the American military attaché in

Warsaw, apparently found fault with an article Marguerite wrote for the *Baltimore Sun*. He said that while the material reflected "the role she was playing," it contained passages that might reflect badly on the United States.[5] Even today, the details of Marguerite's mission—and the role she was playing—are not known. Could MID have planned for Marguerite to get caught in order to peek behind Cheka's thick curtain of secrecy? Churchill's arrangement for her to receive Associated Press credentials after Russia had expelled AP correspondents was a flagrant—and seemingly needless—provocation. And, despite being refused a visa, Marguerite made no effort to enter Russia secretly. For nearly two months, she left a trail of stories documenting her travels. Then, once allowed inside Russia, she took risks by attending meetings without authorization and associating with suspected dissidents. MID knew in late March 1919 that Bolsheviks in Switzerland had alerted Russian authorities that the woman posing as a reporter for the Associated Press and *Baltimore Sun* was an American agent, yet they professed they were unable to warn her.[6]

If the aim was to have her infiltrate Cheka by being captured, the United States probably received unexpected help from a mole in either the State Department or MID. Mogilevsky had obtained the report Marguerite wrote about Hecker. A week after her arrest, the Russians also received a copy of a coded telegram that Undersecretary of State W. L. Hurley sent to L. Lanier Winslow in London confirming Marguerite was an American spy.[7] Suspicion fell on a captain in MID's propaganda section as the source of the leak, but he was never prosecuted.[8]

Now that Cheka knew she was an American agent, a complicated game ensued. The Reds did not want the U.S. government to know she was giving information to Cheka, so they continued to allow her to file her news stories and possibly even innocuous intelligence reports. Meanwhile, Marguerite knew her freedom depended upon satisfying Cheka that she was working on behalf of the Bolsheviks. The safest means to serve two masters was to feed Mogilevsky information on Western Socialists. While Americans might have seen little difference between Bolsheviks and other Left-leaning parties, the Cheka was anxious to suppress the Socialists who posed a real threat to the revolution by attracting workers to their party. The danger of the Socialists became evident in August 1918 when Fania Kaplan, a Socialist Revolutionary, shot and seriously wounded Lenin as he was leaving a worker rally at a Moscow factory.

To succeed in her role as a double agent, Marguerite needed both luck and skill. Before her arrest she did not send any documents to MID, expecting she would report her findings in person to Churchill once she returned to the United States. Now that her stay in Russia was indefinite, she devised various schemes to get information to American officials, usually sending oral or written messages through journalists or businessmen she deemed trustworthy. Ten days after her arrest, she slipped two reports to officials in Berlin. One was a five-page economic report on conditions in Russia, and the other a list of Americans held by the Russians.[9]

A few weeks later Marguerite managed to hand a Latvian diplomat a report prepared by an American engineer who had witnessed the disorganization and decay of Russian factories. Although she didn't name the source, he likely was Royal Keeley, who had been invited to Russia by Lenin to provide technical assistance but was put in prison when his reports were not to the Bolsheviks' liking.[10]

On another occasion Marguerite confided to Jewish aid workers, who passed the information to the U.S. authorities. One worker, Harry Kagan, told MID that Marguerite initially introduced herself to him as a wire service correspondent but, after he gained her trust, told him she was a Secret Service agent. Kagan gave a lengthy report to MID, but Marguerite was not likely the source of his information. He relayed that the Bolshevik government would not last because of growing dissatisfaction in the working class. Marguerite, however, had determined the Reds were entrenched in power and likely to remain.[11]

Marguerite's most important conduit for information, at least initially, was Francis McCullagh. Both had been arrested on Good Friday, along with Dr. Karlin. As in other instances, their accounts of their arrests and incarceration do not completely align. Marguerite wrote that both were released the day after their capture. McCullagh, however, said that he was held in solitary confinement for three days and then brought before Mogilevsky and another Cheka agent for rigorous interrogation. McCullagh was able to persuade his captors that he was a British journalist, and they allowed him to leave, but not before the Reds offered him the opportunity to stay and write favorable stories about Russia.[12]

Marguerite was fortunate that Cheka permitted McCullagh to leave Russia a week after his arrest. She surely told him the details of her interrogation and that the Reds knew she was an American agent. She would have told him that she could not leave the country and that Cheka was forcing her to provide information on foreigners. And she also would have warned him that there was a leak and that he needed to be careful.

When he returned to England, McCullagh relayed a cryptic report to the U.S. State Department on April 17, 1920, that included information he and Marguerite had gathered on Russian propaganda plans and Bolshevik agitators who might try to enter the United States. The report also contained inexplicable statements that American spymasters might have understood but would confuse the Russians if they read them.

The first part of the document described efforts of the Third International, the world organization of Communist parties, to disseminate Bolshevik propaganda. Its tactics included sending agitators with fake British passports and counterfeit money. The document then named some of the suspects and briefly described their activities. In one case McCullagh relayed a warning from "an American Secret Service agent" that the United States should not admit a technical expert who might instigate Bolshevik activities. Further along in the report, he wrote of American "agents" who warned of other businessmen and journalists, including *Chicago Daily News* correspondent H. J. LeMarc, who "would not make a desirable American citizen."[13]

Halfway through the six-page document the author mentioned Marguerite, describing her as "a highly educated and enterprising American lady journalist who does her best to inform the outer world correctly about Russian conditions, but is unable to do so owing to the fact that the censor allows only favorable news concerning Bolshevism to pass. Mrs. Harrison intends to leave Russia in a week or two, probably by way of Reval." Certainly, McCullagh knew that Marguerite was not simply an "enterprising American lady journalist" and that she was not permitted to leave Russia. The message might have been meant to alert American authorities that Marguerite was trying to escape, and some later news reports referred to her attempt to bribe her way out of the country. But it is also possible McCullagh's information on Marguerite was meant to fool the Bolshevik mole he knew was leaking government documents to the Reds.[14]

In the following weeks, Marguerite told several American and British visitors that she was unable to leave Russia, and the word reached the *Baltimore Sun* in mid-May. The newspaper initially discounted the reports, however, because Baltimore friends and family told the paper they had received recent letters from her that gave no indication of trouble. When the newspaper received her first article from Russia, an editor's note that accompanied its publication downplayed her problem of getting out of the country: "Mrs. Harrison is still in Russia. She is all right and in good health, but apparently finding it more difficult to get out of the country than she did to get in. Other Americans, it has been reported in recent dispatches, have been having the same trouble."[15]

Marguerite had succeeded in gathering valuable information on American prisoners, suspected Bolshevik agents, and the economic and political conditions inside Russia, but extracting her from the mission proved a difficult task. Certainly by May 1919 the Associated Press as well as officials in the State Department and MID realized the seriousness of her predicament. The Bolsheviks held about thirty Americans at this time. Some were businessmen, such as Kodak executive Samuel Hopwood, who was working in Moscow when the Bolsheviks seized power. Others were Socialists, such as journalist Albert Boni and engineer Royal Keeley, who went to Russia to see the Communist experiment.[16] Some were in prison, but others, like Marguerite, lived in apartments, hotels, and guesthouses where they were carefully watched. They were valuable bargaining chips the Bolsheviks could use in their negotiations for diplomatic recognition and food aid.

Officials at MID held to the slim hope that the Associated Press would be able to extricate Marguerite by demanding the release of its correspondent. She sent word to AP bureau chief Collins that she wanted him to call her back from this assignment, saying she believed she was in danger. He sent the cable she requested, but apparently it was never delivered to the Russian Foreign Office. In late May she sent word through a British army captain that she feared for her life, but the military attaché in London could offer no help except to suggest that the Associated Press lodge a protest for the return of its correspondent.[17]

While she awaited rescue, Marguerite assumed the role of a double agent and kept watch on the foreigners she encountered. A U.S. Central Intelligence Agency report, written many years after Marguerite was in Russia, described the work of a double agent as "one of the most demanding and complex counterintelligence activities in which an intelligence service can engage."[18] The double agent allows a country to gather valuable material on how the enemy operates its spy network, yet always there is great risk that the opponent will use the agent to feed disinformation. The report notes that the psychological profile of someone who undertakes the work of a double agent is not unlike that of a con man. Its description of double agents is worth noting because Marguerite possessed many of these characteristics:

They are unusually calm and stable under stress but cannot tolerate routine or boredom.

They do not form lasting and adult emotional relationships with other people because their attitude toward others is exploitative.

They have above-average intelligence. They are good verbalizers—sometimes in two or more languages.

They are skeptical and even cynical about the motives and abilities of others but have exaggerated notions about their own competence.

Their reliability as agents is largely determined by the extent to which the case officer's instructions coincide with what they consider their own best interests.

They are ambitious only in a short range sense: they want much and they want it now. They do not have the patience to plod toward a distant reward.

They are naturally clandestine and enjoy secrecy and deception for its own sake.[19]

A week after her release from prison, Marguerite received a telephone call. "Bonjour, madam," the soft voice said. "I would like to see you this afternoon. Meet me in the Alexandrovsky Gardens at four o'clock." She knew immediately that the voice belonged to Mogilevsky and that she had no choice but to meet him in the small park in the shadow of the Kremlin wall.

"Any news?" he asked.

And so the game ensued. Marguerite tried to distract him with harmless gossip about foreign Socialists and to steer the conversations toward political theory and life in America. Surprisingly, she found herself enjoying the verbal duels. "Gradually there grew up between Mogilevsky and myself a curious sort of camaraderie," she recalled.

Her attraction to the man charged with recruiting foreign agents is perplexing. Marguerite knew very well that one of the reasons American commanders distrusted female agents was that they believed they might fall in love with the targets of their espionage. Marguerite was confident that she was intelligent enough not to fall into such a trap and that she could use her rapport with the Chekist to gain valuable information. She may have underestimated Mogilevsky's ruthless devotion to the Bolshevik Party.

At thirty-five, Mogilevsky had been a Communist half his life. He could be charming and solicitous, yet as a former chairman of a local revolutionary tribunal, he had overseen the executions of untold men who opposed him. Marguerite idealized his devotion to Communism: "He never spared himself, but worked literally night and day in the service of the Cheka. I do not think he was cruel or bloodthirsty, but he was ruthless. Brought up under the Imperial government, he regarded the Cheka as a necessary part of the administration. It was inconceivable to him that any government could exist without an elaborate espionage and counterespionage system, and he regarded the Terror as the inevitable consequence of a state of civil war."[20]

In the spring of 1919 a Polish military offensive against Russia temporarily diverted Mogilevsky's attention and gave her respite from his weekly inquisitions. At this time she met some of the anarchists who had been deported from America in December on the ship *Buford*. After landing in Finland the group had been forced to march across the border to Russia. Among them were Emma Goldman, repeatedly jailed for distributing incendiary propaganda, and Alexander Berkman, who had attempted to assassinate steel magnate Henry Clay Frick. Berkman became a lodger next door to Marguerite in the Kharitonyesky guesthouse, and they had long conversations about Socialism and prison reform. Marguerite wrote sympathetically about him in her memoir, calling him one "of the gentlest, most courteous and kindliest individuals it has ever been my pleasure to meet." When he became ill, she cooked for him, gave him medicine, and changed his compresses.[21]

Marguerite also said she liked Emma Goldman, noting her honesty, humor, and intelligence as well as her growing disillusionment with Russia. Eventually the Bolsheviks assigned Goldman and Berkman the task of organizing a revolutionary history museum, and they left Moscow. "I missed them greatly," Marguerite wrote.[22] But the report McCullagh relayed to MID showed a different line of thinking. Although it is not clear whether the views are his or Marguerite's, the document warned that Goldman and Berkman were dangerous radicals who had joined an organization in Petrograd aimed at creating a Bolshevik revolution in America.

As the weeks wore on, Marguerite's hopes for getting out of Russia faded. Believing she inevitably would be imprisoned, she became even more reckless.

She befriended the owner of an illegal restaurant, met with members of the Socialist and anarchist opposition parties, and patronized the outlawed street market, which frequently was raided by Bolshevik troops.

America had no control over her work, but Mogilevsky's spies followed her everywhere. She believed her room was bugged although she never found the device. At times, though, she enjoyed matching wits with the Cheka, and took pride in giving them the slip or leading them to a suspect completely in sympathy with their cause. She described the spring and summer of 1920 as "a horrible waking dream," and yet, looking back, she felt no regret "for it was during this period and the long months in prison that followed that I had some of the most wonderful experiences of my life, and began really to learn something about Russia."[23]

In early June a delegation from Great Britain, including philosopher and writer Bertrand Russell, arrived in Moscow to gather information that might lead to resumption of trade between England and Russia. The Bolsheviks touted the visit as a great sign of solidarity between British and Russian workers and set about showing off the best of their country, including a boat ride on the Volga River to see villages in southern Russia. Some journalists were to follow the entourage, and Mogilevsky told Marguerite she would be with them to keep watch over the delegates. She readily agreed to go, hoping to slip information to the British representatives.

Marguerite and the delegates traveled by train from Moscow to Nizhny Novgorod, where they boarded a boat to travel down the Volga to Saratov. The tour was carefully managed, and the delegates were given every comfort. Brass bands and red banners greeted them in the villages where they stopped. They toured schools and plants and listened to endless speeches extolling the solidarity of Russian and British workers and the overthrow of oppressive capitalists. To Marguerite, it was obvious that the tour was being used to boost the morale of the Russian peasants who were told that the British visit signified world recognition of the Bolshevik movement. Eventually the delegates themselves caught on to the ploy and demanded that they be allowed to talk with villagers and make independent investigations. The Reds relented, but as only one delegate spoke Russian and the peasants were suspicious of foreigners, the British did not gather much information. Marguerite, however, managed to win the confidence of the locals, who told her that the reorganization of the rural economy had left much farmland fallow. She realized that it would not be long before famine consumed the country.[24]

Of the two dozen British delegates on the trip, Bertrand Russell most attracted Marguerite's attention. Perhaps she was drawn to him because of their shared aristocratic background, or maybe she had been given instructions to follow him. But while other members of the delegation toured children's homes and hospitals, those two took walks alone in the country. Russell had come to Russia excited to see Communism in practice, but, as the days passed, he grew increasingly disillusioned. "The time I spent in Russia was one of continually increasing nightmare," he wrote. "Cruelty, poverty, suspicion, persecution formed the very air we breathed."[25]

The Russians had given the delegates the best accommodations, but Russell noted with disgust that villagers were drawing drinking water from a river flowing with refuse. He was bothered by swarms of malaria-carrying mosquitoes and flies that blackened the tables. Russell told his companions that he had heard shots during the night, but the more ardent Communists in the delegation assured him the sounds were merely cars backfiring. Russell, a lecturer at Trinity College, was particularly horrified at the conditions he found of academics—poets dressed in rags and professors who looked like tramps. "I felt that everything I valued in human life was being destroyed in the interest of a glib and narrow philosophy," he wrote.[26]

One member of the delegation, a Quaker named Clifford Allen, became seriously ill with pneumonia on the Volga trip, and Russell gave a vivid account of the man's suffering. "He had a very small cabin and the heat was inconceivable," he wrote. "The windows had to be kept tight shut on account of the malarial mosquitoes, and Allen suffered from violent diarrhea. . . . Although there was a Russian nurse on board she was afraid to sit with him at night for fear he might die and his ghost seize her."[27] A Russian doctor said he did not believe Allen would live two days, but those on the excursion, including Marguerite, nursed him as best they could. Calling Marguerite a "charming woman," Russell described how she cared for Allen "with more skill and devotion than was shown by his old friends."[28] Allen survived the trip and lived many more years, serving as a member of the House of Lords.[29]

Aside from describing the hardships the delegation encountered, Russell offered insight into Marguerite's own travails. He learned that she was an American spy who had been caught and was being forced to work for Cheka. Quite possibly she told him so herself on their solitary walks. He wrote: "She was in obvious terror and longing to escape Russia, but the Bolsheviks kept her under very close observation. There was a spy named Axionov . . . who watched her every movement and listened to her every word. . . . On the night-train he shared a compartment with her, and on the boat, whenever anybody spoke with her he would creep behind silently."[30] Interestingly, Marguerite does not mention in her memoir that Axionov, the administrator of her guesthouse, was on the voyage or that she was followed.

The evening after the delegation returned to Moscow, the chief censor met Marguerite at the Foreign Office in the Metropole Hotel. "You are just the person I wanted to see," he told her. "We have received an application from a woman colleague of yours who wishes to come to Russia as correspondent for the *New York World*. I wonder if you can tell me anything about her?"

"What is her name?" Marguerite asked. "Is she an American?"

"No, an Englishwoman. Her name is Mrs. Stan Harding."

Marguerite was shocked. She had not heard from Harding since she left Berlin in August 1919, and for all she knew the woman was decorating flats in London. Marguerite was determined to stop Harding from entering Russia, although the reason is not clear. Harding later said Marguerite feared that Harding would report her as an American spy. But the Russians already knew that. More plausible is Marguerite's explanation that she believed the Russians would arrest Harding because they knew she had helped Marguerite gather intelligence in Berlin. It is possible Marguerite had already identified Harding as a spy in her effort to give Cheka a report on foreign agents.

Marguerite recalled that she told the censor that Harding should not be allowed into the country because she was not a serious journalist. She then tried to get word to Harding not to come to Russia. She relayed the message to several correspondents and may have told Bertrand Russell, who said he warned Harding against going to Moscow when he saw her in Reval, Estonia, as he was returning to England.[31]

But Harding refused to change her mind. Like Marguerite, she was adventurous bordering on reckless. She had once told Marguerite that she planned to escape from Germany by swimming the Rhine.[32]

Marguerite's father,
Bernard N. Baker,
was a Baltimore
shipping magnate and
civic leader. *Courtesy
Jonathan Kinghorn*

Marguerite's maternal
grandfather, Elias Livezey,
was a real estate developer
who taught Marguerite
to question authority.
*Courtesy Catonsville
branch of Baltimore
County Public Library*

Ingleside Estate, Marguerite's childhood home.
Courtesy Catonsville branch of Baltimore County
Public Library

Marguerite Harrison with husband, Tom, and son, Tommy. *Courtesy Nancy Harrison*

Col. Ralph Van Deman, head of the Military
Intelligence Section, 1917–18. *U.S. Army*

Merian Cooper, 1920. He credited Marguerite with saving his life in Russia. He later recruited her to accompany him on a mission to the Middle East. *Photo courtesy of L. Tom Perry Special Collections, Brigham Young University*

Solomon Mogilevsky, head of Cheka foreign intelligence service, recruited Marguerite to be a double agent. *Photo by the press bureau of the Russian Foreign Intelligence Service,* Military Industrial Courier *(March 23–29, 2005): 11*

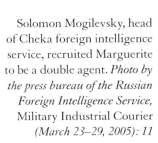

Marguerite Harrison in *Grass*, 1925.
Photo courtesy of Milestone Films

Marlborough Churchill, director, Military Intelligence Division, 1918–20, hired Marguerite to be the first female foreign intelligence agent. *NARA*

Albert Ritchie, 1926. Ritchie was Marguerite's brother-in-law and the longest-serving governor in Maryland. According to family legend, Ritchie and Marguerite had an affair. *Library of Congress*

Marguerite Harrison on the Russian/Polish
border, February 1920. *Photo published in*
Baltimore Sun *Aug. 1921*

Lubyanka Prison, circa 1920. *Public domain image from*
Wikimedia Commons; original source unknown

Senator Joseph I. France (R-MD) traveled to
Russia and persuaded Lenin to release Marguerite
in exchange for food aid. *Library of Congress*

Marguerite Harrison (circa 1930s). *Keystone View Company*

Joseph S. Ames, 1919. Ames was Marguerite's father-in-law.
He helped her become a foreign agent, but later expressed
doubts about her accounts. *NASA*

Senator Joseph I. France (R-MD) traveled to
Russia and persuaded Lenin to release Marguerite
in exchange for food aid. *Library of Congress*

Marguerite Harrison (circa 1930s). *Keystone View Company*

Joseph S. Ames, 1919. Ames was Marguerite's father-in-law.
He helped her become a foreign agent, but later expressed
doubts about her accounts. *NASA*

Merian Cooper, Marguerite Harrison, and Ernest B. Schoedsack
in Angora, Turkey. *Photo courtesy of L. Tom Perry Special
Collections, Brigham Young University*

Marguerite Harrison shares a meal of broiled wild goat with tribesmen
in the Taurus Mountains during the 1923–24 expedition to the Middle
East. *Society of Woman Geographers, Library of Congress*

Stan Harding, who accused Marguerite Harrison of falsely denouncing her as a spy to Soviet authorities. *Photo from the* Underworld of State, *Stan Harding, George Allen & Unwin Limited, 1925*

Frank Kent, editor of *Baltimore Sun* who hired Harrison. Photo circa 1940. Harris & Ewing photographer. *Library of Congress*

Arthur M. Blake, Marguerite's second husband, was
an aspiring actor. *Photo courtesy of Academy of Motion
Picture Arts and Sciences Margaret Herrick Library*

Marguerite Harrison in Turkey during the 1923–24
expedition to the Middle East. *Society of Woman
Geographers, Library of Congress*

Marguerite Harrison, 1960. *Society of
Woman Geographers, Library of Congress*

After hearing positive reports from Leftist journalists such as Lincoln Steffens about the Communist regime in Russia, Harding made up her mind to see it for herself. She dismissed stories about the Red Terror as capitalist rumors and sought a newspaper assignment to report from Russia. The *New York World* gave her the job in June 1920, and Harding quickly traveled to Estonia to apply for permission to enter Russia. Harding made no secret of her Left-leaning political views, knowing they made it more likely she would get a visa.

She soon received permission to enter the country. Mogilevsky called Marguerite with the news. "Mrs. Harding is coming to Russia. I am going to Petrograd to meet her." He continued: "And she will stay with you and I shall expect you to find out why she has come."

Marguerite wondered that herself. Was Harding coming as a newspaper reporter or was she an agent of the British secret service? Whatever the answer, Marguerite knew that the Reds already had enough information about her work in Germany to arrest her.

Harding had anticipated an uncomfortable journey from Reval to Moscow and was surprised when she boarded the train and was given a comfortable Pullman sleeping car. "There were even flowers in my compartment," she later wrote. She soon met the man who provided them: Solomon Mogilevsky.

He had told Marguerite he was going to meet Harding in Petrograd, but Harding said he boarded the train at Reval. Accompanying him was another official, who was introduced as her interpreter. Harding described Mogilevsky as medium tall with a slender build, close-cropped dark hair and "regular and not altogether unpleasing features; a skeptical mouth, and suspicious eyes which followed one's every movement."[33] She had no idea he was a member of the Cheka presidium. Throughout the trip, he impressed her with his courtesy, and when they stopped at the last station in Estonia, she said, "He gallantly bought me a box of strawberries."[34]

When the train crossed the Piusa River into Russia, Harding noted a red flag, six inches square, that marked the border. "We had a larger one, but the rain washed it white," her translator told her. Harding loved the understatement of the symbol. For the rest of the trip, she occupied herself reading a book on Soviet proclamations, which included one she vividly recalled: "All living beings are freed from their shackles."[35] Unbeknownst to her, however, she already was a prisoner of the Cheka.

Delegates of the Third International were on her train, and when they stopped in Petrograd, the representatives visited the president of the city's Soviet council. Harding was not allowed to go with them, however. Instead her translator escorted her down Nevsky Prospect, which was framed by boarded-up shops and crumbling houses. The people she saw in the street did not have the appearance of revolutionaries. "There was nothing about the men and women one passed in the Petrograd streets to suggest that this was a liberated people which had thrown off an age-long oppression," she wrote.[36] Harding began to have doubts about Bolshevism.

Other passengers spent the night in a hotel, but Harding was forced to sleep on the train with Mogilevsky and her translator. Then, when they arrived in Moscow the next day, they took her to the Kharitonyesky guesthouse and told her she would have to share a room with Marguerite, who was out that morning but would be returning before evening. Harding became uneasy. She noted the armed sentries who checked the passports of anyone who arrived or left. She heard someone in felt slippers creep down the hall when she opened the door in her room. "There was a fog of suspicion in the corridors," she later wrote. Kharitonyesky, she later learned, was the "House of Suspicion."[37]

Marguerite arrived that afternoon, and the two women had barely greeted one another when Mogilevsky abruptly announced that the authorities wanted to move Harding to a "more central lodging." Harding asked to rest a bit, and Mogilevsky agreed. Alone with Marguerite, Harding asked her if she knew why she was being moved. Marguerite replied: "I don't want to seem to wish to talk to you. Things are getting critical," and left the room.[38]

Marguerite wrote that when they were alone, Harding shocked her by saying: "My dear, I am going to get us both out of this mess."[39] Marguerite wondered if Harding had heard she was unable to leave Russia. Bertrand Russell and the British newspaper correspondents that Marguerite had contacted to warn Harding not to enter Russia might have told her. Could she have plotted with her Socialist friends to somehow rescue her?

Marguerite left Harding and rushed out of the room to find Mogilevsky pacing the hallway. "Why are you waiting here?" she asked him. "It surely cannot have anything to do with Mrs. Harding. You know as well as I that we have not communicated since we were together in Germany. She is very well known as a journalist and there is no reason for you or me to suppose that she is engaged in any other activity."[40]

"My dear lady," Mogilevsky answered, "I traveled with your friend from Petrograd and she did not suspect my identity. She was rather indiscreet and I learned quite enough from her to justify her arrest without anything you might be able to tell me."[41]

Marguerite was baffled about why he had brought Harding to the guest-house, but then she understood. Mogilevsky lacked proof that Harding was a spy and he needed Marguerite to supply the evidence. Whatever Marguerite told him, he seemed satisfied. Mogilevsky returned to the room where Harding sat sipping a cup of tea. He apologized for hurrying her along, then helped her put her bags into the waiting car. Harding recalled what happened next: "In a few minutes we reached the Lubyanka Square. Mogilevsky, turning to me, said, 'Madam, I have to tell you that you are arrested.'"[42] In time Harding learned that Marguerite was a double agent who had denounced her as a British spy.

Marguerite said she immediately reported to a British correspondent Harding's arrest so her government could be notified. Two days later, she delivered to her a food package at the Lubyanka prison, the first she would send twice a week until her own arrest in October.

In her account, Harding said most of her aid packages were stolen although, knowing that Marguerite helped the Red Cross, she wondered if she had sent her any. "Did she say to herself: 'There is Stan Harding whom I am doing to death: I must send her some biscuits'?"[43]

Marguerite wrote that she saw Harding one more time in Russia. Mogilevsky summoned Marguerite to his office and told her that when she left she would pass Stan Harding in the corridor. He ordered Marguerite not to speak to her. By now Harding blamed Marguerite for her arrest. In the hall, Harding, escorted by a soldier, stared angrily into Marguerite's eyes, but neither woman spoke. The encounter was part of Cheka's psychological game to elicit a confession.[44]

Harding later wrote that Mogilevsky wanted to strike the same kind of arrangement with her as he had with Marguerite: She would spy for him in exchange for her freedom. He told her the Bolsheviks had allowed her to enter the country to trap her into giving them information on the British intelligence network. The primary evidence they had against Harding was Marguerite's statements that she had been a British spy and assisted her in gathering intelligence when they both were in Berlin. Harding believed Marguerite had set the trap to spare herself.

Harding wrote her account of her Russian imprisonment and her relationship with Marguerite while in the midst of a highly public campaign to win compensation from Marguerite and the U.S. government for her suffering. Marguerite had told the Russians that Harding was a spy and repeated the allegations in her autobiography, but the British woman denied any involvement with the intelligence service.

Harding was placed in solitary confinement and subjected to repeated interrogations during which she struggled to convince Mogilevsky that she had come to Russia only to report for the *New York World* and satisfy her curiosity about Communism. Whether Mogilevsky really believed Harding was an agent was irrelevant. Like Marguerite, she could be recruited as a Cheka spy or used as a hostage in the Russian negotiations for economic aid.

The Reds held Harding for five months—most of that time in solitary confinement in Lubyanka. She later described the torturous conditions: She spoke almost no Russian when she first arrived and was allowed no books or paper. The cells were infested with lice, and typhus was rampant. At night, she heard the sound of car engines that were meant to drown out the screams and shots that followed in the courtyard below her window. Like McCullagh, Harding heard unnerving sounds, "shrieks of unearthly agony," uttered by those going mad in isolated cells. Prisoners appealed for interrogations to relieve the terrible solitude. Harding repeatedly went on hunger strikes to demand an end to solitary confinement. She saw herself as a victim of both the Bolshevik secret police and the anti-Bolshevik secret service—and she blamed Marguerite for her suffering.[45]

Marguerite knew it was only a matter of time before she, too, would go to prison, but she tried to push thoughts of her inevitable arrest from her mind. She continued to file censored reports to the Associated Press, and she went to plays, operas, and ballets. She took a certain pleasure in watching the comings and goings of the inhabitants of the guesthouse, some of whom must have wondered about the American woman who remained there permanently. She had no summer clothes with her, but a representative from the Jewish Joint Distribution Committee gave her two silk shirts, one of which she fashioned into a hat. The Jewish aid worker Kagan gave her soap and toothpaste. Workers with the American Relief Administration supplied her with food.[46]

The meeting of the Third International that summer brought new visitors to the guesthouse. Delegates from all over the world who sought a worker paradise descended on Moscow, and the occasion was celebrated with parades, meetings, and theatrical performances. Cheka authorities told Marguerite to stay away from the delegates, but she nevertheless saw a great deal of them, including representatives from Turkey, China, and Persia. A delegate from Afghanistan struck a courtship of sorts.

"You got a husband at home?" he asked her.

"No," she told him.

"You find a man here?"

"No."

"You young and you look healthy. I got plenty wives in Afghanistan, but here it is very lonely. I don't want Russian woman—I always wanted English woman. We marry now, what you say? We stay married while I'm here or I take you back to Afghanistan. Fine country. You be first wife."

Marguerite told him she would have to think it over and fled.[47]

Despite Mogilevsky's spies, Marguerite managed to take a weekend sojourn from Moscow to a country dacha with Samuel Hopwood, formerly a manager of the Kodak Company, and his daughters. They stayed with a peasant woman, a widow whose son had been killed in the war, near the Moscow River. Marguerite later recalled that they arrived on a hot Saturday afternoon and Hopwood's daughters suggested they go swimming.

"I'd like to," Marguerite answered. "But I have no bathing suit."

The women assured her that made no difference. They took her to the river and Marguerite was surprised to see hundreds of naked men, women, and children bathing in the water and lounging on the beach.

"If it's the custom of the country, I suppose I can do it, too," Marguerite said. But she asked her companions to move to a more secluded spot where the women undressed. Marguerite recalled the last article she took off was her hat, "but after the first agonized moment, I quite forgot my embarrassment and never enjoyed a swim more in my life."[48]

Marguerite loved the Russians' willingness to ignore conventionality and act and dress as they pleased. "In the streets in Moscow you see long-haired men, and short-haired women, girls without stockings, and on some occasions wearing men's clothes, while the men wear anything that suits their fancy."[49] Bertrand Russell had been horrified at the bedraggled appearance of mathematicians and poets he saw in Petrograd. But Marguerite admired a professor she saw at the

University of Moscow who was barefoot and wearing long linen trousers and a Russian blouse covered by a black opera cape. As a woman brought up with the strict decorum of the Victorian era, she admired the Russians' freedom from social constraints. Ironically, she discovered these insights while she was a virtual prisoner of Cheka.

Her visit to the countryside was a rare exception to weeks of worry and anticipation. She took some comfort in helping provide aid to Americans and British held in Soviet prisons around Moscow. Marguerite prepared packages for about a half dozen civilians as well as two dozen British officers captured by the Reds in Siberia. Every Monday and Thursday she bought provisions at the Sukharevka outdoor market and spent afternoons cooking and assembling the food packages. Money from the British Red Cross could be used only for British prisoners, so she used her own money to aid the Americans. She had brought fifteen hundred dollars when she entered the country, and this she traded gradually on the black market. In addition, she occasionally received money from the Associated Press, and she sold some of her belongings.

One day the woman in charge of distributing aid to French prisoners summoned Marguerite to the aid office where she met a gaunt Yugoslav man who had recently been released from an internment camp. The man carried a note from a Polish prisoner of war who claimed to be an American. The prisoner wrote that he was ill and nearly starving. The French Red Cross was unable to help him because it was negotiating the release of French prisoners, but the aid administrator thought Marguerite could do something.

Marguerite took a look at the note, which was signed by Corp. Frank R. Mosher. He said he had been a pilot in France and then volunteered for the Polish Kosciuszko bombing squadron. He had been taken prisoner when his plane was shot down near Kiev. Marguerite recalled she had met a member of the squadron while she was in Poland. In a moment, she remembered his name: Merian Cooper.

Marguerite didn't know Mosher but agreed to help—secretly. "If Mogilevsky ever suspected that I had any intercourse with Polish prisoners of war, it would have been all up with me at once."[50] She assembled a food package and gave it to the Yugoslav to deliver to Mosher, with an oral message asking what else he needed. The prisoner needed almost everything—clothes, blankets, food, toiletries, and books. He also asked the messenger the name of the woman who was helping him. Marguerite was afraid to put her name in writing but told the Yugoslav who she was. Gradually, she sent the items Mosher requested, and then she received a note, smuggled out on a piece of cigarette paper one and half inches wide and five inches long:

"My name is not Mosher. I am Merian C. Cooper of Jacksonville, Florida, and I met you in Poland. Don't you remember dancing with me at a ball in the Hotel Bristol in Warsaw?"[51] Cooper had taken the name Mosher because he was wearing second-hand clothing when he was captured and that was the name that had been written on the underwear. He knew that if the Bolsheviks suspected him of being a Polish officer he would likely be shot. He asked Marguerite to get word to his parents that he was alive and being held prisoner.

His secret, which only she knew, placed them both at risk, but she continued to send him food and books until he was transferred to a British camp, where she then helped him openly until she was arrested a month later.[52]

Cooper, meanwhile, shuttled from camp to camp until April 12, 1921, when he and two other prisoners, armed only with a single pocketknife, slipped away from a work detail. They jumped freight trains heading west, occasionally seeking help from peasants who fed them along the way. One day they took a turn on a forest path and encountered a lone Red soldier who arrested them at gunpoint. Cooper walked meekly ahead and then bent down, pretending to tie his shoelace. He whirled suddenly and the three prisoners attacked the soldier, pinning him to the ground. Cooper pulled out the pocketknife, pulled back the Bolshevik's head, and cut his throat. They continued their journey until they safely reached the Latvian border.[53]

In late summer 1920 Marguerite met John Reed, the Communist journalist whose stirring account of the Russian Revolution had enthralled her three years earlier. He had recently been released from a Finnish prison and was trying to return to America to respond to sedition charges.

He was in poor health, and Marguerite perceived he was disappointed with developments in Russia. "I think he saw some of the mistakes that were being made in Moscow and felt that he was powerless to prevent them," she recalled. "I frequently saw him at the Foreign Office in the evenings and we had long talks about Communism. . . . He impressed me as an intensely honest, rather fair-minded person, and I always felt that a certain spirit of bravado spurred on by what he regarded as unfair treatment in America pushed him rather farther than he intended to go in his radicalism."[54]

Other accounts portray Reed as full of optimism that summer with the gathering of the Third International. "It is beautiful here now, and everything is going well," he told his wife, Louise Bryant.[55]

The truth about John Reed's final days has been lost in a swirl of propaganda promulgated by both Bolsheviks and anti-Bolsheviks who used his death to promote their own views. Did he grow disillusioned with Communism as Marguerite and others, including Emma Goldman and Max Eastman, said? Or were his complaints simply the usual gripes against bureaucracy? Was he alert until the end of his life? Or did he lose consciousness in his last days, muttering, "Caught in a trap, caught in a trap"? Had Lenin intervened to give him the best medical care? Or, as in another account, did Lenin know nothing of Reed's illness. As one historian wrote, "Other friends and colleagues . . . heard what they wanted to hear—or, in some cases, fabricated it seemingly out of whole cloth."[56]

Some have even speculated that John Reed himself was a spy.[57] Weston Burgess Estes, a MID operative who was arrested in Russia in August 1920, said he had entered Russia posing as a filmmaker in order to rescue Reed.[58] His cameraman, John Flick, said Cheka interrogators repeatedly asked about their plans to take Reed from the country.[59]

Some facts are known: At the end of August, Reed journeyed with members of the executive committee of the Third International to Baku to rally workers in the region. He returned to Moscow in mid-September and reunited with Bryant, who had just arrived from the United States. They enjoyed a week sightseeing in Moscow and visiting Bolshevik leaders, but then Reed fell ill, complaining of headaches and dizziness. Bryant nursed him for a week until doctors determined he had typhus and placed him in a hospital. He struggled for another week and then, on October 17, he died.[60]

Marguerite, who was acquainted with Bryant, visited her to offer her condolences. "John was a real American," Bryant told Marguerite. "I know he would have wanted to be buried on American soil."[61]

Instead, John Reed received a hero's funeral in Moscow. His body lay in state for a week at the Trades Union Hall guarded by Red Army soldiers, and then his coffin was borne through the streets to Red Square. Bolshevik leaders delivered long speeches in English, Russian, German, and French; few seemed to notice when Bryant collapsed in grief. As the coffin was lowered to the earth beside the Kremlin wall, a cold rain turned to snow.[62]

Thousands attended John Reed's funeral to pay their respects to the American revolutionary, but Marguerite was not among them. The day after visiting Bryant, Marguerite was arrested.

She had returned to the guesthouse after working late at the Foreign Office and was getting ready for bed around two o'clock in the morning when she heard a car approach. She was accustomed to hearing automobiles race down the streets at night, a sure sign of an impending raid. She knew a car would stop for her one day. Mogilevsky had repeatedly warned her that he was not satisfied with the information she was providing, and she would be arrested unless she started to work seriously. When she heard the automobile pull up outside, she almost felt relief that the time had come.

There was a knock at her door, but she didn't bother rising from the sofa when she called for her captors to enter. Two soldiers and a well-dressed woman came into the room. "I suppose you have come to arrest me," Marguerite said.

A soldier handed her two slips of paper—one the order for her arrest and the other a search warrant. The soldiers thoroughly searched the room and collected all papers, down to the tiniest scraps. The cache included newspaper clippings, articles, Russian grammar lessons, and even a ticket to the Bolshoi Theatre. Meanwhile, the woman searched her pockets, stockings, girdle, hair, and coat. When they were finished, Marguerite asked if she could take some things with her, and they allowed her to pack toiletries, a change of underwear, cigarettes, chocolate, her bedding role, and her fur-lined coat. She signed a paper affirming the search was properly conducted. Then she calmly got into the car that was waiting to take her to Lubyanka prison.[63]

Nine

THROUGH DIFFICULTIES TO THE STARS

NO AMERICAN WOMAN had ever survived Lubyanka. Now Marguerite Harrison, a Baltimore aristocrat who grew up in a mansion boasting nine bathrooms and a host of servants, faced an indefinite sentence in a prison that had broken hardened spies and revolutionaries. Once accustomed to wearing French gowns and pearls, she had only the linen suit on her back, and her most prized possession was now a fine-toothed comb she used to pull lice eggs from her hair. The debutante who had nibbled pastries at Queen Victoria's garden party now plucked fish eyes from watery soup.

The British and Americans who escaped from Moscow's prisons returned home with horror stories of starvation, torture, and madness. But from the outside, the most notorious prison in Russia looked no more threatening than Harrods department store in London. British agent Francis McCullagh wrote: "Far from resembling a gloomy prison like the forbidding fortress of SS. Peter and Paul, it is light and airy in its style of architecture, and there is not a single iron bar on any of its exterior windows." Baroque columns and Palladian windows enhanced the yellow-brick façade, and the roof was topped with flags and cupolas. Large plate-glass windows facing Lubyanka Square were inscribed with mundane signs such as "Dentist," "Music Shop," and "Bank."[1]

The reason for its disarming appearance was that Lubyanka wasn't built as a prison at all but as an office complex in the center of Moscow. Several of the buildings had once housed insurance companies, including the largest structure at 2 Lubyanka Square. Constructed in 1898, the five-story story building had been the headquarters for the Rossia insurance agency. Its upper floors had served as worker dormitories, and the interior courtyards had provided pleasant areas for the employees to mingle.

After the Bolsheviks seized power, they turned Lubyanka into the headquarters for the Cheka secret police and converted the dormitory rooms into cells for political prisoners. The bedroom windows were whitewashed and sealed, and peepholes were drilled into the doors. In the courtyards firing squads executed the condemned.

Stan Harding, who spent five months in Lubyanka, described it as a place "where the filthy wallpaper hung in tatters, [and] one felt as though one had been kidnapped by scoundrels and locked up in a small verminous room, where one might well be forgotten forever." To her, the psychological torture of Lubyanka was far worse than of Butyrka, a former czarist prison with stone walls and iron bars.[2]

Like most of those Cheka arrested, Marguerite arrived at Lubyanka in the middle of the night. The prison administrators confiscated all her valuables—her money, camera, typewriter, and jewelry, including her wedding ring—as well as notes written in English, French, and German.[3] They meticulously recorded the items in a ledger and then handed her a lengthy questionnaire that asked, among other things, whether she had relatives in the Red or White Army. The entire process was, above all else, orderly and thorough. McCullagh, who experienced the intake procedure when he was arrested, recalled his surprise at how young the Lubyanka guards were, and he surmised they had been former sailors or factory workers. One inspector who searched McCullagh's belongings assumed he was a merchant because he carried six toothbrushes. The Red Army allowed only one toothbrush for every two men, the guard told him.[4]

By the time Marguerite completed the intake formalities and was escorted to her cell, it was nearly six in the morning. Three inmates in the room awoke and immediately peppered her with questions about who she was and why she had been arrested. Two of the women were speculators and the third a young girl accused of trying to help a Hungarian prisoner escape. Before Marguerite could lie down, the day's routine began—sweeping the floor, visiting the latrine, and eating breakfast of weak tea and black bread. In the afternoon the authorities photographed her against a white screen with her printed identification number—prisoner 2961.

On the second day, a soldier appeared and called out curtly: "*Na dopros.*"

Marguerite did not recognize the Russian word, but her cellmates explained that she was being called for interrogation. Soon she was back in Mogilevsky's familiar office.

"Good afternoon, citizeness," he said somberly. "I hardly need to tell you why you are here."

"I can guess the reason," Marguerite answered. "We have been playing a game and I have lost."

Mogilevsky looked grim. He recounted that she was charged with espionage during wartime, a capital offense. He had spared her life because she had agreed to provide information on foreigners. "You gave us a few bits of news, some of them interesting, others absolutely false and misleading, but you never worked seriously," he said. He had discovered that McCullagh was a secret agent, and he knew that she had slipped reports on Bolshevik spies to U.S. officials.

"Do you know that you deserve the death penalty?" he asked.

She acknowledged that she had violated Russian law but at the same time defended her work. "I have not taken sides or mixed in your internal affairs," she said. "My reports have been fair and objective. I do not believe in Communism, but I think that it is an interesting social experiment which deserves a trial."

She reminded him that she opposed U.S. and British intervention in Russia and the Western blockade that was starving the country. Then she accused him of not trusting her reports because he had sent spies to watch her.

"I hoped, but I was disappointed," he answered. "Perhaps, however, you may decide to give us more information later."[5]

Marguerite Harrison, a confessed American spy and the former sister-in-law of the Maryland governor, was a prize catch for Cheka. She was a perceptive observer with extensive government and social connections in the United States, Great Britain, and Germany. She had provided valuable information on Socialists opposing the Bolshevik Party and warned of unsympathetic Western journalists trying to gain entry into Russia. Although she had proven unreliable as a double agent, Mogilevsky still thought he could force her to cooperate.

The Chekist interrogated her on the people she had met in Moscow and the activities of foreigners she knew, but she answered most of his questions with "I don't remember" or "I don't know." Finally, Mogilevsky grew exasperated and ordered her to return to her cell to reconsider her answers. She was in the room only a few minutes when a guard ordered her to pack her bags. She started to put on her coat, but he told her ominously: "You won't need that."

Marguerite then understood her fate was one she feared even more than death: solitary confinement.[6] She dreaded being placed alone in a cell with only her own thoughts. Ever since her husband's death, she had coped with her grief by remaining constantly busy. Now she was placed alone in a dingy room with nothing to do but think.

She described the cell as about nine feet square with a single whitewashed window, a board bed, a small wooden table, and a waste can that served as a toilet. The peeling wallpaper was covered in notes and calendars in various languages, including one in English, and she wondered if the author might be one of the other Americans in the prison. Some messages were desperate, some defiant. A mathematician had worked out geometry problems. An artist had sketched soldiers. The inscriptions had a profound impact on her. She had been raised to command attention. "As I read these records of the prisoners who had been there before me, I began to realize how unimportant I was," she later wrote.[7]

McCullagh, who spent three days in solitary confinement, recalled that the prison superintendent visited him every day and asked a single question: "What is your name?" McCullagh assumed that when he no longer remembered, Cheka would deem him ready for examination.[8] McCullagh was not a weak man. He was a British intelligence officer who had twice before been imprisoned, and he had survived the arduous journey from Siberia to Moscow after the British forces retreated east. Nevertheless, he found the isolation cell nearly unbearable. "Deprived of outer stimulus or of any possibility of exercising itself, the mind tends to prey upon itself, and to become lost in morbid speculations and gloomy thoughts," he later wrote. He unashamedly admitted to turning to prayer for strength to endure the torture.[9]

Marguerite later said that survival in a Russian prison required a person to completely forget personal discomforts and focus on abstract matters of the mind and the spirit. To keep her sanity, she devised a schedule to occupy her time. She awoke each morning when an attendant opened the door and handed her a broom to sweep the cell. She next searched her sleeping bag for bedbugs that had invaded during the night. She asked the attendant to take her to the latrine where she took a sponge bath in cold water. When breakfast arrived, she spread her handkerchief on the table and placed on it the small slice of bread and mug of weak tea. Next came her morning exercise—pacing five hundred times the length of the room and back. Around eleven o'clock in the morning, the commandant checked on her and asked if she had any requests. The first day she asked for paper, pen, and books, but those were denied. After the commandant's visit came lunch—always herring soup and kasha. Like many of the American and British prisoners, Marguerite could not bring herself to eat the soup where fish eyes, tails, and backbones floated in the watery broth.

She devised various amusements to keep busy. She made playing cards out of cigarette boxes, but the guard took them away. She played jackstraws with matches and a hairpin until she grew tired of that. Then she softly sang all the songs she knew and recited all the poems she could remember. She quizzed herself in languages and history. Still, despite her best efforts to stay occupied, "the first day and the succeeding ones dragged interminably," she wrote.[10]

Harding said that unless one has experienced solitary confinement, one cannot know its psychological toll. "People often ask me if the cell was clean and what the food was like," Harding said. "These are natural questions, but they show that whoever puts them has not the faintest idea of the real torture of solitary confinement of this kind." Yes, the food was terrible and the cells were crawling with lice, she said, but the "real evil of this system . . . is that it tends to induce a state of abnormal sensibility in which the shock of each successive second is torment."[11]

After a week in solitary confinement, Marguerite appealed to Mogilevsky to end the torture. She told herself that he was not a cruel man and did not want her to suffer. After all, they had had pleasant conversations discussing French literature and political philosophy. He had shared his story of growing up in a provincial town and his thirst for social justice. He would be reasonable, she believed. So she asked the guard for a pencil and a scrap of paper, and she wrote to Mogilevsky in French requesting to see him. Within a couple of hours he called her to his office.

"You are the only person I can talk to," she told him. "I will be very glad to have you cross-examine me again, although I am afraid that my memory is no better than the last time. If you don't want to cross-examine me anymore, please put me in a room with other people. I can't stand being alone any longer."[12]

Mogilevsky again questioned her about foreign agents in Russia, but her vague replies irritated him, and so he turned her over to his secretary for questioning. Marguerite did not see Mogilevsky again for two months, and she was sorry. "Although we disagreed on many subjects from world revolution to herrings, of which he was evidently fond, for he often had a bowl of our prison soup for his dinner, I took a certain enjoyment in our verbal duels. He was a keen alert mind and he was a stimulating and resourceful enemy," she said.[13]

Marguerite's admiration for Mogilevsky contrasts with the opinions of other American and British prisoners who met him. Harding described him stupid and completely ignorant of conditions in Europe. His only expertise, she wrote, was to hunt and kill people.[14] McCullagh portrayed him as "thin, nervous in manner." Mogilevsky appeared perceptive when he asked McCullagh about a small, incriminating note written in shorthand that had been among the British agent's papers. But after McCullagh translated it—loosely—Mogilevsky was satisfied and asked no more about it.[15]

For her part, Marguerite's description of her captor resembled the way she wrote about her husband. She portrayed both as men who had risen above an impoverished childhood. Of Mogilevsky she wrote: "I had listened sympathetically to his accounts of his early life, first as a small boy with a thirst for knowledge growing up in a provincial town where all but elementary education was denied him, and already smarting under a sense of social injustice."[16]

Yet either Marguerite embellished her description of the Chekist or he did not tell her the truth. Rather than growing up poor, Mogilevsky was born in 1885 into a family of Jewish merchants in Pavlograd in the Ekaterinoslav Province in what is today Ukraine. Jews in Ukraine did suffer oppression, but Mogilevsky was not deprived of an education, and he attended high school. While still a teenager, he joined Socialist Revolutionaries and spent several months in prison until he fled to Switzerland. He studied law in Geneva, where he met Lenin, who recruited him to the Bolshevik Party. Returning to Ekaterinoslav in 1906, he worked as a propagandist in local factories for a year, and then he suspended his party activities in order to finish law school at Moscow University. After the Bolshevik Revolution, Mogilevsky served as chairman of the Ivanovo revolutionary tribunal, with the ultimate power to execute anyone he believed to be an enemy of the state. After proving himself in Ivanovo, he went to Moscow where he soon gained the attention of Felix Dzerzhinsky, who appointed him to head the investigation section of Cheka in 1919. In that role he helped uncover a British plot to oust Lenin. When he met Marguerite, he was in a new position as deputy director of the special section that aimed to create a foreign intelligence service.[17]

One way to recruit spies was to blackmail and intimidate foreigners caught in his web. Mogilevsky repeatedly pressed Stan Harding to strike a deal to spy for him in exchange for her freedom. During five months of imprisonment,

Mogilevsky interrogated her at least half a dozen times, alternating threats of execution with promises of freedom and reward.

After Marguerite's imprisonment, Mogilevsky interrogated her twice before relinquishing her to his secretary, a young officer with a penchant for math problems. Eventually Marguerite provided a lengthy report of her espionage activities. She told of volunteering to catch German spies in Baltimore in 1917 and recounted her work for MID in Berlin. She described the organizational structure of MID into positive (intelligence) and negative (counterintelligence) branches, and she admitted that she had come to Russia to assess political and economic situations and to locate American prisoners. Marguerite named many of the people she met in Germany, Poland, and Russia and offered insights into their political beliefs although—true to her word—she made no mention of either Merian Cooper or Francis McCullagh.

Based upon her signed confession, Cheka listed three charges against her: She had been a spy in Baltimore; she worked for the U.S. War Department in Berlin; and, most serious of all, "she gave information to Cheka in very poor quality," identifying only Stan Harding as a foreign agent. "On the basis of the above mentioned fact she is considered as a hostile and dangerous person to Society."[18]

Cheka officials were sufficiently satisfied with her admissions to move her from solitary confinement. Her new cell, which she would share with six to thirteen other women, was an irregular rectangle that resembled the shape of a European coffin. It was about eighteen feet long, seven feet wide at one end, and ten feet wide at the other. Two windows, one at each end, had been white-washed and sealed with putty, making it impossible for the inmates to see out-side. During the six months she spent in this cell, Marguerite saw the sun only twice, when she was taken out to the public baths. The room was warm, but the air reeked because of the lack of ventilation. Beds were arranged along the walls, and a long table occupied the middle of the room.[19]

When Marguerite first arrived, she found seven other women from various backgrounds, including peasants and aristocrats. One woman, wearing a worn Parisian suit and straw slippers greeted Marguerite. "I see that you are a foreigner," she said in flawless French. "This is very poor hospitality to offer you in Russia."[20]

Marguerite claimed the best bunk in the cell, which was oddly unoccupied. It was next to a window at the narrow end of the cell and provided a little fresh air and a commanding view that was outside of the guard's persistent gaze from the peephole. Soon Marguerite learned about her cellmates. The woman in the Parisian suit had been arrested because of an alleged relationship with a White Army officer. The other inmates included three clerks from the War Office who were arrested as witnesses to a counterrevolutionary plot; a Latvian Communist suspected of being an agent provocateur; the wife of a naval officer imprisoned in the next room; and a sixteen-year-old peasant arrested because she was overheard to repeat a rumor that there would soon be a new revolution.

Over the ensuing months women came and went. The remaining prisoners never knew the fate of those who left. They might have been freed, transferred to another prison, sent to a Siberian work camp, or executed. Marguerite wrote that she knew of only one woman who was condemned to death. The prisoner, whom she called Natya in one published account and Tasya in another, had once been a ballet dancer and stood falsely accused of helping White Army officers. She nevertheless serenely accepted her fate because of another crime that she told Marguerite she did commit. She said she had been a dedicated Communist and a political commissar in the Red Army in Ukraine when one day a White officer was brought to her for questioning. He was the most handsome man she had ever seen, and when she asked him if he had any statement to make, he told her he had done all of which he was accused and had no regrets. He wanted to live like a gentleman, and he could not do so under a Communist system. The woman was overwhelmed by passion and devised a plan to save him. She told him she was leaving the room for ten minutes and that the man could escape if he wanted. But when she returned to the room, he was still there.

"Why didn't you go?" she asked him.

"Look at me," he told her. "I think you are the most wonderful woman I have ever seen. God made you to be loved, not hated. You are throwing away your divine birthright. It is monstrous that you should send men to their deaths, but you will never do it again. I watched your face when we were talking a while ago. You are still a woman in spite of your hideous creed. You love me and you cannot deny it. I knew from the first moment I saw you that you were the woman I had dreamed of all my life. . . . If I die tomorrow you will never forget me and never condemn another man to death."[21]

The woman told Marguerite that the next morning she witnessed the man bravely face the firing squad. She continued another week as the political commissar, but, as the officer had predicted, she could not order another man to death. She pleaded ill and took a leave from her work. "I had committed a crime against the party, and my faith in myself was gone," she said. A few days after relating her story the guards took the woman away, and Marguerite never heard of her again.[22]

The goal for every inmate—aristocrat or peasant, Russian or foreign—was survival. Some prisoners, such as Stan Harding, resorted to hunger strikes to demand better treatment. Many agreed to spy on their cellmates in exchange for increased rations. Only a small number were as lucky as Merian Cooper and actually escaped. No reliable statistics exist for the number of Cheka prisoners at this time. According to one report, 21,697 were held in prison, 7,488 were in concentration camps, 4,139 were in forced labor camps, and 5,491 were held hostage in 1919. Those numbers were surely underreported.[23]

A prisoner's first step to staying alive was to keep as clean as possible in a cell infested with lice and fleas that carried deadly typhus. Three women in Marguerite's cell contracted the disease, and the rest waited anxiously to see if they, too, would succumb. They had no medicine, but the women did their best to care for one another, applying cool compresses to those suffering hysterics, trying to make pregnant women comfortable, and sharing their aid packages with their friends. Once a prostitute suffering from advanced syphilis went mad in the middle of the night and tried to attack the other women with a bottle. The inmates held her to the floor until guards took her away, biting and screaming. Hunger was a constant. According to one estimate, the rations given prisoners amounted to about 750 calories a day, and unless a prisoner received aid packages from the Red Cross or a similar organization, starvation was inevitable.[24] Whenever the women received any extra bread, they broke it into cubes and dried it to consume in lean times.

Survival also meant finding ways to occupy their minds. They softly sang songs so the guards could not hear, told stories, engaged in political debates, and predicted each other's fortunes. Fluent now in five languages, Marguerite also mastered the prison communication of tapping on pipes to send messages to the inmates in other cells. Men who were locked next door managed to poke out a small hole in the wall separating the rooms and the women took turns making friends with the men.

A little over a month after arriving at Lubyanka, word of her incarceration reached Baltimore. The *Sun* reported that Marguerite had been imprisoned for trying to bribe her way out of Russia. The newspaper said that none of her friends or family members had heard from her in six months. Tommy had returned home from Switzerland in July and received a letter in August saying only his mother was well. The newspaper noted the complications of negotiating her release because the United States did not recognize the Bolshevik government.[25] The next day, Albert Ritchie, now governor of Maryland, wrote to U.S. Secretary of State Bainbridge Colby, citing the *Sun* article and asking whether he knew anything more. "Mrs. Harrison has been a life-long friend of mine and I have long been worried about her," Ritchie wrote.[26] Ritchie contacted U.S. officials repeatedly to inquire about Marguerite's welfare and ask if he could help. Newspapers began to speculate that one reason Marguerite might have been captured was because of her relationship to the Maryland governor.

In mid-December the *Sun* published an advance copy of an article that would appear the next day in the *New York World* providing details of her imprisonment. Coincidentally, the *World* was the paper that had hired Stan Harding; although Harding had been released, the article noted similarities of the two cases. The newspaper speculated that both women had been seized as hostages to force England and the United States to recognize the Bolshevik government. The *World* quoted a statement from the Russian government that said Marguerite had confessed to being an American spy and had volunteered to become a double agent in exchange for her freedom. The newspaper, however, called the allegation "preposterous."[27]

Other reporters repeated the Russian allegations, including Louise Bryant, who was a Moscow correspondent for King Features. The British Admiralty intercepted her radio dispatch to the Hearst Newspapers' office in Berlin and sent a copy to the U.S. MID. Bryant related: "As an agent of the Soviets, she [Marguerite] is responsible for the arrest of many of her compatriots. In some cases, she gave correct information, in others absolutely false."[28]

As Christmas 1920 approached Marguerite saw no hope for release. She heard almost nothing of the outside world and no news from her family and friends except one letter from Tommy telling her that he had returned to Baltimore in July and was living with his grandparents. His two-paged typed letter described his year at the Swiss boarding school. He said that during "the first two or three weeks I was pretty blue," but he made friends, played hockey and tennis, and learned a great deal. "I really feel that in no other way could I have gained so much in such a short space of time as I did at La Villa," he wrote. He had taken a job with Barnes-Jackson Grain Merchants in Baltimore and said he planned to go into the shipping business. His closing must have reminded Marguerite of herself: "The winter promises to be one of the greatest we've ever had for gaiety. I'm restless, though. I want to get on a ship and travel."[29]

Christmas was difficult for the inmates who longed to be with their families. A few of Marguerite's cellmates were lucky enough to be released before the holiday, but she and five others who remained tried their best to celebrate. A few days before Christmas they were taken to the public baths, and they found in the street a few evergreen branches that had been discarded by a Christmas tree vendor. From the twigs they fashioned a tree that they decorated with bits of paper, cardboard, and cotton. Their holiday meal included two cans of corned beef Marguerite received from the Czechoslovak Red Cross, two salt herrings, rice pudding, bread, butter, and tea. The guards agreed to keep their cell light on, and the inmates played games until midnight and then sat down to their meager dinner. Afterward they each sang Christmas carols from their home countries. Marguerite sang "O Little Town of Bethlehem" and after the others had gone to bed, hid small pieces of chocolate she had saved from aid packages under their wooden headrests.

Marguerite, never comfortable with organized religion, became superstitious and drawn to mysticism as the months passed. She began to imagine that she could send and receive thoughts and that she could read the minds of the other inmates. She also dabbled in fortune telling and developed a reputation as an accurate prognosticator. On New Year's Eve the women played a game in which each wrote down on scraps of paper possible events: a meeting, a journey, an enemy, a trial, liberty, prison, and death. Each then drew three pieces. Marguerite twice drew imprisonment and then journey—predictions that would come true in the next four years.[30]

In mid-January the Bolsheviks seemed ready to make a deal with the United States to free her. Washington Vanderlip, a negotiator representing the new Warren Harding administration, offered to reestablish trade in exchange for valuable mining concessions in Siberia, port access on Sakhalin Island, and freedom of American prisoners. Mogilevsky summoned Marguerite to his office to tell her she might soon be released, but the Soviets wanted her to make it clear that she had not been mistreated. Marguerite agreed to write a letter to Albert Ritchie telling him she was well.

"Our prison can hardly be named one with such conditions," she wrote cheer-
fully. "It is rebuilt from a hotel and only the windows have bars so the rooms
can hardly be called a prison. My room is quite spacious and light with two big
windows. My bed is located in a corner close to one. I had enough time during
my arrest to take all necessary things with me. Every morning we are met by
Red Army soldier with smile." She went on to lie about the food: "Our breakfast
contains hot coffee, good bread and sugar. . . . Our lunch contains a big piece of
soup from fish, potatoes, vegetables, cabbage and for the second course kasha. . . .
As you can see, we are not starving." She told him of the Christmas celebration and ended by saying that the Reds had the right to arrest her because she
had entered the country illegally. "I have no reason to complain," she wrote.[31] In
another, undated letter to Ritchie, Marguerite asserted that the Soviet government was in control and had implemented "strong and admirable" changes in
Russian society. She told him that the people were clothed and fed better than
before the revolution, adding, "no one has any use for a constitutional assembly."[32]

But the weeks passed, and nothing came of the Vanderlip negotiations. Mogilevsky called her back to his office and told her to write the U.S. State Department asking officials to admit that she was a spy and agree to trade talks in
exchange for her release. Marguerite refused, knowing the State Department
would never acknowledge its agents.[33]

Meanwhile, Marguerite's friends continued to send aid packages and work
for her release. *Baltimore Sun* editor Frank Kent appealed to the Associated Press
for help, and the wire agency asked the powerful London press baron Lord Beaverbrook to lobby Soviet trade minister Leonid Krasin for her freedom. Johns
Hopkins urologist Dr. Hugh Young, a friend of Marguerite's father-in-law, also
appealed to Beaverbrook for help.[34] Joseph Ames, meanwhile, wrote her letters
to bolster her spirits and assured her she had not been forgotten. "I see a great
many of your friends almost every day and everybody is anxiously inquiring
about you," he said. "When you come home, you are liable to receive a city welcome—possibly the Mayor will give you the freedom of the city."[35]

Her friends and family must have been particularly anxious given the news
reports coming from Russia. Some accounts were wildly inaccurate. On January
21 the *Baltimore Sun* and other newspapers quoted Soviet officials who mistak-
enly said Marguerite had been released. In April the *New York Herald* quoted a
Communist organizer who had visited Russia and said Marguerite had been tortured. The article went on to say that she had not seen her "infant son" in more

than year, although Tommy was eighteen. "Broken in health by frequent transfers and Bolshevik inquisitions and savage interrogations, she is a nervous wreck and . . . she has been forced to sign all sorts of documents on promises of release which are never kept," the paper reported. The *New York Times* reported that all of the American prisoners were suffering but that Marguerite's situation was the most serious. According to the article, Marguerite was held in solitary confinement and "barely keeping alive with the rations served." The next day the paper reprinted an excerpt of the same report, adding that the news distressed her friends and family members who had been sending her packages of food and clothing.[36]

As famine ravaged Russia, America's demands for the release of the prisoners became more urgent. Merian Cooper joined the chorus of those describing the horrors of Russian prisons, and he insisted that action be taken to free Marguerite and the others.[37] In early May Cooper wrote to the State Department, volunteering to covertly return to Russia to rescue some of the prisoners. Cooper thought that it would be impossible to reach Marguerite and those held in Lubyanka, but he believed he had a chance of saving Red Cross worker Capt. Emmet Kilpatrick and Thomas Hazelwood, also known as Russell R. Pattinger, an American soldier whom Cheka believed to be insane. Both men were held in numerous prisons, although at the time Cooper volunteered the rescue mission, he probably thought they were held at the Andronievsky prison camp on the grounds of a Moscow monastery.[38]

The Bolsheviks tried to dispel the accusations they were mistreating the American prisoners. A representative of the Soviet Foreign Office told the *Baltimore Sun* in late April that Marguerite wasn't in prison at all but "living in a villa about a fifteen-minute walk from the Kremlin." The same article quoted a cable from Maryland senator Joseph I. France, a staunch supporter of recognizing the Bolshevik government, who said he didn't believe reports Marguerite was being mistreated.[39] Days later the unofficial Soviet foreign office in New York telegrammed the *Sun* to repeat the message that she was well. "Inform Governor Ritchie that his sister-in-law, Marguerite E. Harrison, is in good health. Statement from Associated Press picturing her in dire straits here is untrue. She cannot be released at present in light of her activities as self-confessed spy."[40]

In May the Foreign Office either allowed or forced Marguerite to write another letter to Ritchie describing her Easter celebration. "The supper was wonderful, and I doubt if any people in Moscow fared as bountiful as we," she told him. She defended Cheka's ruthless tactics as necessary. "The Russian people as a whole are weak in civic responsibility and lacking in patriotism— nothing but a strong hand could control the unusual disposition to evade the law, which is not captured to any one party. Without oppressive measures there would be economic and political chaos." She went on: "It is a pity that we in America know so little about Russia. I myself realize that the majority of our people are under the misapprehension as to the real state of affairs. I have been for six months in the most strict prison in Moscow and I have not heard of, or seen, a single act of cruelty or 'Bolshevik Atrocity.'"[41]

The Bolsheviks undoubtedly forced Marguerite to write favorably about her treatment and conditions in Russia, but she gave surprisingly similar accounts after her release. A notable example was her description of the Easter celebration. In her memoir, Marguerite wrote that the Easter table she and her cellmates set "was so beautiful that the guards themselves stared open-mouthed at it every time they opened the door." She described a centerpiece of flowers surrounded by gaily colored Easter eggs, ham, raisin bread, vegetable salad, and pickled herring. Yet that spring Russia was suffering from one of the worst famines in history. As Marguerite had noted on the trip down the Volga the previous summer, fertile fields had been left fallow amid the chaos of the economic revolution. Before it was over the famine of 1920–21 would cost an estimated five million lives. Aid workers reported Moscow residents collapsing in the streets while in the countryside desperate peasants resorted to cannibalism. By summer the situation had become so dire that the Bolsheviks were no longer negotiating contracts for mining and port access but desperately seeking American food. Hunger was so widespread that it is inconceivable that the guards would merely have stared at such a bountiful table unless Marguerite and her cellmates were given special privileges.

Shortly after Easter Marguerite and eight prisoners in her cell were moved to the attic. Prison officials may have learned that they were communicating with the men next door, or perhaps their room was needed to accommodate an influx of prisoners. In any case, they found the new quarters much worse. Not only was the cell smaller but the fumes of fresh paint and the waste pail that had no lid made the women sick. They protested until the guards called the warden, who immediately broke open the window.[42]

Although Marguerite insisted that she was not mistreated, the months of confinement and the poor diet inevitably took their toll. In her May letter to Albert Ritchie, she wrote that she was bothered by chronic bronchitis, but her condition was much more serious. She had contracted tuberculosis. Since winter she had been bothered by a persistent cough and fever, and despite daily exercise and some simple remedies prescribed by the prison doctor, she grew weaker. With release seeming unlikely, she knew her only hope for survival was to transfer to a prison where she could get fresh air. She petitioned several times to be moved, and finally toward June Cheka agreed to send her to the Novinsky women's prison.

On the day of her transfer, a soldier escorted her from Lubyanka into the street, where she stood dumbfounded by the noise of the passing trams and carts and blinded by the brilliant light of the June sun. She searched for the car or cart she expected to take her to the new prison, but it did not arrive.

"Aren't you going to requisition a droshky?" she asked the guard who stood beside her side with a rifle slung over his shoulder.

"I have no authority to do that," he replied. "We will have to walk."

Marguerite could barely stand, and, loaded with her bag and knapsack, she knew she would not make it far. Nevertheless, she agreed to try. "Where is the Novinsky prison?" she asked him.

"I don't know," the boy answered, smiling bashfully.

"Then you must ask someone," she commanded. He only kept grinning stupidly.

Marguerite took charge and asked a man she saw passing in the street for direction. "I am a prisoner and am being transferred from the Lubyanka to the Novinsky prison," she explained. "But my guard has not the faintest idea where it is."

The man showed no surprise at the strange pronouncement. Instead, he gave her directions but added, "You can't walk there. It is at least six versts (four miles) from here and you have a lot of baggage to carry."

Marguerite had no money to pay for a cab, so she tried offering two cans of American corn beef in exchange for a ride. Finally an old man with one leg agreed to take her. She and her guard piled her belongings into his carriage, took a seat in the back, and traveled to Novinsky.[43]

The women's prison had been built about ten years earlier on the site of a former monastery. It consisted of several buildings surrounded by a brick wall.

To Marguerite, it seemed like a "terrestrial paradise." The courtyard included grass plots with flowering shrubs and benches where women sat talking or sewing. Children of the inmates played in the dirt. In the middle of the courtyard was a small white church and behind that a library. The complex included the prison blocks, administrative offices, a hospital, school, workshop, and recreation hall.

Some women who had been with Marguerite in Lubyanka rushed to greet her and ask what had happened to the others they had known. They helped her to a large cell that she would share with eleven others, all but two political prisoners such as herself. She found conditions much better at Novinsky. The prison had clean toilets with modern plumbing, hot water, and baths. The cells doors were open, and the women could go freely about until night. Food packages arrived daily, and political prisoners could even see friends and relatives. The library was stocked with Russian classics as well as a few books and magazines in French, English, and German. The Socialists at the prison were allowed newspapers, which they shared with Marguerite. In the evenings the inmates often engaged in political debates and held musical concerts.

But despite the better surroundings, Marguerite's health worsened. The Novinsky doctors admitted her to the prison hospital, where she enjoyed the luxury of a straw mattress and rations that included dried apples, tinned beef, and a generous portion of rice and wheat cereal. Medical care, nevertheless, was sorely deficient. The prison possessed just one hypodermic syringe and two needles with which the doctor administered cholera vaccine to 248 inmates and gave Marguerite daily injections of arsenic.

Marguerite's roommate in the hospital was a Polish woman accused of espionage. Her attendant was imprisoned for killing her sister. Other hospital attendants were professional thieves, including a train station pickpocket and a prostitute who robbed her clients. Marguerite loved talking with the criminals and studying their psychology. She never grew bored as hundreds of inmates passed through Novinsky on their way to internment camps in Siberia and Arkhangelsk.

Although a prison for women, Novinsky could nevertheless be a violent place. The inmates often beat suspected thieves and spies while the guards pretended not to see. Marguerite recalled that one woman feigned insanity and set herself on fire. The same woman led a mob that nearly beat a suspected spy to death. Fights often broke out on Sundays, which usually was the day women with criminal charges were allowed visitors. If they had violated prison rules, however, their families were not allowed inside the prison and instead climbed a bell tower of a nearby church to shout greetings to their loved ones. The noise was so great the women grew angry when they couldn't hear their relatives. Fights erupted, with scratching and hair pulling.

Marguerite took the violence in stride, but she was bothered by what she termed widespread "sexual perversion." She had been attracted to a girl at St. Tim's and romanticized Stan Harding, but she criticized lesbianism as an "incalculable evil" that she believed grew from segregating the sexes and "suppressing normal instincts." She lamented that Novinsky was not rehabilitating women to make them better suited to live in society.

As summer progressed the famine grew worse and the Bolsheviks more desperate to strike a deal to trade the American inmates for aid. Already a similar arrangement had helped free British nationals, but about a dozen Americans were still unable to leave the country. Marguerite's friends told her she surely would be released soon, but Marguerite didn't dare hope so. "I felt as if I had always been at the Novinsky. I seldom thought of home or family or anything of the world outside," she recalled.[44]

In early June Marguerite's case went to the highest authority in Soviet Russia—Vladimir Lenin. Senator France wrote to Lenin asking permission to enter Russia to discuss the release of the American prisoners in exchange for food aid. France, who was facing reelection in the fall, was especially eager to free one of his constituents. Russian foreign minister Leonid Krasin urged Lenin to approve France's visit, hoping it signaled a turning point in American-Soviet relations. Lenin agreed and met France in Moscow on Friday, July 15. France explained to Lenin the realities of American politics. He had long advocated for diplomatic recognition of the Bolshevik government and restored trade between the two countries, but many Americans abhorred Communism and distrusted the Reds. He told Lenin that he did not believe Marguerite was being tortured and that he thought she indeed was a spy, but he needed to do something to help her because she was a citizen of Maryland and her former brother-in-law was the governor. Lenin promised to talk it over with Foreign Minister Georgy Chicherin and Cheka deputy Jozef Unshlikht and give him an answer by the following Monday.[45]

While he awaited word on Lenin's decision, France visited Marguerite in the Novinsky prison. Marguerite had never met France, but she recognized him from pictures she had seen in the newspaper. Marguerite recalled that her first thought was the senator had become a Bolshevik. Almost at the same time, she thought "perhaps he has come to take me home!"

France told her he was hoping to take her with him the following Monday, but she put the idea out of her mind when he left. Too many times she had been disappointed. Monday came and went without news. So did Tuesday. Then, on Wednesday night, the head of Cheka's American Bureau ordered her to pack her bags to go with him to Lubyanka for her trial, which was to be the next day. The doctor at Novinsky, however, refused to let her leave because she was running a fever. Instead, two guards and attendant searched her and took her papers, including the verses to Russia songs and poems that she had learned in prison.

"What does this mean?" she asked.

"It means you will be deported tomorrow," one of the guards told her.

That night, Marguerite found sleep impossible. She packed her bags early the next morning and said goodbye to her friends. "Suddenly I realized that a close tie was about to be broken," she said. "Prison friendships are about the most real things in the world."

Late the next day, a car arrived and took her back to Lubyanka where she waited anxiously for her release. She at last was taken to the head of the American section and interrogated about the papers the guards had seized. He was especially curious about a crochet piece of lace in which she had stitched the Latin words *per aspera ad astra*—through difficulties to the stars. She persuaded him the words were not a secret code, and he handed her a release order.

"Thank you," she replied numbly.

Senator France was waiting for her to accompany him to Riga that night. The officer told her she would not have time to gather her things because the train was about to leave. She asked that her money be donated to the Red Cross to help children and that her personal belongings be forwarded to her in Riga. As she was making these final arrangements, Mogilevsky suddenly appeared to say goodbye.

"You and I have been enemies, it is true," he said. "But it was all part of a big game. I hope you feel that I had nothing against you personally and also that sometime you may be able to come back to Russia under happier auspices."

"I feel exactly the same way, Citizen Mogilevsky," she answered. "I hope that one day I will return to Russia under different conditions."

Marguerite imagined that Mogilevsky hoped one day to convert her to Bolshevism. She hoped the Communist dictatorship would give way to democratic Socialism. They smiled and shook hands.[46]

Neither could imagine that in sixteen months they would meet again in Lubyanka.

One week after Marguerite left Russia, Mogilevsky assumed command of Cheka's foreign intelligence department charged with recruiting spies to work for the Soviet government abroad. Meanwhile, the men who led America's spy agencies wondered if their prized female agent could still be trusted.

"A LADY WITH A MYSTERIOUS PAST"

MARGUERITE FINALLY WAS on her way home, but she did not completely leave Russia behind. Nine months in Soviet prisons had left her ill, weak, and nervous. She would recover from the physical ailments. More serious, however, were the suspicions that followed her.

Days before she left the Novinsky prison hospital, U.S. Army general Dennis Nolan, who had succeeded Marlborough Churchill as director of MID, wrote to her father-in-law, Joseph Ames, to give him news on Marguerite's condition. He told him that the American military attaché in London had received word from Scotland Yard that Marguerite was working with a British journalist, Morgan Philips Price, a suspected Bolshevik sympathizer. The source also reported that she was a liaison between the Soviet government and Wolff Telegraphic Bureau, a German news agency. Nolan noted that Marguerite might be pretending to help the Soviets in order to "keep herself out of Peter and Paul (Prison) and to obtain provisions," and he cautioned that the information was not confirmed.[1]

As with the earlier newspaper accounts of Marguerite's imprisonment, the intelligence report contained some truth and some inaccuracies. Marguerite had spied for Russian authorities and may have collaborated with Soviet agents, but she had not managed to stay out of prison. American intelligence officials were understandably anxious to know the truth about the extent of her collaboration with the Bolshevik government.

Marguerite later said she remembered little about the two-day trip from Moscow to the Latvian capital, Riga. She shared a sleeping car with Senator France, an arrangement he found appalling. But after almost a year of living in prison cells with strangers, Marguerite considered the bed with its privacy curtains the height of luxury. When the train stopped inexplicably for several hours at the

Latvian border, Marguerite grew nervous, recalling that other prisoners had been forced back to Russia just as they were almost free. She and France were both relieved as their train eventually lumbered on across the border.

U.S. military attaché Col. Worthington Hollyday and his wife met Marguerite in Riga. Even amid a crowd of other passengers from Russia, Marguerite stood out. She was still dressed in the clothes she had worn in prison—the crumpled khaki suit she had on the night she was arrested, a man's shirt that a Jewish aid worker had given her, a cap she had fashioned from a shirt, and men's shoes that were many sizes too large. The newspapers reported that she looked thin and pale.

The Hollydays immediately took her to their apartment, gave her new clothes, and showed her to a bedroom. Marguerite reveled in a long, hot bath in a porcelain tub and lunch served on china plates, although she had little appetite. The first night she could scarcely sleep in the soft bed. She could not believe she really was free. "The next morning I woke with a sense of unreality," she said. "I felt as if I were still dreaming until the maid came in with my coffee."[2]

On her first day in Riga she was inundated with congratulatory telegrams. Tommy messaged that he would be sailing to London to meet her. Joseph Ames and Albert Ritchie offered to wire her money. The Associated Press clamored for a story. Local and foreign reporters waited to interview her—the only American woman to survive a Bolshevik prison. The commotion overwhelmed her. After months of trying to find ways to occupy herself, she suddenly had too many things to think about and too much to do. She managed to cable the *Baltimore Sun* to express her thanks to Senator France for winning her freedom, and she spent the first morning working on reports for MID. Only later that day did she realize the effect imprisonment had on her nerves. When she ventured out to go shopping, she became frightened by the city's noise and the traffic and froze on the curb, afraid to cross the street.[3]

Hollyday forwarded to Washington the reports Marguerite wrote for MID in Riga. They contained names and descriptions of American prisoners and suspected Bolshevik agents and shed light on Marguerite's opinions about the people she had encountered in Russia. She described prisoner Thomas Hazelwood as "crazy and crooked." Others she identified as Bolshevik agents, including the man who had been assigned to guide American negotiator Washington Vanderlip. As for journalist Albert Boni, Marguerite was uncertain. "He is either an agent for our government or playing a big game for himself," she reported. The final name on the list she furnished to Hollyday was Stan Harding. Despite what she had told the Bolsheviks and what she later wrote in her memoir, she did not list Harding as a British spy. Instead she called her an English woman and correspondent for the *New York World* who had betrayed her. "I took her into my room in Berlin, lent her money (which she has never returned); and several times paid her for information," Marguerite wrote. And while Harding alleged that Marguerite had falsely denounced her, Marguerite said it was Harding who had betrayed her: "She testified in Moscow as to my activities in Berlin."[4]

Although Marlborough Churchill no longer directed MID, he was eager to learn the truth about his prized agent, and he asked Hollyday for a "gossipy letter" about Marguerite, Senator France, and the others returning from Russia. Churchill knew, of course, that Marguerite had been forced to work for Cheka. She herself had managed to get word to MID that agents should stay away from her because she had been compromised. Then, in February, the *Philadelphia Inquirer* published several articles by Stan Harding in which she described her imprisonment and blamed an American secret agent she called "Madame X" for falsely denouncing her. Churchill and many outside the intelligence community knew Marguerite was "Madame X." Had Marguerite really become a Red agent?[5]

A few weeks after receiving Churchill's request for information, Hollyday responded. He described France as naïvely enamored of the Bolshevik leaders and poorly informed of the real conditions in Russia. As for Marguerite, he wrote, "She did not ring true to me." He said he found her interesting and reasonable but said, "It is my personal opinion that Mrs. Harrison agreed to say certain things before she was released, and she feels that she is indebted to Senator France to such an extent that she must say the things he wants her to say. Furthermore, she is herself rather involved and is afraid to come out too openly against the Bolsheviks because they have something on her." Hollyday's cryptic allegations about Marguerite being involved with the Soviets are difficult to decipher. His statement about Marguerite being involved with the Bolsheviks indicates he knew she had worked as a double agent, but did he doubt her veracity? He found no fault with her statements that the United States had no reason to fear the Third International and should recognize the Bolshevik government. He also agreed with her that the best way to confront Communism was to show the Russians better alternatives.[6]

His skepticism about Marguerite might have stemmed from the incredible statement she gave to reporters in Riga about her prison experience. Her recital, without emotion and occasionally interrupted by a deep cough, began with a listing of facts of when and how she entered Russia. She made no mention of her role as an American spy or that she had been forced to work for Cheka. She told the journalists that she had been arrested for entering the Russia illegally, for supplying British and American prisoners with unauthorized aid, and for meeting with counterrevolutionaries. She went on to say that the reported horrors and suffering in the Russian prisons were exaggerated. She described the cell where she had been locked for a week in solitary confinement as a "room like a small single room of a hotel" and said "generally speaking the rations were as good as, or better than, the Soviet dining room outside."[7] She told the news reporters, "My only privation was my inability to procure good cigarettes."[8] Marguerite was the first of the American prisoners freed in exchange for American food aid, but a week later when the others followed and told their stories, her statements seemed even more incredible.

Rather than defend their captors and praise the Bolshevik authorities, the other Americans told horror stories about their confinement. Capt. Emmett Kilpatrick, a Red Cross officer left weak from scurvy and lung problems, described a living hell in his basement cell in Lubyanka "with rats and the overflow of a sewer running about his feet." He was confined next to the execution room where "water runs over the floor constantly to wash away the blood," he said.[9] Weston B. Estes, a military intelligence officer who entered Russia under the pretext of being a filmmaker, was imprisoned with Kilpatrick and described filthy conditions in the prison hospitals and long confinement in a basement cell with no windows. Estes had once been a dentist, and he told reporters that he pulled the gold teeth of condemned men in order to send the nuggets to their families. Contrary to Marguerite, who amazingly found an empty bed next to a window when she entered her cell, Estes described inmates fighting over prized beds near windows. He said he was unable to fight because he suffered internal injuries when he was thrown down basement steps after an interrogation, but he held on to his bed made of two saw horses and three boards.[10] Xenophon Kalamatiano, an American agent who had been sentenced to death for his involvement in a plot to blow up bridges near St. Petersburg, described listening to the crack of rifles of the firing squad outside his cell, of undergoing repeated interrogations with little sleep, and of suffering long periods without food.[11]

After four days in Riga Marguerite continued her trip home, passing through Berlin. There, to her surprise, she saw Merian Cooper waiting for her at the train station. Although she had provided him aid packages, she had met Cooper only once, at the dance at the Adlon Hotel in Warsaw more than a year earlier. Nevertheless, she had wondered what had become of him. Hollyday had told her Cooper had escaped from Russia, but she had no idea that he would travel so many miles to see her. Cooper, a Southerner with a deep sense of honor and duty, believed she had saved his life by providing him aid packages. "I would have gone around the world to see you," he told her.[12] Newspaper reporters who heard this, speculated that Cooper and Marguerite were lovers, but she later denied they had any romantic involvement.

Cooper told her he had been formulating a plan to rescue her from Novinsky prison. Working with Polish agents, he had made arrangements to bribe one of the Novinsky guards to bring her to the prison gate. There a Polish operative was to meet her and take her to a wide meadow, where Cooper, flying in from Warsaw, was to pick her up and fly her to safety. "It would have been a much more romantic method of leaving Russia than the one which had fallen to my lot, but I was glad for his sake, as well as mine, that he had never been able to put it into execution. The chances would have been overwhelmingly against him," she wrote later.[13]

Also meeting her at the Berlin station was an old friend, Johns Hopkins physician Hugh Young, who had been in France when he heard news of her release. He and a German doctor examined Marguerite and concluded she was in remarkably good health, aside from nervousness brought on by insomnia and lack of appetite. The *Baltimore Sun*, which published the findings, noted that these symptoms were normal for someone who had gone so long without proper nourishment.[14] Marguerite later recalled that her health was good aside from being undernourished and having "a touch of tuberculosis." She said, "My nerves were as strong as ever, and I was rapidly readjusting myself to a normal existence."[15]

She amazed an entourage in Germany when she marched into the clothing store closest to her hotel and walked out fifteen minutes later with dresses, shoes, and other necessities. The men who accompanied her told a reporter that they had never seen a woman make up her mind so quickly, whereupon Marguerite replied: "They probably had never seen a woman escape from jail with so few clothes, and those a year old."[16] She explained that she was getting ready to meet Tommy in London. "So I must shake off my Russian appearance before then."[17]

Marguerite had regained not only her sense of humor but also her sense of duty. In Berlin she gave the American military observer an account of her imprisonment that contradicted what she had told the newspapermen in Riga. Despite telling reporters that she knew of no atrocities and ate well while in prison, she told the Berlin office that Cheka was routinely executing Socialist Revolutionaries and that the food shortage had become so severe that the Soviets were forced to release criminals from prison. Although she made public statements calling on the United States to recognize Soviet Russia, in her report she said that the Bolsheviks should not be trusted and were bent on stirring up trouble in the United States, England, and Germany.

She also made it clear that she intended to continue her work for the intelligence service. She reported the conversations she had had on the train with Danish representatives about a munitions factory in Helsinki and with Lithuanian Jews about Communism. She told the Berlin office that Senator France had been deluded by Russian propaganda, and she offered to compile a list of the documents he had carried with him. If military officials wanted more information about France, she asked them to let her know what they needed. Then, foreshadowing her next adventure, she told her commanders that the Bolsheviks "have a most wonderful net work [sic] of propaganda centers throughout Asia. They have a map marked with red circles, showing propaganda centers, and red lines showing the principal routes to the centers, which covers all of China, Korea, Tibet, Afghanistan, India, Persia, Beluchistan [Pakistan], etc.—in fact all Asiatic countries."[18] Out of Soviet prison for only ten days, Marguerite was ready to return to service.

The intention must have been in her mind a week later when she reunited with Tommy at a London train station. She had not seen him for two years and still imagined him as a small boy. Instead, she was greeted by a dapper nineteen-year-old man in a dark suit and straw hat who was taller than she. "Hello, Mother," he said matter-of-factly. "Hello, Tommy dear. Goodness how you've grown!" she exclaimed.[19] She recalled that she clung to him as if she would never let go. But, of course, she would and they both knew it.

Marguerite had been liberated only one week when she wrote her first bylined article for the *Baltimore Sun* about her experience. She repeated the earlier statement that the Bolsheviks had reason to arrest her because she entered Russia illegally. She provided a general description of the people she had met and the events she had witnessed. Carefully avoiding any mention of espionage, she said her first arrest in April was related to the Polish offensive, and she repeated that the officers of Cheka and the prison guards always treated her courteously. She wrote that they moved her from solitary confinement after she requested it and that they transferred her to a prison hospital when she became sick with "a bad cold." All in all, she had no regrets, she said. "It was a wonderful experience and well worth the price I paid, which, after all, was the result of my entering Russia uninvited." With the United States having agreed to give humanitarian aid to Russia, she said Americans needed to know more about the country and she promised to provide information in future articles.[20]

In her next piece she wrote that the Bolsheviks were firmly in power, and no other party was sufficiently strong to mount a counterrevolution.[21] In another article she supported the Bolshevik position that a Soviet committee, rather than an American agency, should oversee aid distribution inside Russia. Responding to critics who opposed helping Russia until all U.S. citizens were released, she said that many of the Americans still in the country did not want to leave. In another article she explained that humanitarian relief would help the Russian people settle on the best political system.[22]

Her refusal to publicly criticize her former captors puzzled her friends and family members but did not detract from their joy at seeing her safely out of prison. When she arrived in New York on August 26, 1921, she was met by a crowd of reporters and photographers anxious to speak to the first American who had been released as part of the food-aid agreement. As her steamship arrived, her father-in-law, Joseph Ames; *Baltimore Sun* owner Van Lear Black; and her old friend Mary McCarty stood on the pier to greet her. "I am not a martyr at all, but a very happy woman just returned from a rather uncomfortable, but extremely interesting experience," Marguerite told the reporters.[23]

Senator France, who accompanied Marguerite on the voyage, used the occasion to repeat his position that the United States should immediately recognize the Bolshevik government and establish normal trade relations. The Republican senator was a minority among American leaders in his expressed admiration for Lenin, calling him one of the "outstanding statesmen of his day." Ignoring the famine that was raging through the Volga region, France described the Russian farming community as "reasonably content." He pointed out that nearly all other major nations had recognized the Bolshevik government. "When America knows the truth, which I will tell from Washington, America will demand a reversal of policy, and will insist that Russia be aided on Russia's account as well as on our own," he said.[24]

For a few days Marguerite put aside the questions of world politics to enjoy the reunion with her family and friends. Black offered his new, 140-foot yacht, *Sabalo*, to take her home, and she and Tommy sailed leisurely down the East Coast, stopping to lunch at the seaside resort of Cape May, New Jersey. Black had planned to sail to Baltimore, but Marguerite was so anxious to get home, he docked in Delaware City, and Marguerite and her companions took a car the rest of the way. It was nearly ten o'clock in the evening when she finally reached the stately brick home of her in-laws in the Guilford neighborhood of Baltimore. Waiting to meet her were Joseph and Mary Ames, Albert Ritchie, and a reporter from the *Baltimore Sun*, who recorded the happy reunion. "She looks much as she did before she went to Europe just after the signing of the armistice, and hardly a day older than she looked then," the reporter observed. "She is not at all emaciated and bears no marks of her privations, either physically or in her spirit or in manner."[25]

Marguerite was thrilled to be home, and at first it seemed little had changed. Her in-laws had left her favorite chair next to the fireplace, and the room where she stayed when she visited them was just as she left it. Over the coming days family and friends flocked to see her and tell her the news she had missed during the nearly two years she had been away.

With her release, she was an international celebrity. Newspapers across the United States and in Europe and Canada reprinted the details of her homecoming. A Baltimore minister even compared her to the Apostle Paul, who endured hardship and imprisonment to deliver life-saving messages. "She has brought Russia closer to us," he said. "She has liberated us from intellectual serfdom."[26]

Everyone was excited to hear her accounts of prison. Photographers asked to take her picture in her prison clothes. Reporters wanted to know about the hardships she had endured—the filthy cells, the hunger, the interrogations, and torture. Marguerite repeated her account of prison many times and wrote about her experiences in a seven-part series for the *Baltimore Sun*.[27] But these were not the stories the public expected. She repeatedly insisted that she had been treated fairly, and she defended the Bolshevik government. Prison had liberated her from the social restrictions that had confined her and endowed her with new confidence. "I looked back on my year in prison without horror and without regret," she wrote in her memoir. "It had been a wonderful revelation to me. Through it I had acquired a new sense of values and an indifference to material things. Petty worries and physical hardships would never bother me again."[28]

But Marguerite was eager to talk about more than Russian prison. She wanted to focus on the Russian people and their bold experiment with Communism. Two days after she arrived in Baltimore she made her first public appearance, speaking to the Baltimore Foreign Trade Club. She told the audience that she wanted to discuss the events in Russia and the ways in which Bolshevik leaders were bringing order to the country. Nevertheless, the club's members seemed more interested in an anecdote Marguerite told about a prison hospital attendant who was serving time for killing her sister so she could marry her brother-in-law. The audience chuckled when Marguerite added, "Aside from that, she was a very nice girl indeed." Despite Marguerite's efforts to talk about Russia's political situation, the headline in the next day's paper focused on the prison anecdote.[29]

Marguerite was astute enough to realize that the public would soon tire of Russian prison stories. Even at the dinner where she spoke, she was not the headliner. The event was held to honor the club's president, who was resigning to travel to China, and the keynote speaker was the Chinese ambassador, who expressed hope for closer ties to the United States.[30]

In the ensuing weeks Marguerite tried to stir interest in her experiences by tailoring her lectures to her audiences. When she spoke to the Educational Society of Baltimore, she described Russia's success in fighting illiteracy; before the City Club, she gave her views of Lenin and Trotsky; at Johns Hopkins University, she explained the Soviet educational system; and speaking to the YWCA, she explained the roles of women in Soviet society.[31]

But as the weeks passed Marguerite grew frustrated that the subjects that mattered to her held little interest for her friends and family. The new social season arrived, and they talked about the autumn horse races at Pimlico and the Monday night dances. Society matrons dressed in their gowns, set their tables with the finest china, and hosted teas and bridge parties. They invited the long-lost Marguerite to join them, but she no longer could share in their conversations. How could she relate to her friends' complaints about their servants after having discussed with Mogilevsky the workers' revolution? What could she add to a conversation about bobbed hairdos and finger waves when she had spent nine months combing lice from her hair?[32]

Editor Frank Kent offered Marguerite her old job back at the *Sun*, and she accepted, hoping to rediscover the pleasure she once had covering Baltimore's music and theater scene. But first she needed to go to Washington to meet with Marlborough Churchill. Even though he no longer was in charge of the dramatically downsized MID, she spent a day with him going over reports and files. She was pleased when he told her that she had given MID more information than any other agent and that her reports had always been accurate, fair, and impartial. Gen. Peyton March, the Army chief of staff, dropped by to congratulate her. There is no record of them raising questions about her role as a double agent or statements she had made after returning to the United States.

But Marguerite had questions for them. She wanted to know who had betrayed her. Mogilevsky had shown her copies of her MID reports, and she asked Churchill how the Russians had obtained them. The major promised to try to find out, and he wrote to various officials in the Army and State Department to determine who had access to the reports. For a time, suspicion fell on a file clerk in MID, but then Churchill learned he had been discharged three months before Marguerite sent the Hecker report. Churchill never found the source of the leak.[33] Years later Marguerite inexplicably placed the blame on an article that she said appeared in the *Army and Navy Journal* describing her involvement in the Robert Minor arrest. She wrote that the Soviets discovered she was an agent when they saw the article; however, no such article has been located in the journal, and there are no copies of it in the Russian prison files.[34]

Now that she had admitted to working for the U.S. secret service, Marguerite's espionage career seemed over, but she still wanted to voice her opinions on American policy toward Russia. A few days after meeting with Churchill she returned to Washington for a long conversation with Secretary of Commerce Herbert Hoover, who was overseeing the U.S. aid program to Russia. Although conservatives in the Harding administration counseled against helping the Bolshevik government, Hoover believed the best way to fight Communism was to show the superiority of the capitalist system by providing food and other humanitarian assistance. Marguerite spent several hours with Hoover but left his office disappointed because he opposed recognizing the Bolshevik government.[35]

Marguerite felt increasingly alienated from those people and values she once held dear. A onetime zealous patriot, she blamed officials in the U.S. government for her sufferings in Russia. A committed internationalist, she loathed the nativism that seized America. She hated the Harding administration and was appalled by the resurrection of the Ku Klux Klan. She even began to question the basic principles of American democracy and capitalism. "I was gradually coming to the conviction that the Western world was facing a breakdown of its established institutions," she wrote. Meanwhile, she missed Russia. America's focus on materialism grated on her, and she recalled fondly the philosophical debates she had with fellow prisoners in Lubyanka.[36]

Marguerite was aware that her sympathetic views of the Bolsheviks sparked rumors that she was a Red agent. Some even said she had been Trotsky's lover. Putting aside the outlandish accusations, it seems likely that Marguerite's statements sparked discussions inside MID and the State Department about whether women were suited for foreign service after all. Had Marguerite's judgment been clouded by her emotions? Had she fallen in love with a Chekist?

But if her words cast doubts about the ability of women to work in the intelligence service, she seemed not to care. "I knew that I was regarded by many people as a lady with a mysterious past," she later wrote. Yet she saw some advantages to the questions people had about her loyalties because she believed the uncertainties attracted audiences to her lectures. She was willing to accept the suspicions in exchange for telling them what she really wanted them to know: Bolshevism was not a Jewish plot against Western civilization; Russia's Communist dictatorship posed no real threat to U.S. capitalism; and the United States should recognize the Soviet government and extend aid to the country. Some of her most receptive audiences were in the women's clubs, where the members surprised her with their knowledge and perceptiveness, and in the labor unions, where organizers had a realistic understanding of the limitations of Communism. "I heard more sane and intelligent criticisms of the Soviet government in labor circles than anywhere else," she said.[37]

Meanwhile, life in Baltimore became increasingly unbearable. Not only did she feel isolated from her friends and family, but she was also beset with legal troubles. Her father had died in 1918 without a will, and the courts were still sorting through his complicated estate. She had to provide evidence of gifts from her father before he died while the slow legal process determined how to divide the inheritance among her, Elizabeth, and the young daughter who had been born to Bernard Baker's second wife.

Money was tight. Twenty thousand dollars she had given to investors before she left for Russia had been lost in a stock market slump in 1920. And when she returned to her home at 1206 North Charles Street, she found that it had been ransacked, trunks broken open, and valuable antiques, rugs, and china stolen. A tenant, Delcie Stant, told police she stole about four thousand dollars' worth of items because she didn't expect Marguerite to ever come out of Russia alive. Another boarder admitted to stealing cocktail glasses and cut-glass vases valued at sixty-five dollars. A jury convicted Stant of theft and released her on parole but refused to hear the case against the woman who stole the glasses.[38]

Once a leading figure in Baltimore civic and social affairs, Marguerite longed to escape to a new city. She had finished a book, *Marooned in Moscow: The Story of an American Woman Imprisoned in Russia*, which she called an objective portrayal of Soviet Russia. Largely drawn from the series she had written for the *Baltimore Sun*, the book made no mention of working for MID or of spying on foreigners for Cheka. The reviews were favorable, with critics praising the book as entertaining, insightful, and well written. So in the winter Marguerite decided to make a fresh start as an author and lecturer in New York City.

Sun editor Kent agreed to hire her as a temporary stringer until she could establish her literary career. Tommy decided to go with her and accepted a position with the International Mercantile Marine, the former J. P. Morgan shipping conglomerate that Bernard Baker helped create. They rented two rooms in a hotel on the West Forties, and although their combined incomes did not cover weekly expenses, Marguerite hoped New York would be the anecdote to her restlessness.

She soon accepted several speaking engagements that took her to lecture halls throughout the Northeast and Midwest. During these appearances Marguerite carefully avoided mention of her intelligence work. Once, when a woman in the audience asked about rumors that Marguerite had been a double agent, she replied coyly: "Don't you think that if I had done any secret service I would have stuck to it?"[39]

All the while, she may indeed have been continuing her work as a spy. The lectures brought her in close contact to American Leftists. In January she spoke to a crowd of one thousand people in Minneapolis as part of an effort to raise money for Russian famine relief. She was joined by Senator France, who, although he had lost his reelection bid in November, still spoke in favor of closer ties to Russia.

Her speeches were well attended, and a lecture bureau gave her a contract to tour the United States the next year.[40] Audiences might not have been interested in learning the finer points of American-Russian diplomacy, but they leaped at the chance to see the strange woman who could joke about life in a Soviet prison. The idle curious weren't the only ones filling the lecture halls. Agents and informers from the Justice Department also showed up to hear what she had to say. The woman who had been one of America's most prized agents now became a target of suspicion.

As early as September 1921 an informer went to the Pennsylvania Hotel to observe a meeting of the New York Committee for Russian Relief, where Marguerite was scheduled to appear. Also on the program were Louise Bryant, the widow of John Reed, and Lewis Gannett, associate editor of the *Nation* magazine. Marguerite unexpectedly did not show up, but Bryant told the audience that Marguerite would speak in coming days.[41] In March another informant was in the audience when she spoke at Bryn Mawr College on Russian art and education. The agent concluded that the lecture was "disguised Soviet propaganda."[42]

Raising money for Russia orphans and speaking to college audiences was one matter, but even Marguerite's defenders must have wondered why she spoke at an event sponsored by Socialist magazine *The Liberator*. The magazine, founded by Max Eastman, counted among its contributors revolutionary John Reed. At the time of Marguerite's speech, another familiar Communist was on the staff— Robert Minor, the cartoonist and journalist whom she had helped catch for distributing propaganda in Germany. The program at the Arlington Hall community center in New York's East Village was billed as a "Russian Evening." Marguerite told the audience she was imprisoned for breaking the law and that her stay in Russia was a "highly pleasant one." She went on to speak well of Soviet officials and blamed conditions in Russia on the Western blockade. This time, the agent watching her was not from the Justice Department but the U.S. Army.[43]

Yet even as agents spied her on lectures, Marlborough Churchill contacted her to make a mysterious proposition. Churchill no longer headed the Army's Intelligence Division, but he continued to use his personal connections to secure intelligence information, which increasingly relied on a network of individuals and companies operating overseas.[44] His letter is lost, but Marguerite's reply was placed in her MID file: "Your letter was forwarded here from Baltimore and I received it this morning. I am interested in hearing what you have in mind."[45] Churchill responded, asking her to meet him at the ladies' dining room of the University Cub in Washington, D.C., at one o'clock on May 1. "I will arrange at the same time for the interview which I referred to," he told her.[46]

What was Churchill's offer, and whom was she to meet? One clue is that on the day after she met Churchill, she returned to Washington to see Maj. Robert L. Eichelberger, who had served as the Army's assistant chief of staff with the American Expeditionary Forces in Siberia and had led the American intelligence mission in China. More significantly, he now was helping run America's spy network in Asia.[47]

America's intelligence officials seemed unable to make up their minds about Marguerite Harrison. While Justice Department spies took notes on her lectures, foreign intelligence officers were meeting with her to discuss developments in the Far East. One thing was clear: Marguerite was going abroad again.

Despite her professed longings to return to America and reunite with her son, she could not settle down to life as a writer and lecturer. New York had satisfied her for a while. She even had rediscovered her long-suppressed feminine instincts and dated a few men, who marveled at her exploits. But the excitement did not last. She told the lecture bureau that she needed fresh material and thought a trip to Asia would interest her audiences. For twenty years, Western nations and Russia had vied for China's valuable ports and mineral rights, but eight nations and the United States had recently agreed to the Nine-Power Pact recognizing China's sovereignty. Japan and Korea were beginning to assert their territorial rights. The developing events would be of keen interest to American audiences, she argued, and she persuaded *Cosmopolitan* magazine to commission her to write a series on the Far East.

But in truth, Marguerite had another plan that horrified her family: She was returning to Russia. In her memoir, Marguerite portrayed her second trip to Russia as both an accident caused by fluctuating foreign boundaries and as a spur-of-the-moment decision made after she arrived in Asia. But as early as February 1922 she told an audience she would be going back to Russia, and she frequently told her friends she wanted to see Moscow again. She knew she would not be able to slip in as easily as she had in 1920 when she crossed the Polish border. She was aware she would likely be arrested again if she were caught, and yet she was mysteriously drawn back. "Why, she did not say," the *Baltimore Sun* later wrote. "She was singularly non-committal on this point."[48]

Churchill knew that her Asia trip would bring her to the edges of, if not inside, Soviet Russia. Three weeks after their meeting, he dispatched four identical letters to the military attaches in Canton, Peking, Tokyo, and Chita. His message was as perplexing as her mission:

> This is to advise you that Mrs. T. B. Harrison (Marguerite E. Harrison) will probably visit the Far East in the near future and may ask you for indorsements or letters setting forth the fact that she at one time was employed by the Military Intelligence Division. This is to advise you that, although it is a fact that Mrs. Harrison was employed by the Military Intelligence Division during the war and for a short time afterwards and did excellent work for us, it has not been deemed expedient to give her any letters in Washington, either in this office or the State Department. This decision is based principally on the fact that, if such letters were found in her possession, they would militate against her in the eyes of Soviet authorities.[49]

Churchill went on to add that "Mrs. Harrison is a woman of great refinement and excellent education and thoroughly reliable so far as I know. There is no reason why you should not extend to her such courtesies as may be appropriate, but you should politely decline to give her anything in writing in the way of indorsements or to indicate to anyone except members of the diplomatic service that she was ever in our service."[50]

Marguerite's request for letters attesting to her work for MID was highly unusual. She knew the United States rarely, if ever, acknowledged an intelligence agent. Possessing such documents could be extremely dangerous. And if her trip was merely to gather material for a book or magazine series, she did not need letters saying she had once worked as a spy. Churchill's letters raise other questions: Why did he fear the Soviets might catch her with the documents? Did he suspect she would return to Soviet Russia? Was he beginning to distrust his prized agent? His letters indicate that Washington already had denied Marguerite's request for the documents, and yet he felt compelled to warn the military attaches that she might try to acquire them anyhow. What was he to make of a woman who wanted to go back to Russia a year after being released from a Soviet prison and carrying documents that she had been an American spy? Was her goal to be arrested again? Or were Churchill's letters part of an elaborate ruse meant to confuse the moles he knew were planted within the American secret service? Was she on a mission so secret that only a few high officials were aware of it?

No certain answers have been found. But in the middle of June, less than one year after Marguerite reunited with Tommy in London, she left him with a friend in a small apartment on West Forty-Fifth Street in New York City. She boarded the Canadian Pacific Railway train to Vancouver and days later caught a steamer bound for Yokohama, Japan. On the way she jotted down her reminiscences about women she had met in Russian prison for a series in *Cosmopolitan* magazine. "Each story was basically true," she later wrote.[51]

But telling truth from fiction had become increasingly difficult in Marguerite's world.

Eleven

"A VERY CLEVER WOMAN"

ON BOARD THE SHIP bound for Japan, Marguerite felt free again.

She had tried for almost a year to settle down in America. She had hoped to find contentment living with her son and fulfillment as a writer and lecturer. But wanderlust seized her and would not let go. Asia—Japan, Korea, China, Mongolia, and Siberia—promised exciting new adventures. Here nations fought to control the region's vast resources, and country borders shifted by the week. When she was freed from prison, she had reported to Army and State Department officials that Soviet Russia operated a sophisticated propaganda network in these countries. She soon would learn the extent of the Bolshevik grip on the region.

Marguerite told her family that she was going to the East to write a series for a Hearst syndicate, and in her memoir she wrote that she had a contract with *Cosmopolitan* magazine. But the magazine series never appeared. Her father-in-law said the syndicate refused the articles because they were "too serious."[1] However, the information she collected, including reports on gold extraction, oil reserves, arms shipments, and government officials' views on treaties and summits, was of high interest to American intelligence services. And despite her later insistence that she was no longer spying, she sent at least four reports to American intelligence agencies during the five months she traveled through Asia. She even entertained offers to collect information for a British arms maker, the Japanese Foreign Office, and a Chinese warlord. All the while, her travels drew her closer to Soviet Russia.

But why was she so determined to go back to a country where she had been imprisoned and forced into service as a double agent? Now that the Russians knew she had been a spy, it is inconceivable that the United States would have sent her on a mission to that country again. American spymasters knew that if Marguerite returned, she would certainly be arrested again, creating an embarrassing international incident. Would American officials take that risk?

Or was she on a personal mission to return to a country she loved? Marguerite strangely missed the spirituality she had found in Russia. America seemed to her empty, materialistic, and superficial by comparison. She longed for the life-or-death struggles that had forced her to focus on what was meaningful. She could not find the same satisfaction in America, even with her son.

Or could Marguerite have wanted to return to Russia to deliver intelligence reports to the Soviet secret police, now called GPU? Did the statements she had made over the last eight months defending the Bolshevik government and denying the hardships of Soviet prison mean she was really a Russian agent after all?

In addition to the questions surrounding the nature of the mission are questions of how she paid for the trip. At times she traveled with American diplomats and stayed with them as their guest. But often she was on her own, paying for guides, transportation, meals, and lodging. Marguerite indicated that Hearst paid her in advance, and she made occasional references to buying goods using Mexican dollars, an accepted international currency of the day. In the Mongolian city of Urga (now Ulaanbaatar), she wrote that she expected to collect three hundred Mexican dollars she had ordered from the international firm Anders, Meyer & Co., but chaotic economic conditions prevented her from doing so.[2] Possibly Marguerite spent her own money on the trip. The family had sold the Ingleside estate for $150,000, and most of Bernard Baker's vast stock holdings were sold in 1920 when she was in Russia. Marguerite's share of the inheritance was over $52,000.[3] But Marguerite had said she had lost much of her money in the market downturn and had just a few hundred dollars when she moved to New York with Tommy.

As soon as Marguerite arrived in Tokyo, the wary Japanese assigned an agent, Dr. Matsujiro Honda, to act as her guide and translator. On the whole, she didn't mind the chaperone. Japan was unlike any country Marguerite had visited, and she marveled at its many contrasts. She rode an efficient electric train from Yokohama to Tokyo, yet along the way passed villages of straw-roofed huts. In the city she observed women in kimonos with babies strapped on their backs walking alongside young people dressed in the latest European fashion. Exotic geishas, Japanese flappers, students, soldiers, and tourists mingled throughout Tokyo.[4]

At first Marguerite interviewed Tokyo government and business leaders, including a former U.S. ambassador and a past premier. But after several weeks of attending official lunches, teas, and receptions, she ventured beyond the capital. Interested to learn about the Japanese worker movement and its views on socialism, she traveled to the slums of Kobe, where she interviewed one of the country's foremost labor leaders. After that visit she concluded Japan was too nationalistic to be swayed by international socialism. Even the nation's major labor organizer focused on improving conditions for the unemployed through schools and clubs, not revolution.[5]

In Japan Marguerite for the first time began to seriously consider the roles of women in society. She had not advocated women's suffrage in the United States or fought for equal treatment in the workplace. She had been America's first female foreign intelligence officer, but it was a position she wanted for herself, not her gender. She had never fought for women's rights—or needed to. She had never encountered discrimination that prevented her from doing as she pleased. "Feminism has never appealed to me," she admitted. "And in my various wanderings around the world, I have never cared to study social problems purely from the sex angle."[6]

But in Japan she found the question of women's rights too pervasive to ignore. Marguerite based her assessment of Japanese women mainly upon her encounters with aristocrats, and even among the elites, views varied tremendously. Marguerite described three women who represented the different attitudes about women's roles in Japanese society. One she identified as Princess Oyama, who knew English and European customs. This princess probably was the daughter of Sutematsu Yamakawa, a Vassar College graduate who was the first Japanese woman to receive a college education. Yamakawa returned to Japan, married Army field marshal Oyama Iwao, and assumed the title Princess Oyama. The princess died in the Spanish influenza epidemic in 1919, but her daughter, Oyama Hisako (later Baroness Ida Hisako), fits the description of the woman Marguerite met.[7] The princess was not interested in the women's movement or modern ways. She spent much of her time writing poetry and rarely went anywhere without her husband. She was young and living in a modern atmosphere but "deliberately choosing to remain medieval."[8]

Another woman, Baroness Shidzue Ishimoto, embraced trendy new movements. She took up Margaret Sanger's campaign to introduce birth control and was helping raise money for Russian famine relief. A Socialist and a suffragist, she shocked her friends by dabbling in journalism. Nevertheless, Marguerite believed Shidzue was playing with these projects and movements. "They were new and fascinating toys but not vital problems."[9]

The third woman, Madame Ritsuko Mori, was an actress who worked to open theatrical doors to women. Women had been forbidden to perform on the Japanese stage, but Mori had managed to appear in several roles in the Imperial Theater and helped establish a theatrical school for girls.[10]

Of all the women she met, Marguerite most admired the geishas, particularly those hired to converse with politicians and statesmen. To perform this role well, the women needed knowledge, wit, and charm, Marguerite noted. A middle-class girl aspiring to education and access to power could receive both in a geisha establishment. "If a geisha is ambitious, beautiful and clever, her opportunities are practically boundless," she observed.[11]

Marguerite once was able to peek inside a private club where geishas served as hostesses. After paying two hundred dollars for the evening, she and a group of other foreigners arrived at the establishment and were greeted by geishas who helped them remove their shoes and escorted them upstairs to dinner. The women poured sake and led them in party games throughout the evening.[12]

Marguerite thought the Japanese had a childlike sense of humor. She described a luncheon with a Japanese admiral and an Englishman who represented a large British arms manufacturer. The admiral shrieked with laughter when the Englishman imitated a monkey eating a banana.[13] Yet despite its frivolity, this meeting wasn't just a social gathering. The man who imitated the monkey had provided Marguerite with important information about British trade strategy in the region. He told her the British intended to use the Japanese as middlemen in Siberia to establish trade with Soviet Russia, which England had yet to formally recognize.[14]

Learning of the British plan, Marguerite sent a report to the American military attaché, Lt. Col. Charles Burnett. Her original document has not been found, but in the cover letter sent to Washington with the report, Burnett wrote that Marguerite gathered the information from Maj. Basil Winder, an employee of the British weapons maker Vickers Ltd. Burnett said Marguerite asked that her name not be attached to the document, and he explained how she obtained it. Burnett said Winder "fell head over heels in love with her and while in that state gave up the information contained in that report."[15]

According to Burnett, Winder also offered Marguerite a position with Vickers secret service, presumably working in industrial espionage. Burnett said he advised her to take the job because "I think it would be well for us to know about such ambitious plans and that would seem the best way to find out."[16] Marguerite made passing references to Vickers in her accounts of the trip, but she made no mention of a love affair with one of its agents. She had resorted to subterfuge to elicit information from suspected Bolsheviks. Did Marguerite now abandon her principle that she would never exchange sex for secrets?

Vickers wasn't the only agency interested in employing Marguerite's services. Burnett also said that the Japanese Foreign Office had asked her to send reports on the economic and political situation when she traveled through Siberia.[17] No evidence exists that Marguerite ever worked for Vickers or the Japanese, but the offers testify to how powerful men admired her and valued her services. No wonder she expressed admiration for the Japanese geisha.

The known reports Marguerite sent to the U.S. intelligence agencies while in Asia mostly pertain to economic matters. After spending two months in Tokyo, she traveled north to Sakhalin Island, a territory rich in oil and coal reserves that was claimed by both Japan and Russia. Only one American journalist had been to the island since Japan seized control several years earlier, but the Japanese Foreign Office agreed to allow Marguerite to visit with her guide, Dr. Honda. The Japanese tried to keep Marguerite from the Russian inhabitants at the northern end of the island, but she had the advantage because she spoke Russian and her Japanese monitors did not. She thus found a way to gather some information on the views of the Russian community.

The Japanese were anxious to show off the improvements they had made on the island and gave her tours of a hospital, a school, and a prison. Yet traveling through the region, Marguerite made particular note of the vast natural resources, especially the oil fields. She realized the Japanese needed oil, not only for their industries but also for their growing navy. At the same time, Western nations were beginning to stake claims in the region. Sinclair Oil Company of America was negotiating with Soviet Russia to lease the northern part of the Sakhalin Island, despite Japanese claims to the land.

After visiting the island Marguerite sailed with American military attaché Burnett across De Castries Bay to the Siberian mainland. Within a few days, they were joined by two more Americans with secret service connections—Maj. Philip Faymonville, a military observer, and Edward Thomas, the vice consul at Chita in the Far Eastern Republic. The presence of the group created a stir among the natives who believed the Americans were coming to liberate them from the Japanese. For her part, Marguerite was thrilled to be back in territory that had once been part of Russia. "I had been homesick for the sound of Russian voices, for the broad sweep of the Russian wheat fields, for the homey little villages with their wooden izbas, for the childlike, lovable people with whom I had lived through so much," she recalled.[18]

Sailing toward the city of Nikolayevsk, she looked out of the porthole of her steamer and was mesmerized by the Amur River, glistening like gold and teeming with fish.[19] Vast forests stretched on either side, promising riches of timber, gold, and oil. After a few days the Americans parted company. Burnett, Faymonville, and Thomas returned to Japan, but Marguerite stayed in Nikolayevsk, making plans to sail down the Amur River to Khabarovsk, where she would board the Trans-Siberian Railroad and journey to Vladivostok, the Pacific port city then under the control of the White Army. A coastal route to Vladivostok would have been simpler, but Marguerite was not looking for ease. "I was fed up with security, comfort and easy living," she declared. "In America I had first enjoyed, then been stifled by material comforts. . . . I longed for a freer atmosphere—I craved hardships and adventure!"[20]

In the first leg of the journey, she traveled in a paddle-wheel steamer where she met a mine inspector who told her of the tremendous gold resources in the region. He handed her a report detailing the amount and quality of the gold British and Russian miners were finding, and he described opportunities in the Far Eastern Republic. After she arrived in Vladivostok, Marguerite relayed the report to the American consulate, which forwarded the findings to Washington. In the cover letter the American officer noted that Marguerite "was reported to be a Bolshevik agent."[21]

Doubts and suspicions swirled around her travels.

On the steamship, Marguerite encountered a mysterious ticket comptroller who appeared to be too educated for his position. He told her he had served in the Russian Imperial Army during World War I and had briefly fought with the White brigades in Siberia before joining the Red Army. The man was an excellent singer, and in the evenings Marguerite accompanied him, playing on an aging piano in the ship's saloon. One night she confided to him that she had been in prison in Moscow. His reply surprised her.

"I knew it all along," he said. "It is our business to know everything."[22] Marguerite suddenly realized Cheka's spies reached to the farthest corners of the former Russian empire.

Finally arriving at the Khabarovsk train station, Marguerite squeezed through the crowd, purchased a third-class ticket, and scrambled onto the train. At first she could find no place to sit, but the stationmaster arranged for her to occupy the top berth of a three-tiered sleeper reserved for railroad employees. From her bunk she looked down as strangers constantly streamed in and out of the car looking for seats. One of them stole her typewriter, but she took the loss with "true Russian fatalism," she later recalled. "It was one piece of baggage less to watch."[23]

The trip, which in the old days took thirty hours, took five days because large sections of track and bridges had been destroyed during the civil war. Fighting still continued along the route, and Marguerite had to pass through three armies to reach Vladivostok. The decrepit train struggled over the mountainous terrain. At one incline, the engine balked and the passengers had to get out and push it up the hill and over the top. Along the route, Marguerite saw burned-out stations and peasants standing on charred platforms selling food to travelers. One night bandits boarded the train and robbed passengers in several cars.[24]

As the days passed Marguerite became acquainted with her fellow travelers, many of them soldiers. She shared with them her cigarettes and chocolates and played poker with them in the evenings. But one tall, slender soldier kept to himself. When they were alone, he told her that he was a Serb who had been drafted into the army of the Far Eastern Republic and planned to desert. His goal was to reach Vladivostok, where he hoped to obtain a passport from the Yugoslav Embassy and return to his country. It was a desperate gamble. He could be shot as a deserter, captured by the Japanese, or executed as a Bolshevik spy.

Marguerite could be coldly analytical and detached from her friends and family, but she also could be soft-hearted in dealing with those she perceived as less fortunate than herself. When she was freed from Russia, she had asked that her money be donated to help children. Another time she put dollars in the hand of a beggar sleeping in the street. On the train she bought a ticket for an elderly peasant woman who had been robbed. Looking at the Serb soldier, she remembered her grandmother Baker, who had harbored Confederate spies in Baltimore during the Civil War. She agreed to aid the soldier, and that night she helped him burn his identification papers.

When the train approached a checkpoint near the Ussuri River, the soldier secretly disembarked to travel on foot, bypassing the sentries. The other passengers got off the train, showed their passports, and continued their journey on horse-drawn wagons. The travel was excruciatingly slow under the scorching Siberian sun. Swarms of mosquitoes, gnats, and flies pestered the passengers, and near the Manchuria border, guards had to fire shots to scare robbers away from her wagonette. But Marguerite was happy. "The gypsy in me had responded to the call of the road, and I could have gone on indefinitely thus," she wrote.[25]

As she reached the neutral zone between the Far Eastern Republic and the territory occupied by the Japanese army, the Serb soldier reappeared. The Japanese allowed him to enter their territory, but they warned Marguerite that the White guards would not be so lenient. The monarchist troops were on the lookout for Bolshevik spies and had just shot several suspects in recent days. Marguerite began to doubt the wisdom of helping the unknown man.

Just as the Japanese warned her, the White Army proved a more difficult obstacle. The officers boarded the train, locked the doors, and inspected all of the passengers' documents. Marguerite's papers were in order, but the guards were suspicious of the Serbian soldier and an elderly woman who had lost her ticket. Marguerite told the officers their train had been beset by robbers who stole the documents, and she vouched that the Serb had been an Imperial soldier. Nevertheless, the White guards arrested all three of them and marched them to the staff headquarters. The old woman cried and pleaded to the saints, but the officers were unmoved. The three would have to spend the night in detention, the soldiers said. Marguerite then took charge. "I have no intention of doing anything of the kind," she said firmly. "You are detaining me without any justification whatever. I demand to see your commanding officer."[26]

The young soldier reluctantly sent for his colonel, whom Marguerite described as an educated and reasonable man. Again Marguerite showed an amazing talent for getting out of tight situations. She persuaded the colonel that the old woman and Serb could be trusted, and he released them.

When they reached Vladivostok, Marguerite breathed a sigh of relief that she had seen both her charges through to their destination. It was now the end of August. The Japanese army was evacuating the city, and the Russian monarchists were about to assume control. Marguerite called the unsettled time a "bubble." The new government had almost no money, and the people had no jobs.

They tried to lose their sorrows in alcohol, drugs, and prostitution. Everyone, even schoolchildren, bought Lotto cards for a ruble, hoping their luck would change.[27]

The most serene person she encountered was a Japanese general, Tachibana Koichiro, who was overseeing the troop withdrawal. In a long interview he described the plans for the Japanese munitions and told her that he planned to sell the weapons to Chita. If he could not reach an agreement with the Far Eastern Republic, he would destroy them, he said. Marguerite went straight to the American consul to give him the information, which was sent to the State Department in Washington. Although the United States had withdrawn its troops from Siberia two years earlier, America had reasons to worry about the weapons. The United States did not want the arms to fall into the hands of the Bolsheviks. Besides, American weapons makers were trying to strike their own deals selling rifles to the White Army.[28]

In Vladivostok Marguerite reunited with Major Faymonville, the military observer, and Edward Thomas, the Chita vice consul, who were eager to hear about her experiences on the Amur River. American military attaches were keeping watch over the turbulent region, which promised vast business potential despite political instability. The agents asked her to write about her observations and included her report along with one they sent to Washington.[29]

Yet, even as the State Department was accepting her information, new suspicious arose that caused leaders in Washington to urge their men to be cautious when dealing with Marguerite. On August 21 the *Guardian* in London revealed that she was the woman who had denounced British journalist Stan Harding. Although those with knowledge of the case knew Harding had accused Marguerite of betrayal, until then, her name had not been revealed publicly. Now, in addition to rumors that she was a double agent, came word that she was to blame for an innocent woman's imprisonment.[30] Within days the news reached Asia. The English-language paper *The Japan Advertiser* published Marguerite's photograph and a front-page story headlined, "Mrs. Harrison Called Red Agent." The lengthy article misidentified Harding, calling her Star Baker, but recounted the alarm Japanese officials felt over having spent a month cavorting with a purported Bolshevik spy.[31]

Immediately the charges d'affaires of the Japanese Embassy in Washington called on Dewitt C. Poole, head of the Russian division of the U.S. Department of State, demanding to know whether the reports about Marguerite were true.

Poole told the representative that the State Department did not believe she was really a Russian spy but added the department would take no responsibility for her because "she was a very clever woman and one could not always know just what she was about."[32]

The newspaper article also alarmed the U.S. State Department representatives in Peking, who expected Marguerite to arrive there soon. A representative wrote to Washington asking whether he should seize her passport in light of the report.[33] Again officials sought to quell the concern. In a coded telegram Undersecretary of State William Phillips replied to Peking: "Department doubts very seriously truth of allegations that the person in question is a Soviet agent and suggests only an attitude of discreet reserve on your part." Interestingly, Phillips gave the Peking office permission to aid Marguerite's travels. "Her passport now reads for Japan, Siberia and China and may be amended upon application to include all countries," he wrote.[34]

Even though officials in the State Department said they did not believe Marguerite was a Bolshevik spy, the head of U.S. Army Intelligence urged his subordinates to exercise caution in dealing with her. Col. Stuart Heintzelman had received the report Marguerite gave Burnett on British plans for Siberia, and he sent a warning: "Extreme caution . . . should be taken in dealing with your informant. . . . No written documents of any kind whatsoever should be given, and confidential oral information should be carefully guarded." Heintzelman repeated Churchill's concern for what could happen if Marguerite would be caught with documents from the Army's intelligence unit. He emphasized that the information she gave Burnett was voluntary. "The subject is probably a patriotic American, but has learned so much inside information in many countries and has had such frequent personal contact with many different national leaders that quite unconsciously may someday make a most serious mistake."[35]

Marguerite made no mention of the revelation she was the mysterious Madame X who had betrayed Stan Harding or of suspicions the newspaper articles aroused. After a week in Vladivostok, she set out again, this time headed for China. She traveled by a coastal steamer to Korea, where she observed a nascent nationalist movement brewing in opposition to the Japanese rule and glimpsed the work of American missionaries trying to convert the natives to Christianity. On the whole, Marguerite disapproved of the American missionary presence in Asia. She detested the smugness of the workers who were sure that their religion was superior to that of the natives. "I have always felt that religion is the instinctive effort of humanity to put certain universal truths into symbols to answer man's eternal questions as to the meaning of the universe," she wrote. "The various faiths in the world have translated these aspirations into the languages best suited to the culture and degree of civilization of the people who have adopted them, and they a contain a measure of truth. Why teach a man to be a Christian when his mentality remains that of a Buddhist? Why abolish idolatry among simple savages before they become sufficiently civilized to find a more enlightened expression for their religious beliefs?"[36]

Arriving in Mukden, Manchuria, she sought a meeting with the de facto dictator of the region, Chang Tso-lin. She soon encountered the slight man dressed in a long, black satin coat and small skullcap. He had never been interviewed by a woman, and he offered her a cigar. Their conversation centered on an upcoming trade summit in Changchun between the Japanese and Russians. Chang made it clear that he would have something to do with the trade arrangements because goods would have to pass through his district.

Marguerite had agreed to cover the summit for a Japanese newspaper, and Chang asked her to deliver a personal message to the Russian representative at the conference, Adolph Joffe: Manchuria must be included in any trade agreements.

A few days later, Marguerite arrived in Changchun. Only a handful of journalists were at the Changchun conference—a reporter from the Associated Press and one from the *Japanese Advertiser*, which a few weeks earlier had alerted its readers to the charges that Marguerite was a Bolshevik spy. Marguerite found the week-long summit a rather dreary affair, although not without intrigues as businessmen attempted make lucrative deals with the Russian and Japanese representatives. Ultimately the two countries failed to reach an agreement. The Russians refused to negotiate until the Japanese had left the Sakhalin Island, and Japan would not agree to evacuate until Russian paid compensation for the destruction of Nikolayevsk.

When the conference concluded, Marguerite slipped north to Harbin, which she described as the "center of Russian intrigue in the Far East." The town on the Sungari River contained a mix of people, including American fur traders, merchants, refugees, arms dealers, and Bolshevik agents. In her books Marguerite described her visit to Harbin as brief but productive, although unlike the other cities she visited, she gave no specifics of whom she met. She seemed to have been primarily interested in conflicting claims against the Chinese Eastern Railway. After an unspecified amount of time, Marguerite returned to Mukden to give a report to Chang, who quizzed her intently on the personalities of the Russian and Japanese negotiators at the trade summit.[37]

From Mukden Marguerite traveled to Peking, where donkey carts, rickshaws, and an occasional automobile kicked up the dust of wide city streets. She described the month she spent there as a "continual round of parties and entertainments" with Americans, Russians, and Chinese, but she conceded she could glean only a superficial view of life in the complicated country.[38] By now it was mid-October, and she was due to return to the United States for a lecture tour in November. But rather than making preparations to travel home, she began to solidify plans to enter Russia.

She applied to the Russian Embassy in Peking for a visa, making no effort to hide her previous imprisonment and expulsion. Several Russian officials, including Adolph Joffe, who had returned from the Changchun conference, told her the government would probably grant her visa request.[39] She planned to travel to Chita and await word there on her application. But she walked into a trap. On October 9 Genrikh Yagoda, head of the Foreign Office of the GPU, ordered Chita officials to arrest her as soon as she arrived.[40]

Again Marguerite chose an arduous route to her destination. Rather than traveling by train from Peking to Chita, she decided to pass through the Mongolian capital, Urga. She had no visa for Mongolia, so she planned to journey to the Chinese city of Kalgan, 125 miles northwest of Peking, where she hoped to find a car to take her to Urga. Then she would need a way to get to Verkhne-Udinsk, where she could catch the Trans-Siberian Railway to Chita.

No one in Peking could advise her how to make the journey. It already was October, and winter was not far off. She realized it was extremely unlikely she would make it back to New York in time for her November lectures. "It was a foolhardy and senseless undertaking from many points of view, but I deliberately closed my eyes to that fact," she later admitted.[41]

Marguerite made the dubious assertion that her reason for traveling to Urga was to investigate Bolshevik claims that they were not interfering in Mongolia, despite its strategic importance in the region. She journeyed to the Chinese city of Kalgan, where she found few foreigners aside from the British and American consuls and representatives of the Standard Oil Company. But, as she had hoped, she found an Englishman willing to drive her north to Urga. He wouldn't be leaving for a few days, however, so Marguerite decided to join a group of Americans and Englishmen on an excursion to the countryside. Five passengers and the Chinese chauffer crammed into a Ford for the one-hundred-mile journey. Just leaving Kalgan proved to be a difficult as they inched through the streets packed with carts, camels, goats, and sheep. A frightened sheep tried to jump into the car, and a bullock's horns became stuck in a lunch basket on the car's hood. At the city gate a Chinese guard argued heatedly with the chauffer over the amount of a toll until one of the passengers produced five Mexican dollars to settle the dispute.

Marguerite spent several days in the countryside visiting a ranch owned by an American who was breeding racehorses, a dairy farm run by a Swiss, and a Tibetan monastery. Returning to Kalgan, she discovered her English driver was preparing to leave the next day for Urga. It took three rickshaws to carry Marguerite and her luggage to the Kalgan gate of the city's wall, where she was met by the English fur trader, his Russian chauffer, and another passenger, a Methodist missionary. Their new Dodge was already loaded with bags and boxes. Marguerite's luggage was added to the pile, and she squeezed between the boxes to take her place in the back seat next to the missionary.

She spent the first night at a mission and by noon the next day she was crossing the vast Gobi Desert. Passing caravans and sheep herds, they arrived the second night in a village that was composed of two houses, a telegraph station, and an inn with one guest room. The Englishman slept in the car; the chauffer, the missionary, and Marguerite were assigned to the one room in the inn. As Marguerite slipped off her shoes and into a dark silk kimono, the missionary looked aghast. He grabbed his bedroll and started to leave. "I think I'll go outside," he said. "I've never slept before with a lady." Marguerite persuaded him to come back, arguing that he would freeze outside and that sleeping in the same room with a woman was "not such a terrible experience."[42]

Two days later the group reached Urga, where she spent ten days living with an American fur trader and his wife. She interviewed the prime minister, who told her he looked forward to the day when Mongolia would become a Soviet republic. Urga fascinated and repelled her. The city was a collection of lowlying, non-descript buildings dominated by a white Buddhist temple. Mangy dogs ran through the streets and the outskirts of town, where they devoured dead bodies that were left outside to rot and threatened the living. She heard the story of a Russian soldier mauled to death by a pack after he fell down in the street drunk.

Marguerite, who was so fastidious about hygiene that she carried a rubber bathtub with her, was shocked at the dirtiness. She said the Mongolians never bathed, and they were covered with parasites, which they refused to kill because of the Buddhist belief that all life was sacred. They changed their undergarments only once a year and never their outer clothes until they fell to pieces. The long sleeves of their rich Chinese brocades were caked in grease and dirt. When they needed to relieve themselves, they stopped where they were. "Walking through the streets you are constantly obliged to circumnavigate a Mongol lady or gentleman squatting peacefully with the wide folds of his or her garment tucked up under their crooked elbows," she recalled.[43]

Near Urga she toured a city populated by red-robed lamas and theological students. On the edge of the religious site stood a cluster of yurts inhabited by prostitutes who served the monks. Once they became too old for the profession, the women became nuns, and Marguerite saw many of them, with shaven heads and wearing filthy saffron robes, walking through the streets and stopping to gossip with their neighbors.

Marguerite eventually became accustomed to the sights and smells of the Urga streets, but she found little to do in the evenings, aside from playing poker with other foreigners. Once she attended a cultural program featuring a one-act play, a Japanese geisha dancer, folk songs, and an exhibition by a sorceress, but Marguerite complained she could barely see the entertainment because she sat behind a row of Mongol princesses "whose huge headdresses with their dangling gold ornaments completely shut off the stage."[44]

Although the people fascinated her, Marguerite's objective was to understand the political and economic currents moving through the country. Chinese, Japanese, Mongolians, and Europeans mixed in Urga, but the Russians vastly outnumbered the other foreigners. She learned that most Mongolians were not even aware of the Bolshevik Revolution, but they generally had high regard for the Russians. And the Soviets had many reasons to cultivate relations with the Mongols. The country not only offered untold natural resources, especially gold and oil, but also provided an important strategic position in the event of conflict with China. "While Mongolia is relatively unimportant commercially to the rest of the world, particularly to the United States, it may be destined to play a role out of all proportions to its size and economic importance in Far Eastern politics," she concluded.[45]

As she prepared to leave Urga, her American hosts urged her to reconsider her plan to go to Chita. The political situation in the Far Eastern Republic was in a state of flux, and travel was not safe. Moreover, the rivers that she would need to cross had not yet frozen. But Marguerite would not be dissuaded. Soviet officials in Urga gave her a visa to Chita, and the Russian consul who lived near the Far Eastern Republic border town Kyakhta invited her to be his guest. With such assurances, Marguerite believed she would have no trouble aside from the hardships of traveling in a wild territory with winter approaching.[46]

She found a Russian frontiersman named Kosakov willing to take her to Chita. On a cold November morning he arrived at her hotel with a doubtful troika—one horse that was a twenty-two-year-old veteran, an unbroken colt, and a horse lame in its hind legs. Shrugging off the protests of her friends, Marguerite climbed into the carriage and set off with harness bells gaily jingling. They climbed through steep hills and descended valleys, passed goat herds and ponies, but saw few people along the way. At night, they stayed at small inns and houses. At one they arrived just moments after the hostess had severed a finger on a piece of sharp tin. The woman was groaning in pain, and her children shrieking in hysterics. Marguerite calmly retrieved a first aid kit from her bags, dressed the woman's wounds as best as she could, and helped her make dinner for the guests. That night her bed was a narrow bench in a room she shared with several Russian travelers.

On the third day they drove through a blizzard, struggling to see the roads and river crossings in the piling snow. It was already dark when they reached the remote post station. There were no guest rooms or bed, so Marguerite took off her shoes, slipped on her kimono, and crawled into her sleeping bag on the floor. She rested just a few hours when Kosakov awoke her at two in the morning to continue the journey. In the cold, quiet night, Marguerite marveled at the northern lights that danced in the sky. Packs of wolves roamed nearby, but game was plentiful in the region, and they did not menace the travelers.

After four days Marguerite reached the border of the Far Eastern Republic. Without hesitation, the guards on the Mongolian side waved her onward. In a few miles she encountered a sentry from the Far Eastern Republic, who allowed her to proceed to the first town, Kyakhta. Marguerite passed by ornate, brightly painted houses with large courtyards. Birch trees lined the main street, and a beautiful white church with gold domes was perched on a hill above. Yet almost all the homes and stores were empty. Rich merchants who once inhabited the town had fled or been killed in by the Reds, Whites, or Chinese.

With no lodging in Kyakhta, she proceeded to the next village, Troitskosavsk. The Russian consul offered her a room, but it was not heated, so she accepted Kosakov's offer to stay with him and his wife in their three-room log house. She spent a week with the couple waiting for the rivers to freeze so she could continue her journey northward to Chita. "I knew that I would not be able to get back to the United States in time to keep my lecture engagements, but I did not care," she recalled. "To tell the truth, I was enjoying myself immensely, I did not mind the cold or the discomforts, I was not homesick, lonely or afraid. This vagabond life had a curious fascination for me. I did not want to go home!"[47]

Marguerite arrived in Troitskosavsk as the town was celebrating the fifth anniversary of the Russian Revolution. She attended speeches, concerts, theatrical performances, and banquets marking the occasion. On her final night in the town, she regaled local officials with stories about her adventures in Russia in 1920, including her time in prison. "They particularly enjoyed the latter," she noted.[48] Likely some of the Russians knew she soon would be in prison again.

The Russian officials kept a close eye on Marguerite after she crossed the border into the Far Eastern Republic. While she perceived the attentiveness as hospitality, it is likely they followed her because of orders from Moscow. The Russian consul, Shakov; Cossack commanders; and a political commissar shadowed her throughout her stay in Troitskosavsk. When Marguerite and Kosakov resumed their journey to Chita, they were joined by an armed Cossack soldier carrying diplomatic mail for the Russian consulate. He also may have been sent to escort Marguerite, but he proved a handy companion. Along the way he spotted a band of robbers hiding under a tree. Marguerite held the reins of the horses while the Cossack and Kosakov shot at the robbers, scaring them away.[49]

The weather had turned quite cold, but Marguerite was dressed warmly in a fur-lined coat and goat-skin boots. During the day she and her two companions lived on tea, rye bread, and meat dumplings called *pelmeni*. When they stopped in the evenings, she slept soundly, even when she had to share the floor with other travelers or, occasionally, livestock and vermin. They lodged among Old Believers, a sect that eschewed modern conveniences and adhered to customs dating back centuries. Marguerite and the other travelers had to eat at a separate table and were not allowed to smoke in the homes. One night Marguerite persuaded her host to let her sit by the stove and blow her cigarette smoke up the chimney. "He kept crossing himself all the time and saying that he was committing a sin."[50]

When she at last saw the rooftops of Verkhne-Udinsk, Marguerite felt a mix of sadness that her adventure was nearing an end and relief that the hardest part of her travels appeared to be over. She expected to board the Trans-Siberian Railway in Verkhne-Udinsk and travel to Chita, where she would meet Faymonville and Thomas.

Entering the town, she at first paid little attention to the red banners that hung in the streets. She assumed they were simply left over from the Revolution anniversary celebrations the previous week. But when they stopped at the guesthouse that had been recommended to her, the landlady curtly told them she had no rooms for rent. The answer was the same at the second and third houses they tried. Finally Marguerite went to a general store named American Trading Company, where the Danish owner told her all the guesthouses were afraid to take her in. Communists had seized the municipal government. They were confiscating the houses and arresting suspected spies.

Marguerite at last found a Jewish woman willing to rent her a room. But minutes after Marguerite arrived, the political police knocked on the door and ordered everyone inside to appear the next morning before the Revolutionary Tribunal. Local officials were sure to suspect her of espionage.

Realizing the danger, she asked her Cossack companion for help. He knew of a place the Communists were not likely to look—the town's brothel. Marguerite reluctantly agreed. The proprietor offered her a room with a secure lock, and Marguerite tried to ignore the sound of revelry coming from the adjoining rooms.

The train to Chita would not leave for two days. Marguerite continued to hide at the brothel while trying to figure out what to do next. She did not know whether the Communist uprising had been confined to Verkhne-Udinsk or had swept through the entire Far Eastern Republic. Her worries grew when the next night a suspicious-looking man knocked at her door saying he was a local newspaper reporter who wanted to know her political views.

The Cossack who was with her during the interview became nervous. He left the room and returned after a few minutes, saying they must leave for the train station at once. Marguerite threw her belongings into her bags and they hurried through the deserted streets to the station where they spent the night waiting for the train.

When Marguerite boarded the train for Chita, she was still unsure whether the Communist takeover was confined to one town or had spread to the larger region. At the next station, she bought a newspaper and learned the truth: the Far Eastern Republic had been dissolved and was now part of Soviet Russia.

Marguerite realized her situation was precarious. She telegrammed Thomas, the American vice consul, and asked him to meet her at the station in Chita. She believed she would be safe under his protection. When her train pulled into Chita on Saturday, November 18, Thomas and Faymonville were waiting. They told her they thought she would be safe, but she nevertheless spent most of the day in their apartment.

The next day she felt confident enough to accompany the Americans to a dinner with officials of the former Far Eastern Republic and Russians who now were in control of the country. The Russians, including the former foreign minister, teased her about being back in Soviet Russia. Trying to dispel her worries, Marguerite asked them to check on her request for a visa to enter Russia.

On Tuesday, November 21, her Cossack friend returned to ask her for copies of photographs she had taken along their journey. They were walking to a studio to have the film developed when suddenly a Red Army soldier stopped them in the street.

"Hands up!" he ordered, pointing a revolver toward them.

Marguerite obeyed, half wondering whether she was being robbed. The soldier took the Cossack's handgun and then turned to her: "Are you Citizen Garrison?" he demanded to know.

"Yes," Marguerite replied.

"You are arrested," he said.[51]

RETURN TO RUSSIA

MARGUERITE'S ACCOUNT of her Asian travels and her subsequent capture and imprisonment strains credulity. The trip around the edges of Soviet Russia had posed obvious risks, but she later wrote that her capture completely surprised her. By her account, she said she believed overzealous local officials in Chita were just taking precautions in detaining an American visitor in the wake of the Soviet coup. She was confident she would be able to clear up the confusion as soon as she showed them her documents permitting her to enter the Far Eastern Republic. She tried to stay calm, even though the soldier pointed the gun at her head as he ordered her and the Cossack into a waiting carriage. They drove to the prison on the outskirts of town, and her hopes evaporated. This was not a local jail but one run by the Russian government political department—the GPU. The political police in Moscow had ordered her arrest. The charge: espionage.

Marguerite had talked herself out of tight situations before, so she tried to save herself by feigning outrage as she had with the White guards on the train to Vladivostok. She argued that it was not her fault the country had fallen to Soviet Russia. "My passport is visaed for the Far Eastern Republic and is quite in order," she said forcefully. "I am not responsible for your change of government."[1]

Under interrogation by a GPU official named Bogdonov, Marguerite recounted her trip through Asia and insisted she was working purely as a journalist. With somewhat tortured reasoning, she argued that America had no reason to spy on Russia because the two countries were not at war. She added that she had supported and continued to support Soviet Russia.[2]

Her captors would not be swayed. The commandant told her she would be sent on the next train to Moscow, where officials would reveal the details of the charges against her. He did, however, allow her to notify Thomas and Faymonville of her arrest and permit them to bring her personal items and all her documents. She thought the papers would prove she was a journalist and not a spy. Churchill's refusal to give her documents attesting to her previous employment with MID proved fortuitous. Even though the Russians knew her past, such papers would only have made matters worse and, at the very least, embarrassed the United States. As it was, her detention created a new headache for the American government, which still had no diplomatic relations with Soviet Russia.

Thomas telegrammed Washington immediately to let his superiors know that Marguerite had been arrested. He said he had demanded from the head of the Far Eastern Republic Revolutionary Committee an explanation for why she had been detained. The Chita official had expressed surprise and regret and told him there probably had been a misunderstanding and she would be released immediately. But two days passed, and then the administrator sent Thomas a brief note telling him the orders for Marguerite's arrest had come from Moscow. There was nothing he could do.[3]

GPU had been following Marguerite's movements throughout Siberia, looking for the opportunity to nab her. The collapse of the Far Eastern government made little difference. Moscow officials had ordered Chita political police to arrest her even before the coup. They couldn't touch her when she was in the diplomatic quarters with Faymonville and Thomas, but when she stepped into the street alone with the Cossack soldier, they seized the opportunity.

Yet despite the accusations of espionage, Marguerite was not treated as an enemy of the state. According to her account, the commandant told her the cells in the prison were crowded and uncomfortable, so he instead placed her in a small room behind his office. A sentry was stationed at the door, but the door was kept open, allowing her to watch what went on in the commandant's office. The first night, the assistant commandant visited her and noticed the smell of gas coming from a small stove in her room. He ordered the guard to move her bed into his private office and brought her a quilt and pillow. "This will make you a little more comfortable," he said.[4]

Marguerite described the assistant commandant as "more like a friend than a jailer."[5] While she awaited the train for Moscow that was due in three days, the prison administrators allowed her to buy food and to keep her luggage. When the time came for her to depart, they allowed her to take all of her money and any personal items she wanted.

Thomas and Faymonville came to the station to see her off. Marguerite, usually stoic under the most trying circumstances, nearly broke down as she departed. "At the time of my former arrest I had welcomed it as a delivery from an intolerable strain and the inevitable consequence of my own actions," she later wrote. "I had at least done something to deserve it. But this time I was innocent, and I could not understand why the old charges had been revived against me. I knew perfectly well that there was some motive behind it all which I could not fathom. It was baffling and disheartening."[6]

The express train that departed Chita on Friday was scheduled to arrive in Moscow eight days later. But once Marguerite and her captors boarded the train, the guard announced a change in plans. He told her he had not received the proper travel papers. At the next station on the outskirts of town, he received orders to take her to Novonikolaevsk, the administrative center of Siberia.

Marguerite understood that the unexpected detour might be a ploy to lose her within the GPU matrix. Faymonville and Thomas expected her to arrive in Moscow on Saturday, December 2. When she did not show up, the Russians would claim they did not know where she was. The American Relief Administration (ARA), the only connection between the United States and Russia, would not be able to find her. She imagined she would face a secret trial and then "oblivion."[7]

An employee of the local political police tipped off Thomas that Marguerite had been taken to a station outside of Chita, but he did not know what had happened to her.[8] While Thomas tried to investigate, Joseph Ames was seeking answers of his own. The State Department had alerted him of Marguerite's arrest, and he hurried to Washington to meet Assistant Secretary of State Alvey Adee and Dewitt Poole, head of the State Department's Russian section. Ames asked directly whether his daughter-in-law had been spying for the U.S. government when she was caught. Poole told him he "could assure him definitely she had no connection whatever with the State Department" and that he would be "exceedingly surprised, in view of what has happened in the past, if she had any official American connection whatever."[9]

What plans did they have to rescue her? Ames asked. Poole calmly told him that Marguerite knew the risks of traveling to the unstable Far Eastern Republic and that her capture had created "a very complicated situation." Poole said he could ask officials with the ARA to press for her release once Marguerite reached Moscow. In the meantime, all they could do was wait.[10]

The Russians continued to extend unusual courtesy to Marguerite during the four-day journey to Novonikolaevsk. They placed her in a first-class compartment on the train, and the guards allowed her to go to the restroom alone after she promised she would not speak with anyone or try to escape. She ordered her meals from the restaurant car and passed time playing cards with her guards.

But when they reached Novonikolaevsk, the conditions changed when she was escorted to a log house that served as a prison. Marguerite had spent months in Lubyanka during the famine, she had slept with livestock on earth floors in Siberian cabins, and she had stepped around Mongolians relieving themselves in the street, but this prison was far worse than anything she had seen before. She passed through the kitchen, which reeked of "half-rotten vegetables, putrid meat" and "dirty human beings." She was taken to a poorly heated cell that was crawling with vermin. "So little light came through the boarded windows that I was at first hardly able to see the other occupants—four women lying on plank beds without pallets or any other covering, but their own clothes," she recalled. Marguerite distributed a few cakes of soap and food to the women and gave a warm coat to one clothed in a thin cotton dress. As it turned out, she stayed only a few hours in the prison. A guard arrived and told her she would be traveling on to Moscow that night.[11]

The new guards who accompanied her to the train station were not so amicable as the ones who had escorted her from Chita. One kept a pistol pointed in her back as they boarded the train. Marguerite chatted amiably until he finally put away the gun, but the trip would not be pleasant. The next day one of her guards awoke with a fever and a badly swollen face. She gave him some aspirin and swabbed his face with antiseptic, but his condition grew worse. She and the other guard tried to find a doctor, but three days passed before they found one in a town where the train stopped. The doctor diagnosed the guard's affliction as erysipelas, a contagious and sometimes fatal skin infection, and said the man should be hospitalized. But no one was willing to take the chance of allowing the guard to leave his prisoner. While the poor man writhed in agony, Marguerite and the other guard had no choice but to continue to share the train compartment with him and care for him as best they could until they reached Moscow.[12]

She arrived in the capital on Sunday, December 3, and Marguerite was amazed at the city's transformation since she had last seen it sixteen months earlier. Foreign aid and Lenin's New Economic Policy, which relaxed some of the more draconian measures of state communism, had made life better. Tramlines were operating, and the streets and sidewalks were cleared of snow. Marguerite's guard suggested they go to a nearby restaurant for a cup of tea while they waited for a car. Inside the tables were covered in white cloths, and the buffet offered a variety of sandwiches, fruit, and pastries. Waiters in black coats and white aprons took orders from well-dressed patrons.

But while the city outside had changed dramatically, Lubyanka was much the same. Marguerite endured the familiar intake procedure with its lengthy formalities, and she answered the same questionnaire about her affiliations. She thought she even recognized some of the guards. After completing the paperwork, she was moved to a detention room. There she waited for four days, but no one questioned her or told her of the charges she faced.

In the evening of the fourth day, guards ordered her to pack her bags, and she was transferred to Butyrka Prison, where she once had delivered care packages to American and British inmates. Unlike Lubyanka, Butyrka seemed like a prison, with high cement walls and stone floors. Marguerite was placed in a cell with eleven other women and began again the prison routine. She awoke to the sound of a gong at seven each morning and was led out into the corridor to wash at a long trough. She then returned to the cell and received the day's food ration. Provisions were better than they had been two years ago, although the prison still served the unappetizing herring soup. The inmates were allowed to sing, dance, and play games to pass the time, and Marguerite renewed her practice of telling the fortunes of the guards and prisoners around her.

A week passed, but she still was not interrogated. Then a guard ordered her to pack her belongings. She hoped the ARA had won her release. Instead she was returned to Lubyanka, where she waited another day in the detention room. By now she was feeling ill. The stress of not knowing the precise charges and evidence against her and the uncertainty of her fate began to take their toll. She asked to see the assistant commandant to find out what would happen to her. He told her she would be sent to the inner prison. Guards escorted her through the familiar corridors of Lubyanka and carefully searched her bags before taking her to an attic room just around the corner from the cell she had occupied in 1921.

This time the room was clean, prisoners were allowed to bathe every two weeks, and Marguerite was allowed to purchase items from the outside with the money she had brought from Siberia. But discipline was stricter than before.

Everyone in the cell lost the privileges to obtain books and cigarettes after one girl went on a rampage and broke a bed and windows.

Marguerite wrote two accounts of her second imprisonment. In both, she described being interrogated repeatedly by a man named Roller. In these sessions, which lasted two to four hours, he tried to make her confess that she was spying in Siberia. He forced her to read a diary she kept in the Far East and frequently interrupted her to ask for more details. Finally he told her that the date had been set for her trial. The proceedings would be held in secret, although she would be permitted a court-appointed lawyer. If found guilty, she could receive the death sentence or, at the very least, three years in the gulag.[13]

In her second account she added startling new details. She said weeks passed without interrogation, and she feared she would be locked away and forgotten. Then, just before New Year's Day, she was summoned to the offices of the Presidium where she confronted her old nemesis: Solomon Mogilevsky. Now stationed in Tbilisi, Georgia, he had returned to Moscow to offer her another chance to work in Russia as a spy.[14]

Documents in the Federal Security Bureau Archives offer yet a third version of the events surrounding Marguerite's second imprisonment. While numerous pages in the file remain sealed, it is clear she did not languish months or even weeks awaiting questioning. Roller cross-examined Marguerite on December 11, just a little over a week after she arrived in Moscow. According to the report, she described her travels through Asia and insisted she was not spying but instead collecting material for the Hearst syndicate. She admitted to meeting with Maj. Robert L. Eichelberger and other officials in the State Department before she left the United States, but she said these were informal meetings to help her understand the countries where she would be traveling. The file of her second imprisonment makes no mention of Mogilevsky.[15]

So what really happened? Did Mogilevsky orchestrate her capture and then fly from the Caucasus to persuade her to stay in Russia as a spy? Did the plan to recruit her as a Russian agent explain the unusual courtesies extended to her following her capture? Did he really have a romantic interest in her as she suspected? If so, why did she omit such a sensational anecdote from her first account of her capture? On the other hand, why would she invent the story? Marguerite sometimes erred in reciting the details of her adventures. Occasionally she omitted crucial facts, such as not revealing in her first book, *Marooned in Moscow*, that she worked for MID. But there is no evidence in any other case in which she completely fabricated a story.

The Mogilevsky meeting becomes more credible in light of the positions Mogilevsky and her interrogator, Roller, held at the time. The interrogator known as Roller mentioned in her memoirs and in Russian documents was most certainly Karl Frantsevich Roller-Chelek, an Austrian who defected to Soviet Russia in 1920 and became a special agent for Cheka. In 1922 he was assigned to counterintelligence, including recruiting foreign spies. Unknown to the Russians, Roller was actually a Polish spy.[16]

Mogilevsky, meanwhile, had continued to rise through the ranks of Cheka. Within days after Marguerite's release from prison in 1921, he had assumed control of the Foreign Department, helping create and expand Russia's spy network in Europe. In 1922 he helped foil an attack against Russian delegates at an international conference in Genoa. But with the reorganization of Russian intelligence operations and the creation of GPU in February 1922, Felix Dzerzhinsky inexplicably appointed Mogilevsky to oversee internal troops and intelligence operations in the Caucasus. Such a post far removed from Moscow would appear to be a demotion, although his work for GPU remained vital: His job was to recruit foreign spies.[17] Could Marguerite, the agent who had brazenly told Van Deman that she could persuade Communists to provide evidence against Robert Minor in Germany in 1919, have concocted a plan to turn Mogilevsky into an American agent? That mission would obviously have been a closely guarded secret, but one worth the risk Marguerite took in exposing herself to capture.

Marguerite faced three charges—the old espionage charge, entering the country illegally, and a new spying charge. She was completely cut off from the outside world. Unlike the first imprisonment, when she received aid packages, this time she heard no news, received no letters. Many years later, Marguerite's son said the Soviets pressed her to become an agent in the United States. "They put tremendous pressures on Mother," Tommy Harrison said. "They grilled her over and over, day after day. They kept stressing, 'We've got you. Nobody knows where you are,' making her feel helpless. They were ready to do anything to get her to sign up to work as a Soviet agent in the United States, but she wouldn't do it."[18]

Roller interrogated her for hours at a time and threatened her with imprisonment and death if she did not confess. She recounted that Mogilevsky, however, promised her a comfortable salary and life with her son in a new, dynamic country, if she would agree to work as a Russian spy. Under the stress, Marguerite's usually robust health and indefatigable spirit faltered. She had no appetite and barely the energy to rise from bed.

Throughout this time, her relatives struggled to persuade U.S. officials to fight for her freedom again. "The government must be very tired of Mrs. Harrison, but there she is," Ames wrote to Christian Herter, assistant to Secretary of Commerce Herbert Hoover. "The family will be most grateful to you for anything you can do. You and the A.R.A. are in fact our only hope."[19] Albert Ritchie, took a more diplomatic approach, thanking the ARA for its "kindness and interest in her case."[20]

In truth, ARA officials gave the family only tepid assurances, while privately debating among themselves whether they should help at all. "Having rescued her once from the Soviet authorities, I do not see that we are under any obligation to again get her out of the jail since she has deliberately put her head into the lion's jaws," Herter wrote to an ARA official. He said he did not believe Marguerite was in any danger and he was not willing to make a formal request for her release, although he begrudgingly agreed ARA officials in Moscow might make inquiries "in order to show that we are interested in her fate."[21]

Edgar Rickard, the American director of the ARA agreed. "Mrs. Harrison has evidently shown some indiscretion," he replied. "I think it would be a mistake for the A.R.A. to voluntarily inject itself into this Harrison business unless we are specifically requested to do so." Rickard cynically added a handwritten notation: "Perhaps Senator France might get her out?? He claimed he did it before."[22]

Harrison's arrest clearly was an embarrassment, and it couldn't have come at a worse time. Stan Harding and the British press were now loudly demanding that the United States make amends for the actions of its agent, who they said had sent an honest journalist to Lubyanka. Harding was proving to be a very formidable foe. She insisted on a public apology and compensation for her suffering. When an American military attaché in London offered to pay her if she kept quiet, she told newspapers and vowed not to be bought with hush money.[23]

The British Foreign Office also took up Harding's case as part of its negotiations of a trade deal with the Soviets. Great Britain insisted that Russia pay Harding and the widow of a British man who had been shot as a spy. The lengthy trade talks kept the issue in the headlines for months until Russia finally paid Harding three thousand pounds in August 1923 to settle the dispute.[24] In the meantime,

Harding recruited well-known British journalists and human-rights activists to her cause, including Bertrand Russell and Labor Party leaders in the House of Parliament to pursue her claim against Marguerite and the U.S. government.[25]

Marguerite had just started her Asia trip when the controversy erupted, but as the accusations mounted, Ames and Ritchie came to her defense. "A great injury has been done an unfortunate woman," Ames said.[26] Ritchie declared: "To anyone who knows Mrs. Harrison the whole thing is absurd and inconceivable. It is entirely impossible for one of her high character and honor to be guilty of such a thing."[27]

Privately, however, the family wondered whether Harding's accusations were true. In December 1922 Ames wrote to his old friend Marlborough Churchill to ask whether he knew any details about the case. "I am very anxious to be in a position to deny with all conviction her charges and I can say this with a better conscience if I am absolutely sure myself," he said.[28]

The Harding controversy placed the United States in the awkward position of having to respond to public accusations that one of its spies had been a Bolshevik agent while at the same time explaining how she had ended up in the hands of the Russians again. ARA officials clearly blamed Marguerite for her predicament and resented having to petition the Soviets again for her release. State Department representatives, however, realized the American public would be outraged if she were harmed and urged the ARA to help.

"As I understand it, we have no confirmation of her presence in Moscow or that she is alive," Dewitt Poole, head of the Russian section at the State Department, wrote to Herter in the Department of Commerce. "If she has been killed or seriously mistreated, the fact will out eventually, of course, then there will be a pretty to-do. You, of course, have all this in mind. Can you suggest anything to do which has not already been done? The situation rather worries me."[29]

As Marguerite had feared, no one was sure what had happened to her after she left Chita. Thomas apparently was unable to confirm whether she had been taken from the train at the station outside the city. U.S. officials and news reporters assumed she had been sent to Moscow, but no one knew for certain she had arrived. ARA officials repeatedly pressed the Russian government for answers, but weeks passed without a response.

Then, the day after Poole urged Herter to keep trying to find out what had happened to Marguerite, there was surprising news: Soviet authorities announced that they would deport her within days. What accounted for the sudden turn of events? Why, after weeks of refusing to provide any information about her at all, did the Soviets suddenly acknowledge they held her and would soon let her go?

Marguerite said she was surprised at the announcement. According to her account, Roller had informed her in early February that she would soon face trial. Under the Soviet system, she was assumed guilty unless she could prove otherwise. Marguerite resigned herself to the prospect of a long imprisonment. Then on February 17, a few days before the scheduled proceeding, she was summoned to the office of Baron von Pilau, head of the GPU foreign espionage section.

He rose as she entered. "Citizen Harrison," he said. "I know that you will be glad to hear that I have an order for your release."

Marguerite was not sure she heard him correctly and thought she might be hallucinating.

"You are free, citizeness," he repeated, handing her the discharge paper.

Shaking, Marguerite reached out to take the paper. "I thought I was to be tried in two weeks. I don't understand," she said.

"Don't try to understand," Pilau said abruptly. "I am not at liberty to tell you anything about the circumstances of your release. The only condition attached to it is that you will cross the frontier within a week. That will give you sufficient time to obtain the necessary permits to leave the country."

A guard escorted her back to her cell and stayed with her until she packed. A few minutes later she was standing outside in Lubyanka Square.[30]

Marguerite later explained the astonishing turn of events. She said GPU had arrested and detained her for two months without the knowledge of the Russian Foreign Office.[31] Then Col. William Haskell, director of the ARA in Russia, discovered she was in prison.[32] In one account she said a Russian worker for the ARA happened to see her in the prison, alerted Haskell, and he then demanded that the Foreign Office release her. The division between the Soviet secret police and the Foreign Office was not without precedent. Harding said that while she was in Lubyanka, she repeatedly asked to speak to the head of the Foreign Office, who had granted her permission to enter the country, but Cheka refused, saying the Foreign Office had nothing to do with her case.[33]

But contrary to what Marguerite said, Haskell did not suddenly learn of her imprisonment and demand her release. ARA officials had known for months that the Soviets held her. By Haskell's account, he was having dinner with Maxim

Litvinov, head of the Western section of the Foreign Office, when the Soviet official told him Marguerite soon would be released. According to Haskell, Litvinov said that her freedom was "entirely due to the American Relief Administration," although there is no evidence Haskell worked very hard for her freedom.[34]

Ames offered a different version of what transpired. In a letter to Poole he explained: "I have been irritated by the attitude of the A.R.A. . . . Their first cablegram to their agent in Moscow was cautious, to say the least, and naturally did not produce the faintest result. Finally—through personal influence out of Washington—I had a real cablegram sent and there was immediate action on the part of the Soviet authorities. I think I might have saved two months if I had only thought more quickly and I had not believed so credulously what the A.R.A. in Washington told me."[35] How had Ames won her freedom? Writing to Herter in the Department of Commerce, Ames said that George S. Jackson, a Baltimore grain exporter, had interceded on Marguerite's behalf. Jackson's wife, Annie, was a third cousin of Marguerite's husband, Tom.[36]

Records in the Russian archives provide yet another explanation for why Marguerite was set free. A document notes she was released because of bad health and because she denied the spy charges.[37]

None of these accounts completely explains how Marguerite, held secretly in Lubyanka for two months, won her freedom. Just as bewildering were the terms of her release. In 1921 she was given just minutes to catch a train headed to Riga. At that time she left her belongings at Lubyanka, and a Cheka car raced her to the station just as the train was about to leave.

This time officials in GPU gave her one week to arrange her affairs and allowed her to stay with the family of a woman she had met during her first imprisonment. Marguerite said she became friends with the woman, Evgenia, at Novinsky prison, and that they had kept in touch over the years. Marguerite described her as an art lecturer who worked for Trotsky's wife. Evgenia had been imprisoned for two years and after her release had sent aid packages to Marguerite, although Marguerite did not mention her in her accounts of the first imprisonment. Evgenia seems to have been a member of the Russian intelligentsia and was living fairly comfortably despite the recent upheavals caused by the Bolshevik revolution. She resided in a seven-room apartment in Moscow with her mother, father, a married brother, his wife, four children, and an uncle. By combining the incomes of the adult members, the family lived well enough to even employ two servants.[38]

Marguerite stayed with the family for a week while she waited to secure the necessary documents to leave the country. Although she had been ordered to leave Russia, the Soviets seemed to expect her to still apply for a passport. During the week, Marguerite met Haskell with the ARA and stopped by the Russian Foreign Office. She also had the chance to observe the changes in Moscow. Theaters and cabarets flourished. Shops sold luxury goods, furs, and even American shoes. Bookstores proliferated, and newsstands sold French fashion magazines. Banks had reopened. When she was discharged from prison, she received six hundred gold rubles (about sixteen hundred dollars in today's money)—presumably the money she had with her when she was arrested. She was allowed to deposit it in a Russian bank and order a transfer to a bank in Riga, where she would withdraw it when she arrived.

She credited the Bolsheviks for bringing stability to the country. "I admired the tenacity and courage which had enabled the Soviet leaders to bring order out of chaos and to establish their autocracy on a firm basis," she wrote. At the same time, she missed the optimistic spirit that had been prevalent in the early days of the revolution. "It had been stamped out by bureaucracy," she noted.[39]

Marguerite lingered in Russia until the last possible moment. On February 24 she boarded the diplomatic express train and crossed the Latvian frontier fifteen minutes before her exit permit expired. "There was something final about my departure this time. I felt that I would never see my beloved Russia again," she wrote.[40]

Marguerite arrived quietly in Riga this time. She did not confront the gaggle of reporters and photographers clamoring to hear her story. "I was no longer 'good copy,'" she said. "My first experience had been unique. This was a repetition. . . . The only dramatic feature of the situation was the reason for my arrest, and that I kept to myself."[41]

In Riga, U.S. envoy Frederick W. B. Coleman questioned her about her experience. "She talked at considerable length but without much sequence," Coleman reported. "She impressed me as unreliable and her information superficial." Marguerite expressed the opinion that the United States should recognize Soviet Russia, and she warned Coleman that officials should not allow an American journalist named Elizabeth Harrington, who was then in Harbin, to enter Russia, presumably because she might be arrested. And then Marguerite revealed surprising information about her interrogation: Her Soviet captors had been aware that she had met Eichelberger before she left for Asia.[42] When Marguerite arrived in Berlin, she told a military attaché the same story. Not only did the Soviets know she had talked with Eichelberger, they "repeated this conversation almost verbatim."[43]

Had a mole again leaked information to the Russian secret police? Unlike Marguerite's intelligence reports, which could have been seen by numerous clerks and couriers, only a few people would have known exactly what she and Eichelberger said in their meeting. American diplomats were doubtful about her claim. "This information is passed on for what it is worth," Coleman said. Marguerite made no mention of this possible leak in her writings, and there is no evidence the Army or State Department investigated the allegation. American officials were becoming increasingly skeptical about Marguerite's information.

Within days Marguerite's health had recovered sufficiently to allow her to again take an interest in political affairs. The French had seized the Ruhr valley in response to Germany's failure to meet its reparation obligations. After Marguerite arrived in Berlin, she decided to investigate the situation herself in hopes of gathering new material for her lectures. She traveled to Essen, where she spent two days observing the French making mass arrests and the Germans organizing resistance to the occupation. Marguerite's sympathies lay with the German workers even though she knew that put her at odds with the views of most Americans. "I was thoroughly disillusioned and thoroughly disheartened by the attitude of the American public toward European problems," she wrote.[44]

Marguerite returned to New York on March 22, 1923, on board the steamship *President Monroe*. One of her first actions was to give a statement to the *Baltimore Sun* urging the United States to recognize Soviet Russia. America was missing trade opportunities and allowing Germany to gain an economic foothold in the country, she argued. "Unless the United States acts soon, we shall lose out in trade relationship," she said.[45] The next day the newspaper reported her assertions that Soviet Russia would survive despite Lenin's deteriorating health. "There is a stabilized government administered by men as able as Lenin," she said.[46]

Now that she was back in the United States, she had to respond to Harding's allegations of betrayal. Marguerite told her family that she had not denounced the British woman. She said the Russians knew of Harding's work with her in Germany and had set a trap that would make Harding believe Harrison had told them she was a spy. The records of Marguerite's interrogations, however, show that she did, in fact, provide information on Harding at least twice. In the statement of charges from her first imprisonment, Mogilevsky wrote that she gave Cheka information of a "very poor quality" only pointing to one person who was a real agent—Stan Harding.[47] During her second imprisonment Marguerite told interrogators that she had assumed Harding was a spy in Germany. "While Mrs. Harding was not explicit as to her exact status at the moment, she stated that she was asked by the British 'to talk things over and discuss the situation' and thus, coupled with the fact that she had continued her active and intensive political works and infestations long after she had ceased the work as a correspondent, convinced me double as to her role."[48]

In mounting her defense against Harding, Marguerite again pressed the Army to acknowledge that she had worked for MID. She believed the military attaché in London had said as much in a conversation reported by the British journal *Truth* in February. According to the article, Col. Oscar Solbert offered to pay Harding an unspecified amount of money if she dropped her public campaign against Marguerite. "America will protect its agents. Mrs. Harrison did very good work for us during the war," the article quoted Solbert.[49]

Marguerite believed his comments now justified a complete acknowledgment that she had been an American spy. Churchill presented her position to Col. William Naylor, arguing that the Army owed Marguerite for the suffering she had endured after having twice been the victim of alleged leaks from American agencies. Although the Army had tried to conceal her employment to protect her, "in her opinion matters have come to such a pass as she would prefer to have our connection with us known," Churchill said. "If she feels this way about it, I can see no objection and would suggest that either you make a statement concerning the matter, or since her activities cover the period when I was Director of Military Intelligence, that you authorize me to make such a statement."[50]

Marguerite met twice with Naylor, urging him to acknowledge her work with MID, but he refused. Writing to Churchill, Naylor explained: "It was very difficult for me to arrive at this decision for it was extremely hard to divorce the purely personal side of it from the official." According to Naylor, Marguerite had seemed resigned that the Army would not give out a statement regarding the Harding matter "but was quite insistent upon getting a statement setting forth her alleged activities concerning M.I.D."[51] For almost a year Marguerite had been trying to get the Army to publicly say she had been a spy, but why? When Naylor refused, Marguerite issued her own statement to the newspapers.

Referring to Solbert's comment that she had "rendered valuable service to the American government," Marguerite set out her defense. Although not explicitly stating that she was hired to spy in Berlin, Marguerite said she gathered information for news articles and forwarded reports to MID. She described how she met Harding in Germany and learned that she was sending intelligence reports to the British government. Marguerite went on to describe Harding's help in infiltrating Leftist organizations in Germany, work that the Bolsheviks then used as evidence against her once she entered Russia. Marguerite wrote that she pleaded with Mogilevsky to not arrest Harding but that he refused her entreaties. She said she saw Harding only once after her arrest when they passed in the hallway of Lubyanka, an arrangement Cheka designed so Harding would believe Marguerite had denounced her.[52]

After Marguerite's statement, Harding began to blame not only Marguerite but the American spy services as well. She wanted a public apology for a system that had led an American agent to denounce an innocent journalist. Newspapers, meanwhile, picked up on the theme of journalism ethics and stressed the evil of allowing intelligence agents to pose as journalists. "An ugly blow at honesty and independence in journalism was struck by the combination of secret agent and special correspondent which some ill-advised American authorities evolved," the editors of the *Manchester Guardian* wrote. "But the main thing is the light thrown on this case should make the vicious experiment impossible of repetition."[53]

Having issued her statement, Marguerite hoped to put the controversy behind her. Other matters were concluding too. It had taken five years, but her father's estate was finally settled. In the spring of 1923 Baker's remaining assets were sold and the taxes paid. That April Marguerite received $2,576, plus a painting of Napoleon and the King of Rome valued at another $1,000.[54]

Marguerite moved into an apartment in the Hotel Schuyler in midtown Manhattan with Tommy, now twenty-one, and resumed her lectures and writing. She told herself that this time she would settle down for good. Her family was wary. "I do not know that I will ever unravel the mysteries connected with her because I never ask questions," Ames wrote to Herter in the Commerce Department. Ames said that Tommy had written to George Jackson to thank him for helping win his mother's release. "In the letter he said that he hoped that in as much as his mother had an apparently incurable desire to get into jail, he hoped she would select an American one the next time."[55] To Dewitt Poole, Ames wrote: "I have no idea as to Mrs. Harrison's plans, but if I ever learn the truth about her experiences and her projects, I will let you know."[56]

Marguerite wrote about her Asian adventures in a book, *Red Bear or Yellow Dragon*. She resumed giving lectures on world events. But after a few months she grew tired of New York. She felt driven to go "somewhere—anywhere." She recalled lying in bed and hearing the sirens of the ocean liners enticing her to travel again. "I could stand it no longer. I made up my mind that I would have to go somewhere before the summer was over."[57]

Marguerite told herself that her son respected her compulsion to travel the world. "He had always understood with a wisdom far beyond his years the impulse that was forever driving me to wander over the face of the earth. Nothing could have held me back during those wander years of mine, but it would have been only natural if my son had drifted away from me. I would have had no one to blame but myself. However, even when we were separated for long periods we never lost the sense of contact and distance had never seemed a barrier between us."[58]

So Marguerite began looking for another way to escape New York. She sent queries to magazines and was awaiting an assignment when she ran into her old friend Merian Cooper, who had just returned from a trip to Abyssinia in northern Ethiopia. In the two years since they had last met, Cooper had been indulging his passion for adventure. He had worked briefly as a reporter for the *New York Times*, then joined an expedition sailing the world in a search for ape-like people purported to be the "missing link."

Cooper also had been working as an American spy. Just before leaving for his voyage on the *Wisdom II* in September 1922, he dashed off a hurried note to Army major J. L. Collins offering to collect intelligence as he journeyed through Asia, Africa, and the Middle East. "I am going to the East—Archipelago, India, Persia, Abyssinia, Egypt, Tripoli, Morocco and Algiers on a private yacht and will travel in the interior—whole trip about two years. My purpose is to do magazine work and travel books. I have thought that perhaps I might be of some service to the government. If I can get you any information, please wire me immediately in detail what you wish."[59]

In their response, Army commanders noted that they could not assign him any particular mission, but they did want to use his services. They urged him to make direct contact with the military attaches in Peking and Manila and provided him with reference letters to show local officials.[60]

When Cooper reconnected with Marguerite in the spring of 1923, he had a new mission. He was planning an intelligence operation to the Middle East and already had enlisted the help of his friend Ernest Schoedsack, a former Army signalman who had been the cameraman on the *Wisdom II* expedition. He wanted Marguerite to join them. As a cover story, they would make a movie about nomads who travel for survival. It would be a dangerous trip that would take them to the doorstep of old friends and enemies. One of the Americans working for U.S. interests in the region was former Russian spy operative Robert W. Imbrie, now charged with establishing an espionage network in Southern Russia. His adversary in Tbilisi, Georgia: Solomon Mogilevsky.

DESERT DRAMA

MARGUERITE HARRISON, Merian Cooper, and Ernest Schoedsack kept the Middle East mission secret their entire lives. They wrote books and articles, and they gave lectures and interviews about the expedition. But they never revealed that while documenting the epic journey of a Persian tribe's search for pasture, they were gathering intelligence for the U.S. Army.

For years film critics and historians described their 1925 film *Grass* as a missed opportunity. Schoedsack captured spectacular footage of the Bakhtiari tribe as the nomads hiked barefoot over a snow-covered mountain and herded their animals across a raging river in search of summer pasture. Yet the movie lacked a coherent narrative, critics complained. The first half of the film focused on Marguerite as a woman fed up with civilization who goes searching for a "forgotten people." In the second half of the movie, she virtually disappeared as the story shifted to the tribal chief and his son.

Historians also pondered why, for decades, Marguerite, Cooper, and Schoedsack told conflicting stories about the journey, even disagreeing on such fundamental points as who conceived of the movie and who paid for it.[1] Marguerite wrote in her memoir that she and Cooper came up with the idea one day when they were discussing travel films.

"Isn't it strange," Marguerite recalled saying, "that no one has ever made a travel film on purely dramatic lines?" Cooper agreed, pointing out nomads who must travel for survival.

"Listen, Merian," Marguerite said. "Why couldn't we make a new sort of travel film, based on the struggle for existence? It could be absolutely authentic in every particular. We wouldn't need a story if we could find people whose daily lives contained all the elements of drama. Let's try it."

"I'm on," he replied.[2] Marguerite said Cooper was short of money, so she paid the entire ten thousand dollars for the trip. Schoedsack called Marguerite's account a "damned bunch of lies."[3] He said he and Cooper came up with the project when they were returning from the *Wisdom II* expedition. He said he traveled to the Middle East while Cooper went to America to raise money for the expedition. Schoedsack recalled that when they reunited in Paris some months later, Cooper brought not only ten thousand dollars but also, "to my dismay, a lady journalist, Marguerite Harrison."[4]

Cooper told yet another story. He said Dr. Isaiah Bowman at the American Geological Society in New York helped him locate the tribe. "Dr. Bowman helped me to pick out what he and I both considered the most formidable migration in the world of which we knew—the Spring migration of the Baba Ahamadi [Baba Ahmadi] Tribe of the [Bakhtiari] of Persia." Cooper said he and Marguerite split the cost of the trip.[5]

The explanation for these inconsistencies is as simple as it is shocking: In trying to keep the true nature of the expedition secret, the three were ensnared in lies and contradictions.

The evidence that *Grass* was an intelligence mission is found in a handwritten notation on a letter Cooper sent to the U.S. Army intelligence service in 1940. After World War II began in Europe, Cooper knew that the United States would join the fight. He proposed undertaking a fact-finding mission for the Army under the pretext of making a film. He wrote: "I successfully led two expeditions on my own initiative as the one I suggested to you." In the margin someone, presumably the recipient, Gen. Sherman Miles, wrote: "Grass, a movie project but really to obtain information for us."[6]

Marguerite's version of how the movie began probably contains a kernel of truth because she acknowledged that before they left on the expedition, they received advice from U.S. State Department Near East expert Harrison G. Dwight, who had grown up in Persia and Turkey. She said he told them to try to film the Kurds in Turkey but that if they could afford more time and money, they might also consider the Bakhtiari in Persia, who migrate each summer to the mountains in search of grass.

The real purpose of the mission may never be known. At the time they planned the journey, the area was rife with intrigue. Mustafa Kemal Atatürk had just defeated the British and Greeks and was in the process of establishing an independent Turkey. Both the West and Russia sought to win Atatürk's loyalty in those early days of his reign. Meanwhile, Britain, America, and Russia competed to control the region's vast oil wealth. The intent to film the Kurds and the Bakhtiari point to the mission as one to enlist alliances to help America gain access to the oil fields.

It seems likely that Cooper asked Marguerite to join the expedition because he knew she was a talented linguist who had proven capable of working in harsh conditions in Russia and Asia. Another clue that she was an integral part of the team is that the index to her MID personal file contains three entries marked "training"—on March 28, 1923, April 6, 1923, and May 5, 1923—immediately before they departed for the Middle East and more than two years after she officially ended work with the agency. The actual documents, however, are not in her file. Is it possible she received language training on those dates?

Decades after the expedition, Cooper and Schoedsack portrayed Marguerite as a burdensome accomplice. Cooper said he felt obliged to take her on the trip because she had saved his life in Russia and because she was helping fund the expedition. Schoedsack said he adamantly opposed taking her along, a view that even made its way into Cooper and Schoedsack's most famous collaboration, *King Kong*. In a scene written by Schoedsack's wife, Rose, heroine Ann Darrow asks first mate Jack Driscoll, "I guess you don't think much of women on ships, do you?" Driscoll, a character modeled after Schoedsack, replies, "No they're a nuisance."

In an interview with film historian Kevin Brownlow, Cooper and Schoedsack credited Marguerite's bravery even as they criticized her work on the *Grass* project. "Looking back on it, it was a hell of a trip for a woman to be on," Cooper said. "She had to act tough. This was a very dangerous trip."

"I'll give her credit for that," Schoedsack agreed. "I always give her credit. There's just one thing about it. She didn't belong there."[7]

Cooper said Marguerite nearly ruined the movie by wearing unrealistic costumes and thick layers of makeup. He grumbled about her white riding breeches and said he was irritated by her propensity to leave the production to investigate political developments. "Marguerite could never understand when I said we'd have to sacrifice everything to make a picture," Cooper said.[8]

If the men seemed dismissive of her contributions, Marguerite's light-hearted retelling of the expedition provided even more ammunition to her critics. She described showing up at the dock in New York looking as though she were setting off for a European cruise. She sported a new hair wave and had packed in her duffle bag and two suitcases riding clothes, an evening dress, makeup, and her ever-present rubber bathtub. Marguerite explained that she had always tried to keep up appearances, even when she was a prisoner in Russia.[9]

The success of the mission depended on creating a realistic cover operation. The problem, however, was that the three knew practically nothing about making movies. Thirty-year-old Schoedsack was the most experienced of the group. After graduating from high school he had roamed around California, sleeping on park benches and working odd jobs, including as a deck hand on a boat and as a road surveyor, until he discovered his gift and passion operating a camera in Hollywood. When World War I began, he enlisted as a signalman to film the war. He later recalled that he was not issued a helmet or a gas mask and so wasn't allowed to film scenes close to the battle.

When the war ended, Schoedsack ended up in Vienna, aiding refugees who were fleeing Russia. There he encountered Cooper, whom he described as "wearing one French boot and one German one, and he was wearing a U.S. Navy sword." Cooper was on his way to Poland to fight against the Russians.

The two reunited in February 1923 for the voyage to northern Africa, which marked the start of a partnership that would create *King Kong*, *Chang*, and *Mighty Joe Young*. But in the fall of 1923 Schoedsack was so low on funds that all he could contribute to the *Grass* expedition was his skill and a hand-cranked camera.[10]

Cooper, also thirty, had been a newspaper reporter, soldier, and pilot, but his great aspiration was to be an explorer charting the Earth's vanishing wilderness. Although he had enlisted Schoedsack's help on the *Wisdom II* voyage, they had used film to merely document their travels. They had not attempted to tell a story that time. When he set out on the *Grass* expedition, he had seen only three or four movies in his life. He nevertheless became the film's director.[11]

Marguerite had seen hundreds of movies in her position on the Maryland movie censorship board, but she knew little about how they were made and even less about acting. The early scenes of the film show her wearing heavy makeup and vamping for the camera.

The men's complaints about Marguerite nearly ruining the film may not have been genuine, but there appeared to be real tension among the team members. Marguerite bristled at Cooper's sexist views about women, which she described as "a compound of southern chivalry and Oriental contempt." She went on to say, "He had inherited the idea that 'nice' women were made to be set on pedestals and worshiped. On the other hand, he was convinced that they were brainless creatures fit only to mind home and bear children." Although newspapers reporters had once hinted that they had been lovers in Poland, she dispelled that rumor. "He never thought of me as a woman at all and that was why were able to get on together, for although I had never considered myself a feminist, I suppose I was instinctively one, as are most women who have had to make their way in the world. We had furious arguments about women but they were never personal. To him I was simply a boon companion, a business associate, and the person to whom he claimed he owed an eternal debt of gratitude for saving his life in Russia."[12]

Marguerite described Schoedsack, called Monty or Shorty by his friends, as "a young giant, six feet five in his stocking feet" with "a friendly grin, and a mop of curly brown hair." She noted his Midwestern sensibilities and gruff exterior but added, "he had a heart of gold and the sensitiveness of a true artist. I have never seen anyone who was more responsive to beauty in all its forms."[13]

They set out to film *Grass* at a time when the West was keenly interested in the Middle East. Inspired by the writings of British adventurers, including spies T. E. Lawrence and Gertrude Bell, tourism to the region thrived. In addition to the cultural fascination with the area, the American, British, French, German, and Russian governments were also interested in the politics and resources of the region.[14] The British first established a foothold in the Middle East to gain access to India. Their discovery of oil in Persia in 1908 fueled even greater involvement and sparked intense rivalries among the industrialized nations. In 1923 the region was a cauldron of political intrigues as Turks, Persians, and Arabs struggled to assert their independence while Western countries and Russia sought alliances for their own benefit.

Cooper and Marguerite, now forty-four, departed New York on the French ocean liner *Lafayette* on August 4, 1923. In noting their sailing, the *New York Times* made no mention of movie plans and instead reported that the two were going to Turkey and Persia to collect information for magazine articles.[15] After meeting

Schoedsack in Paris, Marguerite left the men in France buying film and supplies while she went on to Constantinople to make arrangements for permits to film in Turkey.

She arrived just as Mustafa Kemal Atatürk was establishing control over the country. The Turkish nationalist movement had fascinated Marguerite since her girlish flirtations with the Young Turk Reshid Sadi Bey in 1900. When she entered Constantinople in late 1923, the dreams of an independent Turkey were beginning to be realized. Atatürk had defeated the Greeks and proclaimed the creation of the Turkish Republic. The transformation was exciting, yet the upheaval complicated American interests in the region. Turks were wary of foreigners, especially those speaking English, fearing they might try to aid the rebellious Kurds or Armenians.

As part of his nationalist plan, Atatürk moved the country's capital from Constantinople to Angora. So when Marguerite arrived in Constantinople, she could find no one in authority who could issue permits for the Americans to travel farther into the country. A representative of the Foreign Office told her there was nothing she could do until permission came from Angora.

While she waited, Marguerite socialized with American expatriates and studied Turkish, which she found surprisingly easy. She was satisfied to observe the political events unfolding around her, but when Cooper and Schoedsack arrived they were disappointed to learn she had not concluded the arrangements for them to proceed to the Kurdish-occupied lands. After another week of waiting, the trio began filming in Constantinople.

They staged Marguerite's arrival at the Golden Horn and filmed scenes of her being mobbed by baggage handlers as she stepped off a steamer. They passed time in Constantinople filming street scenes, including a dancing bear. But as the days wore on, Cooper and Schoedsack grew impatient to reach the Kurds. They favored traveling to Beirut and through Syria to Iraq, where they hoped to connect to Kurds in the northern part of the country. Marguerite implored them to wait, wanting to observe developments in Turkey.

Just as she was about to give in to the men's demands, the Turks granted permission for them to proceed to Angora. Their progress was fleeting, however. When they arrived in Angora, the foreign minister told them firmly they would not be allowed to take pictures in Kurdistan. The Turks were suspicious about the filmmakers. "I believe they thought we must be British spies trying to get across to see some starving Armenians or start trouble in Kurdistan," Schoedsack later recalled.[16]

Cooper and Schoedsack thought they should journey south to Adana, but Marguerite persuaded them to wait until she had secured an interview with Mustafa Atatürk. She met him at an art exhibition and later noted, "We did not discuss politics, but rather his plans for the New Angora, and his model farm which he hoped would prove a practical example to his countrymen."[17]

Just before the Americans were scheduled to depart Angora, the mission was interrupted when Cooper suddenly took ill. In writing about the incident later, Marguerite never specified the ailment, and Cooper never mentioned it in his own recollections of the trip. She described the problem as a chronic complaint that became acute and required immediate surgery. Schoedsack and Marguerite wanted to return to an American hospital in Constantinople, but Cooper refused. "I have never seen any other man who so reveled in personal discomfort or who got such a grim satisfaction from physical suffering," Marguerite later wrote. "He insisted that the operation should be performed in Angora and went to the Turkish Military Hospital, a dilapidated building on the outskirts of town."[18]

The food was poor, and the hospital lacked morphine and other drugs to ease his pain. Flies and mosquitoes swarmed Cooper's stifling room. Bandages were in short supply, and the dressing on his wound was rarely changed. Schoedsack and Marguerite worried Cooper wouldn't survive the ordeal, but he was soon well enough to travel.

They hired a driver and interpreter to help them cross the Salt Desert of Anatolia. They traveled in a covered wagon, in which Marguerite slept at night while the men slept underneath. Along the way, they filmed the scenes they encountered—a camel caravan, an oasis, merchants squatting around a campfire.

In Konya on Christmas Eve they recreated a sandstorm. Such storms didn't occur during the winter, but the filmmakers devised a novel solution. They bought several dozen sacks of bran and hired locals to toss it into the wind. "We were enveloped in a cloud of bran; it got into our mouths and noses and covered us from head to foot. I almost choked to death and for days I brushed bran out of my hair, but the effect was highly realistic," Marguerite recalled.[19]

The three spent Christmas Eve sleeping on the floor at a roadside inn. A stable was adjacent to their room, and Marguerite could hear the animals rustling in the straw. A donkey peered over the low board partition separating their room from the stable. The air was permeated with the smell of the animals, straw, and manure. Looking through a small hole in the roof, Marguerite saw a single bright star, and she imagined the scene as though it were two thousand years ago in Bethlehem.[20]

Cooper described their Christmas celebration the next day. Marguerite decorated a lemon tree with blue beads and the men pulled crumpled dinner jackets from their bags and wore them over their flannel shirts. They hauled out a portable phonograph that they had brought as a gift for a local chieftain, put on a jazz record, and danced down the hall, Cooper leading the way carrying a three-foot-long cigarette holder like a drum major baton.

They flung open the door to the room where they would dine. Cooper described the scene: "A woman in low-necked European dress, a big Spanish comb in her coiffed hair, standing by a table, blazing—to our candle and lantern accustomed eyes—with the light of four oil lamps. Could this society woman be the Mrs. H of caravans and khans?"[21]

They waited weeks in Konya for permission to travel to Adana. At last Turkish officials said they could proceed, but only by train directly to the city. The filmmakers were disappointed because they had planned to shoot a scene of Marguerite traveling through the Taurus Mountains. Despite the orders from the Turkish government, they refused to give up the idea. They pretended to accept the requirement that they travel to Adana by train, but when they stopped at a station in the mountains, the Americans disembarked with their interpreter.

A shopkeeper agreed to let them spend the night in his store and help them find horses to continue their journey. Luckily, a hunter stopped by the store and volunteered to lead them through the mountains to his village. As they left, a snowstorm descended, hiding their tracks from the authorities, who were searching for them.

They remained in the mountains for three weeks, shooting scenes of Marguerite plowing through the snow with her pony and capturing film of their guide stalking a mountain goat. When he killed the animal out of camera range, they cleverly recreated the scene. They put the goat's carcass on a ledge and tied a rope to it. When the mountaineer pretended to shoot the animal, helpers below yanked on the rope and the goat fell.

One day, while filming in the mountains, Schoedsack, Cooper, and their guide were caught in a blizzard. Heavy, wet snow soon was as high as their waists, and the guide cried to Allah to save them. Schoedsack, who was the tallest, took the lead and forged the path through the piling show, navigating from tree to tree until they found a stream that led to a road.[22]

At last they reached Adana, but they said they never found a tribe suitable to film. Marguerite described the natives they encountered as a "squalid, moth-eaten lot."[23] They made up their mind to press on to Persia fifteen hundred miles farther in hope of finding the Bakhtiari. Marguerite began to study Persian, and Schoedsack and Cooper set about making arrangements for tickets and permits.

The new plan took them by train to Aleppo and then by car to Bagdad, where they arrived at the end of February. Marguerite was disappointed in her first view of the city, which she described as a straggly collection of ugly, semi-modern houses arranged along unpaved streets. But while lacking aesthetics, Bagdad held no shortage of intrigues. Keeping watch over it all was one of Britain's most unusual spies, Gertrude Bell.

For decades Bell had worked for the British intelligence service in the Middle East while pursuing her passion for archaeology. She was smart, energetic, and engaging. During World War I she was assigned as a political officer in the British Army's Expeditionary Forces in Mesopotamia. With her extensive travels in the desert and her knowledge of local culture, she gained the trust of the Arab leaders, including Iraq's King Faisal I, to whom she became an influential adviser.[24]

Not surprisingly, Marguerite was eager to meet this extraordinary woman, who turned out not to be what Marguerite imagined. "I pictured her as a hard, masculine type of woman," she recalled. Instead, she found "a slender figure in a smart gray velvet frock which looked as if it had just come from Paris. A daintily manicured hand was stretched out to meet mine, and I looked into a pair of keen gray-blue eyes set in an oval face with regular features, crowned by a mass of softly waved, perfectly dressed hair."[25]

They first met in Bell's cluttered office and continued their discussion over dinner that evening. The two women had much in common. Both had been born into privileged families, sought adventure in foreign lands, and written popular accounts of their travels. And both were spies.

After Bell's death of an apparent suicide in 1926, Marguerite wrote about their first meeting in Bagdad. Marguerite had come to Bell seeking information and her help in arranging a meeting with King Faisal. But it was Bell who adeptly quizzed Marguerite over what she had seen and heard in Turkey, trying to glean the Turkish views on a boundary dispute with Iraq. "It was a beginning of a warm friendship between us," Marguerite wrote.[26]

Bell also was impressed with Marguerite. She wrote to her father: "I had a dinner party in the evening to meet a Mrs. Harrison, an American traveller and writer and an exceptionally brilliant woman."[27]

According to Schoedsack's account, he traveled to Mosul still seeking the Kurds while Marguerite and Cooper remained in Bagdad.[28] It was during this time that a lawyer from Cairo named Ibrahim Chahine knocked unexpectedly on Marguerite's hotel room door. Chahine wanted to tell her about the views of Sunni Muslims toward the secular reforms occurring in Turkey. His purpose, it seemed, was to influence American opinions about Middle East developments, which were in flux as religious and secular parties competed for dominance. After listening to the lawyer and taking careful notes of the meeting, Marguerite sent a report to the American consul in Bagdad, who immediately forwarded the information to Washington.[29]

Schoedsack returned from Mosul and reported the region was too unsafe for filming. Although Marguerite makes no mention of going to Mosul, she wrote a detailed article for the *New York Times* that made it seem as though she were there. Her account of the region's oil production includes vivid descriptions of the workers, the city, and the surrounding nature, which she described as "a barren, absolutely treeless country, beautiful for only a few months in the Spring, when the hills are covered with poppies, wild hyacinths and cyclamen."[30]

Finally giving up on the Kurds, the Americans looked for another tribe they could film. British intelligence officers in Bagdad, including Bell and Sir Arnold Wilson, advised them to try the Bakhtiari, the same tribe Harry Dwight had suggested a year earlier.

The Bakhtiari, who lived west of the Zagros Mountains, each spring undertook an arduous journey in search of grass for their herds. The trip was filled with the drama pitting man against powerful forces of nature—a raging river, snow-covered mountains, and barren deserts. But the Bakhtiari weren't just simple, poor herdsmen. They also owned the largest oil fields in Persia.

In 1924 the tribe was locked in a dispute with the central government in Tehran over control of the oil fields, the right to negotiate concessions with foreign governments, and the tribe's refusal to pay taxes on their oil profits. Any country or company looking to gain access to Persian oil would benefit from getting to know the Bakhtiari. The interactions the three Americans had with the British officials raise intriguing questions. England, through its Anglo-Persian Oil Company, held a monopoly over Persian oil at the time and had no desire to share that wealth with America. At the same time, Marguerite, Cooper, and Schoedsack relied on British advice and hospitality numerous times. If for no other reason, the film project might have been necessary to deceive the British so the Americans could gather intelligence about the oil fields.

Cooper and Schoedsack were thrilled with the prospect of reaching the Bakhtiari. But it was already mid-March, and they hadn't much time because soon the tribe would be setting out on its journey. Cooper and Schoedsack sailed immediately down the Tigris River for Basra, hoping to catch up to the Bakhtiari at their camps before they departed. Inexplicably, Marguerite chose a slower and more dangerous route, traveling through the desert with George Fuller, the American vice consul at Shiraz. At Kut-el-Amara she boarded a ship to Basra and then crossed the Tigris River into Persia, where she reunited with Cooper and Schoedsack.

The three stayed in Khorramshahr as guests of the Anglo-Persian Oil Company. Company officials agreed to help them find the Bakhtiari, allowing them to take the company steamer to Ahwaz, where a British political officer found them a car to take them to Shushtar, where the Bakhtiari princes were camped.[31]

In Shushtar the governor of the region received them cordially and arranged for them to stay with a rich merchant while he sent word to the Bakhtiari. The next day a young man in a European riding outfit showed up speaking impeccable American English. He told them he was Rahim Khan, a nephew of the Bakhtiari chief. The young man had studied at the American College in Beirut and dreamed of seeing New York. He readily invited the filmmakers to the Bakhtiari camp, where the tribal leaders would hear their request.

As they rode to the camp, Rahim Khan boasted of his family's wealth. His uncle received about $65,000 a year from oil leases to the Anglo-Persian Oil Company, he told them. He went on to explain that the proud tribe acted independently from the Persian central government and paid no taxes, even though the shah was insisting on their allegiance. Their cousins, the Lurs, were rebelling against the central government, and the Bakhtiari were considering joining them.

After a day's ride they arrived at the camp on the banks of the Karun River, where they saw scores of black, brown, and yellow goatskin tents. Rahim escorted them to three adjoining tents. One, furnished with rugs and cushions, was to be their meeting room. Another with a camp bed was to be Marguerite's bedroom, and the third was for Cooper and Schoedsack. The Americans quickly washed, and Marguerite changed into a dress she had brought with her. Shortly, the chief arrived.

Cooper and Schoedsack explained their desire to film the tribe's pending migration. When the chief explained that the tribe actually took five routes across the mountain, Cooper and Schoedsack asked to go on the northernmost passage that had never been traversed by a foreigner. The chief laughed at their foolishness. He was going on the easier road, but he agreed to let the filmmakers go with the clans taking the most difficult route.

Two days later Marguerite, Cooper, and Schoedsack returned to Shushtar. This time they traveled on a river barge with the chief who was on his way to meet other Bakhtiari leaders to discuss relations with Reza Khan, the de facto ruler of Persia. Marguerite vividly described the scene as some twenty travelers piled onto the vessel made of inflated goatskins. The foreigners lounged with the Bakhtiari leaders on rugs and cushions beneath a tasseled canopy of crimson satin while servants brought them tea in small glasses.

Then an attendant presented a brazier full of glowing coals along with a number of pipes.

The chief smiled. "You join me?" he asked.

The guests nodded. He opened a bag and took out a pellet of opium, which he placed in a pipe. With silver tongs, he lifted a glowing coal from the brazier and held it over the opium, which began to sizzle and melt. He then handed the pipe to Marguerite. She later recalled:

I drew in a long breath of the sweet pungent smoke, exhaling slowly. . . . The sun was hot, but there was a delicious breeze. We were passing through a rocky defile with huge crags worn into fantastic shapes and shading from crimson to orange. White-winged gulls skimmed the water and the boatmen sang a rhythmic chant, clear sweet, as their paddles guided our craft. The opium soothed my nerves and relaxed my muscles. I felt a delightful sense of peace and contentment, but my mind was wide awake and I was acutely conscious of my own well-being and the beauty of my surroundings. It seemed the most natural thing in the world that I should be riding on a barge of goatskins down a mountain river. Somewhere, sometime, I knew that I had done it before, and the opium was not entirely responsible for the feeling.[32]

They arrived in Shushtar toward evening and spent the next several days waiting to be summoned to join the migration. Schoedsack inspected his camera equipment. Cooper haggled with traders over horses and mules. He later recalled that a colonel in charge of troops of Arabistan—a tall man with a bushy mustache and wearing a cap with a visor—invited the three to dinner. His comfortable dwelling was decorated with Persian prints, and he told them something of the history and literature of his people. Cooper went on to say, "At dinner time, he and Mrs. Harrison chatted together in Russian most of the time."[33] Cooper does not name the colonel or explain how he came to know Russian. Marguerite, despite her love of all things Russian, made no mention of the encounter at all.

At last a messenger from the Bakhtiari arrived and told the three that the tribe was ready to depart. The Americans left Shushtar with their interpreter and a mule driver, riding all day through desolate land to the foothills of treeless mountains. Cooper had chosen to ride a small Bakhtiari horse while Schoedsack and Marguerite mounted sure-hoofed mules. Marguerite recalled hers was an obstinate animal accustomed to walking second in a caravan. If Marguerite tried to slow down or get ahead, the determined mule insisted on returning to his place in line. "Finally, I decided he was one of those individuals who know their place in the world, and that it was useless to argue with him about it," she said.[34]

They spent the first night in a small village where the mayor asked if they had any medicine to spare. Marguerite gave him the few simple remedies she had— boric acid and cathartic pills. An hour or so later, as she was preparing for bed, crowds of women with sick babies and children descended on her room clamoring for help. Many were sick with skin sores and infested with parasites. Pleading for more medicine, they surrounded her and pulled at her clothes. When she told them she had given medicines to the mayor, they howled in protest. Their translator had to rescue her from the mob, and he later found out the mayor had kept the medicine for himself.

The next day they caught up with the Bakhtiari. Rahim, the young prince, assigned them to travel with Haidar, the leader of the Baba Ahmadi clan. Haidar was not happy about having to escort the foreigners, but the chief had commanded him to do so and he had to obey. He gravely escorted the group to where his family was camped. Haidar had recruited several members of his tribe to serve the foreigners. One woman prepared their tea, three others cooked their food, two men carried the camera equipment, and several others provided general labor.[35]

At dinner the first night Haidar asked the foreigners about events in Europe. Possibly thinking about the Bakhtiaris' tense relations with the shah, he asked them how the kings in Europe had been deposed. The Americans told him there were a few kings left, and Marguerite mentioned that one country was ruled by a queen. Haidar then asked, "What does the queen's husband do?"

"Nothing," Marguerite answered. "He has no power."[36]

Haidar smirked scornfully. The Bakhtiari men ruled harshly over the women, who did most of the work around the camp. While the men gossiped with their neighbors, the women milked the sheep and goats and prepared the meals. Cooper and Schoedsack joined the men, lounging around the tents. Marguerite didn't work with the women, but she soon found herself busy giving medical aid to the tribe.

The tribe may have remembered a female doctor from Scotland, Dr. Elizabeth N. Macbean Ross, who had lived with them a decade earlier.[37] Marguerite had no medical training, but they began calling her Hakim Kham, the Lady Doctor, and they trusted she could relieve their suffering. She saw a large number of cases of malaria, venereal disease, eye problems, and skin disorders. She handed out quinine for malaria and boric acid for the eyes. She dispensed castor oil and cathartic pills for stomach troubles.

One woman brought her emaciated son, begging Marguerite to cure him. When Marguerite learned the boy had become sick after swallowing a leech, she was stumped. Then she had an idea to make the boy drink a solution of lukewarm saltwater. The boy vomited the leech and soon recovered. Another time, she was summoned to treat a man bleeding to death after a fight. Marguerite cleaned his wounds, amputated a finger that was hanging by a thread and bound his lacerations with adhesive tape.

Marguerite was so overwhelmed by requests for treatment that she had to establish hours when she would receive patients. But she could not help everyone. Haidar's second wife, who was childless, asked her for medicine to conceive. "God alone can do that," Marguerite told her.[38]

Cooper and Schoedsack admired the freedom of the tribesmen and the physical challenges they endured. Cooper even fantasized about leaving the comforts of modern life and living with the tribe. But having treated their sick and wounded, Marguerite held no such romantic notions about the Bakhtiari. "There was nothing particularly glamorous about their struggle for existence," she later wrote.[39]

During her travels, Marguerite had developed a sense of feminism she once had scorned. She hated the way the Bakhtiari treated their women and was outraged when she caught Haidar beating one of his wives. Marguerite screamed for him to stop, but he only laughed. Later Marguerite treated the woman for two broken ribs and asked Haidar to allow his wife to ride one of his horses, but he refused.

After weeks of preparation, the Bakhtiari migration began on April 17. At first the Americans saw only Haidar's camp of about a 150 people, but in the ensuing days more groups joined them until their numbers reached nearly 5,000 people and 50,000 animals. Clearly this was the epic journey Cooper and Schoedsack had sought to film. Mothers carried babies in scarves or wooden cradles on their backs. Toddlers were tied to the backs of cows and donkeys. The chiefs rode horses, but most of the tribe walked barefoot or in grass-soled slippers. They followed a route that had been set for generations, often breaking camp shortly after midnight so they could avoid traveling in the heat of the day and stopping to rest in valleys where there was grass and water. At night Marguerite slept in a tent guarding the precious film canisters for fear curious tribesmen would open the containers and spoil their contents.

The first major obstacle they encountered was the swift and deep Karun River. The only bridge was hundreds of miles away, and they had no boats. But the men inflated goatskins bound together to form rafts capable of carrying six to eight people at a time. The tribe launched the rafts at a bend in the river where they twisted and turned in whirlpools until oarsmen steered them to the other side. The crossing was slow and dangerous. It took nearly a week to move the tribe to the other side. Schoedsack's remarkable footage of the crossing shows the drama of tribesmen struggling to herd their animals through the rapids.

As the migration progressed, Marguerite's appearances in the film became fewer. Cooper and Schoedsack instead began to focus their story on Haidar and his young son, Lufta. Sometimes Marguerite didn't see her colleagues for days.

When she did appear on camera, she still tried to look her best. She carried a makeup case in her saddle and applied touch-ups when the broiling sun caused her makeup to melt. At night she bathed and washed her clothes in what water could be spared, although she later noted she shouldn't have bothered. Film critics later commented that she looked too clean for a woman on such a difficult expedition.

About halfway through the forty-six-day journey Marguerite became seriously ill with malaria. For three days she was bedridden, battling a fever that reached 106 degrees. Even the rough Haidar was worried and halted the migration. The khans visited her each day asking what they could do to help, and when she ran out of quinine, the tribe returned tablets she had given them. At the peak of the fever Marguerite struggled to give herself a sponge bath in cool water. "When it was over, I nearly fainted, but my temperature had gone down." By the fourth day, Marguerite was able to be lifted on her mule and continue.

One great obstacle remained before the tribe could reach the grassland: the 15,000 foot mountain Zardeh Kuh, or Yellow Mountain.

When the Americans saw the steep, snow-covered peak, they could not imagine how the tribe and their animals could possibly ascend. They watched in amazement as Haidar and his men, barefoot and with their robes tucked up to their waists, used picks and shovels to cut a two-foot-wide trail through the ice and snow. It took the men four days to forge the trail to the summit, and each day Cooper and Schoedsack went with them to film the ordeal.

Then, just as the tribe was about to start up the mountain, the Americans' mule driver became as stubborn as his animals and refused to go farther. Only reluctantly, after they told him he would likely be killed by hostile tribes if he turned back, did he agree to continue. Schoedsack and Cooper again hurried to get in front of the migration, leaving Marguerite and the fearful mule driver to climb with the rest of the tribe.

Marguerite's recollection of the trip echoes the description Cooper gave years earlier, including a description of an old man hobbling on two sticks carrying a toddler on his shoulders and a little girl carrying a baby calf. Scenes in the film show Marguerite leading her mule close to Haidar and his son.

They climbed all day, and Marguerite spent the night on the summit shivering in her sleeping bag, thinking of the tribesmen, many barefoot and clothed in thin robes, sleeping nearby on the ground. The next day, she walked and slid joy-fully down the other side of the mountain, at last reaching the valley of the grass. Carpets of wildflowers spread before them. Birds were singing. Their journey was at its end.

Marguerite was not sorry to leave the Bakhtiari, whom she called "hard, treacherous, thieves and robbers, without any cultural background, living under a remorseless feudal system, crassly material, and devoid of sentiment or spiritu-ality."[40] By contrast, Cooper romanticized the nomads. "Every day, every hour if they will, they can thus touch paradise by the hundred and one gifts of nature."[41]

After a few days' rest, they rode on to the nearest town, where they sent a tele-gram for a car to take them to Tehran. It took them nearly two weeks more to reach the Persian capital. Tehran, with electric lights, trams, and movie theaters, seemed like the "acme of civilization," Marguerite recalled.[42]

But dark and violent forces swirled in the city as British, Americans, and Rus-sians vied to form alliances that would give them access to Persia's fabulous oil wealth. For years the British had dominated the market through the Anglo-Persian Oil Company and supported rulers who would do their bidding. But by 1924 many proud Persians had grown dissatisfied with the British influence and had invited American firms, Standard Oil and Sinclair Oil, to bid for concessions.

Added to an already volatile mix, the Soviets also began to assert their interest in the region. The Bolsheviks had temporarily abandoned their ambitions in Persia, but—now stronger—the Soviets were looking to reclaim their rights to an old concession in the northern part of the country. Tensions among the three nations were so profound that Cooper wrote about it in the *New York Times* as soon as he reached Paris, describing the forces aligning against the United States: "It is . . . the Russian aim to prevent American capital from building a railroad across northern Persia. England, too, is fighting the Americans in this, and the British Government is using a loan made to Persia in war time as a very effective weapon. If Americans get the concession, the British will demand repayment of the loan."[43]

As head of the border troops and Soviet Russia's GPU spy operations, Solo-mon Mogilevsky actively tried to stop U.S. investment in the region. In late 1921 he ordered the arrest of John Bigelow Dodge, an American entrepreneur and cousin by marriage to Winston Churchill, after Dodge began seeking oil conces-sions in Tbilisi, Georgia. Mogilevsky charged Dodge with being a British spy, attempting to buy nationalized oil fields, and bribing Soviet officials. Dodge was lucky to escape the firing squad and merely face deportation. Unlike Marguerite's expulsion, in which she was given a week to stay with friends before leaving the country, Dodge was held in jail until his ship arrived and then escorted on board by an armed guard.[44]

Marguerite wrote only a few paragraphs about the five days she stayed in Tehran before returning with Cooper and Schoedsack to Bagdad. The highlight of their stay seemed to be a visit to Reza Khan, who a year later would become the Shah of Persia. Writing about the encounter for the *New York Times*, Marguerite described interviewing the leader over tea at his villa in Shimran. At first stand-offish, Reza Khan warmed up to them after she began speaking in Persian to his son, Mohammad, who was destined to become the last shah of Iran. When her Persian faltered, she conversed with Reza Khan in Russian, which he knew fluently. Marguerite told him about their trip with the Bakhtiari, which must have been of great interest to the commander given the uncertainty over whether the tribe would rebel against the central government. Reza Khan told her frankly that the Bakhtiari must submit and pay taxes, either voluntarily or by force.[45]

While they were in Tehran, Marguerite did not stay with Cooper or Schoedsack. The men lodged with American vice consul Robert Imbrie and his wife, Katherine. Marguerite stayed with American financial adviser Thomas Pearson and his mother on the outskirts of the city. The arrangement is perplexing. She described the Pearsons as two friends, yet she and Imbrie had much in common. He had worked as an attorney in Baltimore for a number of years and still had family in the city. After the war, he had joined the American intelligence service and oversaw the American spy network in Petrograd until he was forced to flee the Bolsheviks in 1918.

But there was one notable difference between him and Marguerite: While Marguerite called Communism an interesting social experiment, Imbrie was rabidly anti-Communist. After being assigned to Constantinople, he requested that the State Department send him to a post where he could continue to fight the Soviets. With his brash attitude and tendency to inflate his expense reports, he clashed frequently with his superiors in Washington. One visitor to Angora complained about Imbrie's disparaging statements about missionaries.[46] In July 1923 Louise Bryant told the secretary of state that Imbrie had endangered her life by denouncing her to the Turks as a Communist.[47]

Imbrie was close to resigning from the service when the State Department came up with an assignment that satisfied him: He would open a consulate in Tabriz, Iran, where he would establish a spy network in the Soviet Caucasus. He would be in direct conflict with Mogilevsky, whose job was to recruit and direct pro-Soviet spies in the region.

But before Imbrie could move to Tabriz, the State Department asked him to fill in for the Tehran consul who was taking a leave of absence. He was in that position when Marguerite, Cooper, and Schoedsack arrived. Cooper took an instant liking to the brash young political officer. "Never have I been more impressed with a man, never made a faster friendship," Cooper later wrote. "Clever, honest, true as steel—this was a man I thought." They traded stories about their adventures and discussed the possibility of together exploring Kurdistan.[48] Imbrie readily notarized a letter for the filmmakers on June 20, 1924, attesting that they were the first foreigners to travel with the Bakhtiari during their migration over the Zardeh Kuh mountain trail.[49]

Three weeks later, Imbrie was murdered. His death caused an international uproar and immediately rumors spread about who was responsible. Russia, Great Britain, the United States, and factions in Persia blamed one another for the vice consul's demise. The murder came during an unsettled time when Muslims in Tehran were protesting against followers of the Baha'i faith. Just days before his death, Imbrie had ordered protection for two American Baha'i missionaries. Then on Friday, July 18, 1924, a crowd gathered around a well that the Muslims believed was sacred. A rumor spread through the crowd that Baha'is had poisoned the water. Imbrie, along with his translator and an American oil worker, went to investigate the commotion. When Imbrie started to take pictures of the demonstration, protestors told him to stop. According to some accounts, he obeyed and put the camera away. Other witnesses said he continued to photograph the crowd.

Then one of the protestors, a seventeen-year-old mullah, pointed to Imbrie and shouted that he was a Baha'i. The mob then turned on Imbrie and his companions. They managed to escape to a carriage and flee toward a police station, but an officer stopped them in the street. Soon the crowd caught up, pulled them from the carriage, and began to beat them. Early in the melee, someone ripped off the translator's buttons and insignia that identified him as a consulate employee. The police, under orders not to interfere with the antireligious demonstrations, at first did not try to stop the attack.[50]

Eventually the police rescued the victims and took them to a nearby hospital, but the assailants forced their way inside. Believing the unconscious oil worker was already dead, they resumed their attack on Imbrie. Doctors tried to tell the protestors that Imbrie was not a Baha'i, but the enraged mob paid no heed. They beat him with sticks and even the heavy tiles ripped from the operating room floor. Someone cut him at least once with a sword. Altogether, Imbrie suffered more than 130 blows, yet he remained conscious the entire time.[51] When his wife, Katherine, arrived, she saw his clothes piled on the floor and looking as though "they had been dipped in red paint." Imbrie lingered for four hours until he died from shock around three o'clock.[52]

Confusion and conspiracy theories arose almost immediately. Who had incited the mob? Why had they attacked the vice consul? Persian newspapers and the Russians blamed the British, saying they instigated the religious protests as a way to exert their own authority in the region and maintain their exclusive oil agreements. The British blamed religious fanatics. Still others blamed Reza Khan, who was looking for an excuse to impose martial law and consolidate his power. And still others pointed to the Russians, who had long wanted Imbrie dead because of his anti-Communist crusade. At one time the Soviets had offered the Turks $40,000 for his assassination, and Imbrie himself believed that the Soviets would kill him one day. Imbrie's wife believed her husband was killed for political gain and suspected that the Bolsheviks or Reza Khan played a role.

Imbrie's murder shocked the American government and alarmed the American oil companies, Standard Oil and Sinclair Oil, that were trying to win concessions in the region. The U.S. government demanded restitution. Anxious to mollify the Americans, the Persians agreed to pay Imbrie's widow $60,000 and the United States $100,000 for transportation of Imbrie's body back to America with full military honors. The Persians arrested a dozen of the demonstrators and executed the seventeen-year-old mullah who had first shouted that Imbrie was a Baha'i, a nineteen-year-old soldier, and a fourteen-year-old camel driver who confessed to taking part in the attack. An American official present at the execution of the two younger boys refused their pleas for mercy.[53]

Despite Reza Khan's overtures, U.S. oil companies, already struggling to secure funding for Persian concessions, used the murder as an excuse to pull out of the region. They would not return for a decade.

Devastated by the news of Imbrie's death, Cooper expressed his admiration for the political officer in the introduction to his book, *Grass*.[54] Marguerite, meanwhile, blamed international intrigues, coupled with Imbrie's poor judgment, for the murder. She told a newspaper reporter that she believed the British had fomented the religious riots to discredit Reza Khan, who was trying to develop closer ties to the Americans. She added that Imbrie contributed to his own death by taking photos at the shrine and then trying to flee when the mob turned on him. "Undoubtedly the mob intended merely to punish him, but when he drove away rapidly in his carriage, it was taken as an indication that he considered himself guilty of a grave offense, and he was pursued. The way to invite a Near East mob to attack you is to turn your back and run," she said.[55]

In her memoir Marguerite strangely made no reference to Imbrie's murder at all, merely noting that Schoedsack and Cooper had stayed with the vice consul when they were in Tehran. Marguerite was not in Persia when Imbrie was killed, but she must have seen the rising tensions between the Muslims and the Baha'i that factored in his death. Those religious disputes may explain why Marguerite parted from Cooper and Schoedsack in Beirut and headed to Haifa, where she spent two nights in a Baha'i colony rooming with an American woman. She offered no reason for visiting the colony, which she described as "a queer little backwater of modern life" and whose members included a Japanese samurai, a German, a Frenchman, a Russian princess, and a Danish woman.[56]

After a week traveling in Palestine, Marguerite reunited with Cooper and Schoedsack in Paris, and at the end of August the three sailed for New York. Marguerite returned to find that Tommy was engaged to Margery D. Andrews, the granddaughter of one of the founders of Standard Oil. They wed on October 3, a month after Marguerite's return.

Marguerite, now forty-six, felt herself at loose ends. Less than ten years earlier, she had been a Baltimore society matron hosting luncheons and raising money for a children's hospital. In a brief time she had been a movie and theater critic, a foreign correspondent, a travel writer, and a spy. She had been imprisoned in Russia twice, ventured into the remotest parts of Asia and the Middle East, and interviewed kings, generals, and warlords. All the while, she had continued to feed information to the United States intelligence services.

Now she had no idea what she would do next. "I had no desire to settle down and take up a definite career," she recalled. "I had become a confirmed wanderer and I felt that I could not adapt myself to any prescribed pattern of living."[57]

She returned to writing newspaper and magazine articles about her adventures, and, despite her reputation as an unreliable lecturer, she signed with the Ponds Speakers Bureau to earn money to help pay for the *Grass* production.

At last the film's premiere was set for March 30, 1925. A week before, an advertisement in the *New York Daily News* announced the event in breathless prose:

Grass
From a Story Written by an Angry God
Scenario from the Hand of Destiny
Enacted by 50,000 Human Beings and
Half a Million Beasts
Under a Cynical Sky
Dotted with Doubting Stars
Staged
In a World
Withered by the
Crimson Thumbprint of
Catastrophe
A Tale the Eyes of
Man Have Never
Seen and the Hand
of Man
Not Written[58]

The next day an article in the London *Times* carried news of another encounter with destiny: Solomon Mogilevsky was dead.[59]

EBB TIDE

HER GREAT ADVERSARY WAS GONE. Marguerite felt both relief and regret when she learned that Solomon Mogilevsky had been killed in a plane crash in the Caucasus Mountains. When she left Russia in 1923 she knew that she would never see him again, and she sensed that his death had been no accident. She recalled the myth of Lucifer, who had defied heaven and been thrown into hell. Once a rising star in the Soviet government, Mogilevsky had been extinguished.[1]

As with Imbrie, rumors swirled that Mogilevsky had been murdered by political enemies. According to newspaper reports, he was flying to a conference on March 22, 1925, with two other Soviet officials, including the man who had murdered Czar Nicholas II's only brother.[2] About fifteen minutes after takeoff, their Junkers plane caught fire. Mogilevsky and another passenger tried to jump from the burning craft as it plummeted to the ground, but he died when the plane exploded on impact. The Soviets conducted three investigations but could find no fault with the plane's mechanics and never determined the cause of the crash.

Soviet officials accused Georgian rebels of sabotaging the plane, but some historians believe that Mogilevsky's chief lieutenant, Lavrenty Beria, was responsible. A psychopathic killer and serial rapist, Beria later would become Stalin's KGB chief and oversee the slaughter of millions. In 1925 he was the second in command in the Transcaucasia secret police, and rumors circulated about his dark crimes and the disappearance of witnesses who might testify against him. Some believe Mogilevsky had gathered evidence against Beria and was preparing to send a report to Moscow when his plane went down.[3]

Mogilevsky was buried with military honors at Alexander Garden, near where he had met Marguerite for her weekly reports five years earlier. Beria himself wrote the eulogy: "I do not believe . . . I do not want to believe . . . I will not hear the soft voice of Solomon Mogilevsky anymore," he stated, before turning his attention to his own suitability to succeed him.[4]

Marguerite knew her feelings for Mogilevsky were inexplicable. "Logically we should have hated each other, and yet there had been a certain camaraderie between us," she wrote. "I had always felt a certain unwilling admiration for Mogilevsky. He even had attracted me in a curious fashion."[5] His death liberated her from the psychological grasp he held on her.

Back in New York, Marguerite busied herself making ready for the premiere of *Grass*. Although the movie had been a cover for a spy operation, Cooper, Schoedsack, and Marguerite nevertheless completed the film, which showed incredible scenes of human courage and fortitude. Famous Players, the forerunner of Paramount Pictures, produced the film, and the three creators spent the winter seeing it through to the end. Marguerite tried to help write the narration for the silent film, but she found herself at odds with her partners. She disliked the melodramatic script the editors wrote, complaining that they put artificial speeches into the mouths of simple nomads. She wanted to tell the story of the migration in simple, straightforward language, but she was overruled.

Nevertheless, the film was well received. After a private showing in the Plaza Hotel in late February, the New York *Daily News* hailed *Grass* as an epic comparable to the *Iliad*: "It is a gigantic piece of work that should be heralded as one of the reasons Edison should be proud he invented motion pictures," the movie critic gushed.[6] The film premiered to the public on March 30, 1925, at the Criterion Theater on Broadway and ran for two months. Marguerite, however, went to see it just once. "After that I could not set foot in the theater again. I could not bear to see it on the screen because I loathed the manner in which it was presented," she said.[7]

She amicably parted with Cooper and Schoedsack, leaving them to become Hollywood stars while she resumed writing and speaking. She gave talks throughout New England and the Midwest, lectured and wrote pamphlets for the Foreign Policy Association in New York, recounted her travels in newspaper and magazine articles, and appeared on numerous radio programs.

Although she had observed political and social upheavals in Europe, the Middle East, and Asia and had interviewed some of the most important statesmen in the world, she felt she wasn't given the credit and respect she was due.

She bristled when journalists pestered her with what she thought were silly questions, such as whether she had had a love affair with a Bolshevik commissar, wore lipstick in the desert, or slept with an Arab sheik. She wanted to discuss her views on foreign policy and the events shaping the postwar world, not sensational gossip.

She shared her complaints with a small circle of women travelers, including Blair Niles, who lived among tribes in Southeast Asia; Gertrude Matthews, who had traveled through Africa; and Gertrude Emerson, an Asian expert. They had all suffered the same indignities and, despite their accomplishments, were not allowed membership in the prestigious Explorers Club in New York.

So they decided to do something about it. "Why shouldn't we found an organization composed of women who had done unusual things, and blazed new trails in geography, ethnology, natural history and kindred sciences?" Marguerite asked.[8] Thus, in 1925 they founded the Society of Woman Geographers, which would grow to an international organization whose members included Amelia Earhart, Margaret Mead, and Mary Douglas Leakey.

Marguerite did not take credit for the growth of the organization, but she later said the creation of the Society of Woman Geographers and the Baltimore Children's Hospital School were among her proudest accomplishments.[9] The two organizations stand as witnesses to contrasting periods of her life. The hospital was testimony to her charitable work when women were limited to the domestic sphere caring for home and children. The Society of Woman Geographers provided tangible proof of Marguerite's vision that a woman's sphere was limitless.

Ironically, just as she realized this freedom Marguerite found herself increasingly unhappy. She had been apart from her friends and family for so long that she could not share their interests. "I continually heard references to happenings about which I knew nothing, to books I had never read, to plays I had never seen, to controversies about which I had never heard. My friends had died, married, divorced, remarried, lived through domestic idylls or domestic tragedies, and had accumulated a wealth of memories and experiences in which I had no share."[10]

Tommy was married and living his own life as a New York stockbroker. Albert Ritchie was busy with his duties as governor of Maryland. She occasionally visited her old friend Mary McCarty in Baltimore, but for the first time in her adult life, Marguerite felt lonely. Even more unsettling, she had lost interest in the world affairs that had once absorbed her. "I was perfectly free to do as I pleased and go where I wished, but the prospect of wandering over the world alone did not appeal to me anymore. I craved something that would fill my life entirely and completely without the vaguest ideas as to what it was or where I would find it."[11]

Marguerite had never imagined she would marry again. She had many male friends and some "charming" interludes, but none of these relationships had ever tempted her to give up her freedom and settle down. Then she met Arthur Middleton Blake.

Marguerite gave few details about how she came to know the aspiring British actor other than to say she met him soon after she returned to New York. His resume described him as an Oxford University athlete, slender, broad-shouldered, and with iron-gray hair. He had spent many years in the United States and served in the cavalry during the Spanish-American War. Like Marguerite, he had a talent for linguistics, speaking French, German, Spanish, and Italian.[12] And he, too, was searching for something to give meaning to his life.

When Marguerite found herself falling in love, her first instinct was to flee. She accepted an offer from the Near East Relief Society to write a series of articles on the organization's work aiding Turkish and Armenian refugees. According to her account, the society agreed to pay her travel expenses to visit settlement camps in the Middle East and write articles that would publicize the organization's refugee work.[13] Under the arrangement, she would keep any money she made on articles she sold to newspapers and magazines, but there is no evidence she succeeded in selling any pieces about the trip. It is possible the trip again was a U.S. State Department intelligence mission to a volatile region, although no reports have been located.

She left New York in July 1925 and traveled through Paris before heading to Constantinople. This time she had no trouble getting the necessary permits to proceed to Angora, which she found greatly improved with electricity and new government buildings. The Foreign Office readily gave her permission to tour the farm communities where Turks from Greek territories had been resettled. Then she traveled to Syria to tour the camps where some 45,000 Armenians lived.

Travel was somewhat easier than it had been the year before when she was with Cooper and Schoedsack, but dangers still lurked. On a coastal steamer from Izmir in west Turkey to Syria, she struck up a friendship with an Englishman selling jams and marmalade. When he learned she planned to travel to Aleppo alone, he insisted on going with her. "It ain't no trip for a lady to take alone," he told her.

Touched by his concern, Marguerite agreed to let him accompany her. They disembarked at Iskenderun, then called Alexandretta, which Marguerite described as a "forlorn, dirty town, built on the edge of a swamp." They saw no cars but found a Greek merchant who arranged to get them a car and driver. After several hours a "villainous-looking" Armenian arrived with a battered 1917 Ford, Marguerite recalled.

She and her English companion felt uneasy, but they had little choice. There seemed to be no other cars in the town, and so reluctantly they climbed in, the Englishman in the front passenger seat and Marguerite in the back with their luggage.

They kept a wary watch out for bandits who they knew lurked along the mountainous road to Aleppo. Progress was slow. It seemed every few hundred feet the driver had to stop the car to let the engine cool or to fix some problem. Marguerite began to suspect he was stalling. By the time they reached the top of mountain, it was nearly dark. They then began to descend into a gorge flanked by tall cliffs that Marguerite and the Englishman knew was the perfect spot for an ambush. The jam salesman shook with terror. Marguerite tried to reassure him, but she was uneasy herself. Suddenly three men armed with rifles jumped in front of their car and ordered them to stop.

The driver halted, jumped from the vehicle and fled. *Now we're in for it*, Marguerite thought. She didn't think they would be killed, but she had heard stories of outlaws holding foreigners for ransom or robbing them of all their possessions and setting them loose almost naked. "I wondered inconsequently how we would look arriving on foot in Aleppo, I clad in a chemise, and my English friend in his shirt and drawers," she recalled.

The Englishman crouched in the front seat in fear as the three bandits jumped on the car's running board. One of them attempted to grab the salesman's sample case. Suddenly the Englishman jumped up and punched the robber in the jaw, slid into the driver's seat, and took off with a jolt that threw the bandits to the ground. He sped forward as the assailants fired at them but missed. Marguerite and the Englishman were soon out of range.

When they stopped at last, Marguerite thanked the salesman and congratulated him for his courage.

"I couldn't lose my samples, now, could I?" he said.[14]

Marguerite reached Aleppo safely and visited the Armenian camps outside the city. She described the refugees as being geniuses at both trade and trouble. They had set up shops selling whatever they had and at the same time organized rival societies and political parties. The French who ruled Syria and the Americans with Near East Relief were exasperated with the refugees, whom Marguerite describes as "rarely grateful, always complaining and always stirring up dissension."[15]

Marguerite spent a week in Syria not only visiting the refugee camps but also meeting with French military commanders trying to tamp down rebel forces in the Lebanese mountains. Finally, she boarded a steamer in Beirut to begin her journey home.

This time, she felt a reason to return. She had kept her promise to Arthur Blake to write him every day. At first she had imagined that would be a pledge impossible to keep, but she found it not only possible but necessary to share with him her thoughts and adventures.

For ten years she had traveled throughout the world gathering information for the U.S. spy agencies, but now her interest and energy flagged. Throughout Europe, Asia, and the Middle East, she saw evidence that America's idealistic vision of promoting democracy and self-determination had failed. Regions that once had been ruled by the great powers were fractured and unstable. Whole populations were threatened with genocide and forced to move from their homelands. Yet Marguerite felt almost indifferent to the misery she saw. Arthur Blake had managed to do what Soviet prisons could not: capture her heart. "I had to acknowledge to myself that I was fairly trapped and that I could not escape."[16]

She returned to the United States in the fall of 1925 and quietly married Blake in New Orleans in early 1926. The couple spent six months in Morocco for their honeymoon, although Marguerite didn't completely give up her spy work. While in Morocco she passed along her observations on the Wahhabi Muslim movements to the U.S. consul in Casablanca.[17]

But, for the most part, her spying days were over. Marguerite was often adventurous and unconventional, but she held old-fashioned views about marriage. She still traveled, but now as a tourist with Blake. Once again her name appeared in the society columns of newspapers in New York and Baltimore documenting her comings and goings.

In 1928, while living in Morocco, Marguerite completed her most scholarly book, *Asia Reborn*, which analyzed political and economic developments in Asia and the Middle East. Drawing upon her own observations as well as uncited secondary sources, she argued that America must allow Asia its "right to grow" and discounted racial fears about Asiatic people as unwarranted.

Marguerite's past was still mostly secret, despite the public campaign Stan Harding had waged to out her as a double agent and her demand for restitution. Thomas Johnson, a former correspondent with the *New York Sun*, tracked Marguerite down for a book he was writing about U.S. Army Intelligence during World War I. Johnson knew of her work in Berlin and her role in capturing Robert Minor, and he wanted to know more details. In his 1929 book he referred to Marguerite as Agent Q rather than her MID code name, "B," but she undoubtedly is the woman he described meeting: "It seems so far away now," she told him, with an innocent smile. "Then letting fall her sewing and looking about the cozy living-room, 'And see how domestic I am! I'm sure you won't tell my name, will you?'"[18]

In late 1929 or early 1930 Marguerite and Blake bought a chateau called Beaumanoir near Tours, France. The society reporter of the *Baltimore Sun* described it: "The manor house is nearly three hundred years old and is surrounded by a park, delightful gardens and a high wall."[19] After only a few years, however, the couple found the cost of maintaining the mansion too great and returned to the United States, settling in Hollywood, where Blake tried to break into motion pictures.

Throughout the 1930s the couple struggled financially. In 1935 Marguerite asked her old friend, Merian Cooper, to help Blake find roles in the movies. Ever loyal, Cooper wrote to movie executives at Paramount, Fox Film Corporation, and Metro-Goldwyn-Mayer, including David O. Selznick. They warmly responded and forwarded Blake's photo and resume to their casting departments, but no roles materialized.[20]

In late 1935 Marguerite borrowed five thousand dollars from Cooper, pledging to pay it back quickly as she anticipated the sale of her autobiography. The book, *There's Always Tomorrow*, received good reviews, but her British publisher was forced to pay five thousand dollars to settle a libel suit with Harding, and Marguerite apparently did not reap the profits she had expected.[21]

In January 1938 she wrote Cooper to explain that she was not yet able to repay the loan. "We have no fixed income whatever—only fixed charges," she said, noting the taxes and mortgage on their French estate, which they were attempting to sell. "I make enough from my lectures to help with current expenses, but that is all." She continued: "Arthur is still plugging away trying to get in pictures, but as you know conditions in the industry are not favorable for men who have neither big names or studio contracts." She told Cooper she was trying to sell stories, but with little luck.

Marguerite went on to say she knew she would have the money one day because she would inherit the principal of a trust fund left by her grandfather Livezey. But in the meantime, her aunt Josephine was entitled to the interest on the money. To repay some of the loan, she asked Cooper if she could work as his assistant on his next movie project. "I would receive payment from MGM for such work and I could turn whatever I received over to you. It would make me feel ever so much better," she said.[22]

Cooper declined her offer, and four years later, when she had still not repaid the money, he asked her for a document testifying to the loan. He had returned to the Army Air Forces and was preparing to leave for overseas service when he wrote, "I would like to get my affairs in order and if I ever have to write this off on my income tax or there should arise a time when either you or Arthur should be flush and die in that condition, I should have some kind of record."[23]

A few days later Marguerite sent Cooper the note he requested, pledging that she or her heirs would repay the loan. At her death, the loan had not been repaid, and Cooper's lawyers were forced to seek the money from her estate.[24]

Throughout the 1930s and 1940s Marguerite continued to give speeches about her travels. According to reports she made with the Society of Woman Geographers, she gave more than one hundred lectures a year to clubs and schools. She also broadcast radio shows for the United Services Organization (USO) during World War II.[25]

The lectures again brought her to the attention of America's intelligence services. In the summer of 1941, as war intensified in Europe, FBI director J. Edgar Hoover suddenly ordered his men to open an inquiry into Marguerite. He was concerned that she gave speeches advocating for direct aid to Russia, and he suspected she was a paid foreign agent. Months passed, and when the Los Angeles field office produced a skimpy report rehashing what Washington headquarters already knew, Hoover was furious. "I do not consider this report in compliance with my request," he told the Los Angeles agents. "Your five-page report could have been reduced to one page had you not summarized the material furnished you by the Bureau which obviously the Bureau already had, thus saving the time of the stenographer. Had the Agent spent the time it took him to summarize the memorandum and dictate from it, he might have accomplished some worthwhile investigative results."[26]

Even the bombing of Pearl Harbor weeks later would not deter Hoover from insisting that the California office conduct a thorough investigation into Marguerite's activities. Under pressure, the agents complied. They monitored Marguerite's mail and investigated her bank records. They interviewed her landlady and her neighbors and even contacted retired Army colonel Ralph Van Deman for details about her Berlin service. Spies were sent to her lectures to give a full accounting of what Marguerite told her audiences.

In 1942 she spoke regularly before members of the Los Angeles Women's Athletic Club who paid $1.10 admission to hear her espouse views on the political developments in Europe, Asia, and the Middle East, as war engulfed the regions. Commenting on domestic affairs, she accused California attorney general Earl Warren of furthering his political ambitions by prosecuting a pacifist, and she lamented the racial discrimination she witnessed against black Red Cross workers. Her speeches about Russia touched both the country's history and culture as well as her own experiences as a foreign agent. Pointing to wall maps, she lectured her audiences on subjects as diverse as Soviet railroads and nomadic tribes.[27] She was not above exaggeration. She bragged that she knew Lenin and had spoken with him many times, even presuming to know of his distrust of Stalin.[28] In her memoir, she recounted seeing Lenin give a speech just once, and she never mentioned speaking with him directly.

But, try as they might, the FBI found no evidence that Marguerite was working as a foreign agent or was a Communist. In fact, Marguerite seemed to have no political leanings at all. She was obviously knowledgeable and opinionated, but agents found no record that she had ever even voted.

The FBI report the agents compiled again revealed Marguerite as a complicated and not altogether sympathetic woman. As she had told Cooper, she and Blake were struggling financially and living off his small military pension and her lectures. Agents discovered two bank accounts, one with about $523, of which $500 came from a bank loan. The other was an account with about $80 that seemed to be related to bridge club activities. Agents speculated that she and Blake were supplementing their meager income by gambling on bridge games they played, although the agents stressed that she and Blake were not "card sharks."

The landlady described Marguerite to FBI agents as having a "striking appearance, having an erect carriage, a well-modulated and strong speaking voice, a vivacious manner, and a distinguished appearance with her grey hair and thin features." Marguerite still looked younger than her years. Her landlady described her as about fifty-five, but in 1941 she was sixty-three. The landlady went on to tell the agents that in the five years Marguerite had been her tenant, she had seen her treat Blake "with contempt and cruelty." Blake, while handsome and educated, was not Marguerite's intellectual equal. The landlady said Marguerite "often made him the butt of sarcasm and vitreous tirades." Marguerite's wrath was not confined only to her husband, the landlady said. Once Marguerite's dog got into a fight with a dog belonging to an elderly neighbor. Marguerite "reached out and separated the animals 'in a perfect fury' and had struck the old lady, knocking her to the ground." While noting Marguerite's keen intellect, the landlady said she found her tenant to be unethical and unscrupulous. When a visitor knocked at her door to ask a question about one of her lectures, Marguerite slammed the door in the visitor's face, saying "she could not be troubled with every Tom, Dick and Harry cluttering up her apartment and asking foolish questions."[29]

Given the ongoing investigation into Marguerite's activities, the Los Angeles agents must have been surprised, or at least amused, when on January 20, 1942, Marguerite showed up at the field office offering her services once again for her country. She told the agent who interviewed her that she was a former newspaper woman who had previously worked for the Army intelligence service and that she read and spoke fluently Italian, Russian, and German. This time, however, money, not patriotism or adventure, seems to have motivated Marguerite. "The subject stated she would expect a small remuneration for her services and she was not desirous of securing full-time employment, but that she would occasionally assist the Bureau in any capacity if there was need of her services," the agent wrote.[30] The Bureau declined Marguerite's offer.

On May 3, 1947, Arthur Blake died suddenly in California, never realizing his dream of becoming a motion picture star. Marguerite moved back to Baltimore the following year and rented an apartment on Charles Street to be near Tommy, who also had returned to the city after his divorce and remarriage. As vice president of Terminal Shipping, a cargo shipping agency, he was working in the maritime business he loved.

Marguerite still traveled—almost always by steamer—and occasionally gave lectures to women's clubs. One of her granddaughters, Nancy Harrison, has distinct memories of a woman she considers complicated, even unfathomable. She described Marguerite, whom she called "Granny," as intellectual and cultured. She was an excellent pianist, equestrian, and seamstress. Harrison recalled Marguerite making her a dress from cloth she brought from Africa. Yet Marguerite was not a typical grandmother. She didn't bake cookies or give hugs. Even though she had lost a lung to tuberculosis, she chain-smoked Camel cigarettes, and the nicotine had turned her hair the color of straw. Marguerite never told her granddaughter about her work as a spy, but she did tell stories of her travels that she thought a child would enjoy, such as seeing the large Christ the Redeemer statue in Rio. Marguerite was proud of her travels and only regretted not seeing India, Harrison said.

In her final years, Marguerite lived in an apartment surrounded by family heirlooms and souvenirs of her trips, including a collection of wax seals, a tea set the Russian czar had given her father, lacquer boxes, and a mahogany writing desk. Harrison recalled that Marguerite spent hours reading Ellery Queen mystery novels and playing solitaire. "She cheated," Harrison said.[31]

Her great-granddaughter, Susan Richards, wrote about going to the movies with Marguerite: "Sometimes she'd wrap herself in an enormous musty old fur coat, speckled with cigarette burns, and we'd walk a few blocks to the movie theater, where she'd promptly fall asleep and snore through the entire film."[32]

While unconventional in many ways, Marguerite could be old-fashioned and sentimental. She took no interest in television, and she criticized her daughter-in-law, Jean, for not making mashed potatoes from scratch. One Christmas she gifted Nancy Harrison with Nathaniel Hawthorne's *A Wonder Book and Tanglewood Tales*, which had belonged to Tommy. In her inscription she wrote, "To dear Nancy who likes the Greek stories of Gods and Heroes as her Granny does."

While apparently relishing her role as a grandmother, she could still exhibit the sly charm that had made British and Russian agents fall in love with her. Marguerite flirted shamelessly with Tommy's father-in-law in the presence of the man's wife, Harrison remembered. And as she grew older, Harrison became wiser to the unpleasant aspects of Marguerite's personality, including her selfishness. Harrison couldn't fathom how her grandmother could have had an affair with her sister's husband, Albert Ritchie, or how she could have taken Tommy from Gilman school and abandoned him at a boarding school in Switzerland as she left to spy in Russia. "She just decided she wanted to be a spy and travel," Nancy Harrison concluded. "She didn't want children. She didn't want anything to encumber her."[33]

Yet Tommy remained loyal to his mother, Harrison said. His aunt, Elizabeth Ritchie, once wrote him saying that she would have nothing to do with him if he did not cut off relations with his mother, but he refused. Harrison recalled walking with her father every week to his mother's apartment, although she noted that the only photo he kept on his bureau was that of his grandmother, Mary Ames, and not his mother.

Marguerite remained active almost until the end of her life. Against doctor's orders, she continued to take long trips to South America and Africa. But in 1966 she suffered a series of strokes that left her bedridden for almost a year. At 11:30 p.m. on July 16, 1967, Marguerite died at age eighty-eight. She left a sizable estate, which included Russian and Asian art and more than $100,000 (about three-quarters of a million dollars today) in cash, stocks, and bonds. She bequeathed a number of pieces of furniture to the Maryland Historical Society and her collection of textiles to the Washington County Museum of Fine Arts in Hagerstown, Maryland.[34]

Marguerite had asked that her ashes be scattered in the ocean she loved. Tommy hired a boat in Ocean City, Maryland, to follow his mother's wishes, but a storm prevented him from going out to sea. Instead, he tossed her ashes over a bridge into the Chincoteague Bay where the ebb tide carried them to the Atlantic.

The doctor who attended Marguerite's death filled out the death certificate and gathered details about her parents, age, and place of birth. He asked Tommy what he should write down as his mother's occupation. Tommy must have struggled to sum up the work of the mysterious and complicated woman. She had been a socialite, philanthropist, writer, traveler, filmmaker, and spy, but even those closest to her never knew quite what she was about.

At last he gave the doctor an answer: "Housewife."[35]

AFTERWORD

TAKING STOCK OF ANY LIFE is problematic. A biographer must describe not only a series of events that are strung along a life like beads on a necklace but also the motivations and emotions that form the underlying thread. When a life has been lived partly in the shadows of the intelligence service, the task becomes even more difficult.

Nevertheless, it is clear that, by many measures, Marguerite Harrison was a failure, both professionally and personally. The Russians caught her spying twice and forced her to confess. She not only admitted to her own activities, but also implicated others, including journalist Albert Boni, intelligence officer Weston Estes, and most famously, British journalist Stan Harding. Marguerite was responsible at least in part for their torture and imprisonment.

Those who had doubted women could be trusted as foreign intelligence officers could point to the many mistakes Harrison made during her missions. She left scraps of reports where Stan Harding could find them. She was indiscreet in the way she questioned suspected Bolsheviks. And she developed an emotional attachment to Solomon Mogilevsky that clouded her judgment about his work and his motivations.

Marguerite Harrison also failed to achieve her personal objectives. She said she joined the intelligence service "to make the world safe for democracy." Instead, she was forced to acknowledge that the Allied victory in World War I planted seeds of fascism and genocide. Returning from Russia, Marguerite hoped to persuade American officials to recognize the Soviet government, but the United States did not extend diplomatic relations to the Soviet Union until 1933. And if the *Grass* movie expedition was designed to secure oil concessions for American companies, that, too, failed following the death of diplomat Robert Imbrie.

In her personal life, Marguerite fell short as well. She disappointed her mother, betrayed her sister, and perplexed Joseph Ames, who grew exasperated rescuing his wandering daughter-in-law. Most clearly, she failed her son. She constantly told herself, "I am a bad mother!" and yet she refused to give up her work and travels to be with him. From the age of thirteen until he became an adult, Tommy Harrison was cared for by servants, his grandparents, and the masters of a Swiss boarding school while Marguerite pursued her ambitions as a writer and spy.

Looking back on her life at age fifty-seven, Marguerite believed her most tangible accomplishments had been the founding of the Children's Hospital School in Baltimore and the creation of the Society of Woman Geographers. Both of these institutions survive to this day. The Children's Hospital School, renamed Children's Hospital, operated for many years as a specialist in pediatrics and orthopedic services. Today it has returned to its origins as a school, operating as a career and technology center for disabled children under the auspices of the Kennedy Krieger Institute.

The Society of Woman Geographers has grown to an organization of five hundred women in the United States and twenty-eight other countries. Although no longer the only organization open to women adventurers (the New York Explorers Club admitted women in 1981), the society still supports women explorers through awards and fellowships.[1]

Certainly the hospital and the society have made life better for thousands, but Marguerite Harrison's contributions go far beyond those two organizations. In taking stock of her life, we must remember the newspaper and magazine articles she wrote that helped readers understand cultures and political events in remote corners of the globe. We also should remember the individuals she helped as well—Merian Cooper, the Serb soldier fleeing the Far East Republic, and the sick women and children she treated while traveling among the Bakhtiari.

But of all her contributions, none is more significant than the precedent she set as a professional female foreign intelligence officer. Rather than extracting secrets from unsuspecting lovers, Harrison relied on her linguistic talents and observation skills to collect information. By the time World War II began, the U.S. government no longer questioned whether women could work in the intelligence services. Hundreds of women worked for the Office of Strategic Services as secretaries, clerks, codebreakers, and spies. Some still offered sex for secrets, but more used their language skills and powers of deception to gather information that helped win the war.

Marguerite Harrison was not a hero, even of her own story. But neither was she a villain. Her life was messy and complicated. She made mistakes professionally and personally, but so did male intelligence officers. She became a spy for adventure and personal freedom, but through her tenacity and talent, she liberated other women to pursue careers in the foreign service.

NOTES

PREFACE

1. Marguerite Harrison, *There's Always Tomorrow: The Story of a Checkered Life* (New York: Farrar & Rinehart, 1935), 90.

PROLOGUE

1. This account is drawn from Marguerite Harrison, *There's Always Tomorrow: The Story of a Checkered Life* (New York: Farrar & Rinehart, 1935), 544–54; and C. P. Cox to Acting Chief of Staff, March 5, 1923, File PF-39205, RG 165 (War Department General Staff), Military Intelligence Division, Box 607, NARA, College Park, Md.

CHAPTER 1. FOND OF ADVENTURE

1. Application to Office of Naval Intelligence, September 15, 1918, File PF-39205, RG 165 (War Department General Staff), Military Intelligence Division, Box 607, NARA, College Park, Md.
2. Joseph S. Ames to Marlborough Churchill, undated, File PF-39205, RG 165 (War Department General Staff), Military Intelligence Division, Box 607, NARA, College Park, Md.
3. Marguerite Harrison to Marlborough Churchill, September 21, 1918, File PF-39205, RG 165 (War Department General Staff), Military Intelligence Division, Box 607, NARA, College Park, Md.
4. Harrison, *There's Always Tomorrow*, 20.
5. Tammy M. Proctor, *Female Intelligence: Women and Espionage in the First World War* (New York: New York University Press, 2003), 1–7.

6. James L. Gilbert, *World War I and the Origins of U.S. Military Intelligence* (Lanham, Md.: Scarecrow, 2012), 72.

7. Foster Rhea Dulles, *Americans Abroad: Two Centuries of European Travel* (Ann Arbor: University of Michigan Press, 1964), 131–32. In her autobiography, *The Glitter and the Gold: The American Duchess—In Her Own Words* (New York: Harper & Bros., 1952), Consuelo Vanderbilt Balsan recalls a relationship with her mother that was remarkably like that of Marguerite and Elizabeth. Consuelo's mother forbade her to marry a young man she loved and instead insisted upon her marriage to the Duke of Marlborough. Although Vanderbilt gave in to her mother's demands, Marguerite refused Elizabeth's wishes.

8. Alexis Gregory, *Families of Fortune: Life in the Gilded Age* (New York: Rizzoli International, 1993), 201.

9. Patricia Bradley, *Women and the Press: The Struggle for Equality* (Evanston, Ill.: Northwestern University Press, 2005), 183–84.

10. Patricia Craig and Mary Cadogan, *The Lady Investigates: Women Detectives and Spies in Fiction* (New York: St. Martin's Press, 1981), 52.

11. Marguerite E. Harrison, "Edith Cavell's Lawyer Tells of Belgium's Woes," *Baltimore Sun*, August 27, 1917, 4.

12. Harrison, *There's Always Tomorrow*, 90.

13. Lt. Col. Walter Martin Memorandum for Chief of Military Intelligence Division, September 29, 1918, File PF-39205, RG 165 (War Department General Staff), Military Intelligence Division, Box 607, NARA, College Park, Md.

14. Marlborough Churchill, Memorandum for the Chief, Positive Branch, September 30, 1918, File PF-39205, RG 165 (War Department General Staff), Military Intelligence Division, Box 607, NARA, College Park, Md.

15. Gilbert, *World War I*, 11–28.

16. Capt. Dick Slaughter to Marguerite Harrison, October 17, 1918, File PF-39205, RG 165 (War Department General Staff), Military Intelligence Division, Box 607, NARA, College Park, Md.

17. *Influenza Encyclopedia: The American Influenza Epidemic of 1918–1919: A Digital Encyclopedia* (University of Michigan Center for the History of Medicine, 2016), accessed August 12, 2019, https://www.influenzaarchive.org/cities/city-baltimore.html.

18. "City Celebrates Greatest of Days in Triumphant Joy," *Baltimore Sun*, November 12, 1918, 20.

19. Harrison, *There's Always Tomorrow*, 91–92; and "Diva Sings in Sun Square," *Baltimore Sun*, November 12, 1918, 20.

20. Gilbert, *World War I*, 37; and Report from Anna Keichline regarding Negroes in Philadelphia, February 11, 1919, File 10218-304, M1440, RG 165, Military Intelligence Division Security Classified Correspondence and Reports, 1917–1941, NARA, College Park, Md.

21. Harold A. Williams, *The Baltimore Sun, 1837–1987* (Baltimore: Johns Hopkins University Press, 1987), 157–58.

22. Stephen J. A. Ward, *The Invention of Journalism Ethics: The Path to Objectivity and Beyond* (Montreal: McGill-Queen's University Press, 2004), 214–15.

23. Williams, *The Baltimore Sun, 1837–1987*, 154–55.

24. Harrison, *There's Always Tomorrow*, 95.

25. Marguerite Harrison to Capt. Dick Slaughter, December 2, 1918, File PF-39205, RG 165 (War Department General Staff), Military Intelligence Division, Box 607, NARA, College Park, Md.

CHAPTER 2. FIT FOR A KING

1. "Cyclone on the Atlantic Coast," *Baltimore Sun*, October 24, 1878, 1; and Harrison, *There's Always Tomorrow*, 3.

2. Harrison, 3.

3. Harrison, 3–5.

4. Harrison, 5.

5. Neal A. Brooks, Eric G. Rockel, and William C. Hughes, *A History of Baltimore County* (Towson, Md.: Friends of the Towson Library, 1979), 302; and *Department of Labor Bulletin No. 18* (Washington, D.C.: Government Printing Office, September 1898), 668.

6. Robert J. Brugger, *Maryland: A Middle Temperament* (Baltimore: Johns Hopkins University Press, 1988), 313.

7. Jonathan Kinghorn, *Atlantic Transport Line, 1881–1931* (Jefferson, N.C.: McFarland, 2012), 12, 28, 39, 44, 48, 50, 59–61, 70–72.

8. Harrison, *There's Always Tomorrow*, 10; and "Railroad Collision: Smash up Near Havre De Grace," *Baltimore Sun*, June 22, 1887, 1.

9. The Maryland Club, history, https://www.marylandclub1857.org.

10. Harrison, *There's Always Tomorrow*, 15–16.

11. Harrison, 32–36.

12. Report from Agent D. W. Magee, August 22, 1941, p. 14, FBI File, 100-HQ-40298, NARA, College Park, Md.

13. Harrison, *There's Always Tomorrow*, 18–19.

14. Harrison, 20.

15. "A Fine Suburban Home," *Baltimore Sun*, August 6, 1892, 8.

16. Harrison, *There's Always Tomorrow*, 21–22.

17. Harrison, 22; Mayo Clinic, "Grave's Disease," n.d., accessed August 12, 2019, https://www.mayoclinic.org/diseases-conditions/graves-disease/symptoms -causes/syc-20356240.

18. Christianna McCausland, *St. Timothy's School: A History from 1882–2000*, edited by Leslie Lichtenberg (Parkton, Md.: Neustadt Creative Marketing, 2008), 6–10.

19. McCausland, 6–7, 10.

20. Harrison, *There's Always Tomorrow*, 22–28.

21. Carl N. Degler, *At Odds: Women and Family in America from the Revolution to the Present* (Oxford: Oxford University Press, 1980), 308–15.

22. Radcliffe College, Alumnae register (Cambridge, Mass.: Radcliffe College), 1879–1915, https://iiif.lib.harvard.edu/manifests/view/drs:427986956$90i.

23. Harrison, *There's Always Tomorrow*, 45.

24. Francis F. Beirne, *The Amiable Baltimoreans* (Hatsboro, Pa.: Tradition, 1968), 285–87.

25. Harrison, *There's Always Tomorrow*, 41–42; "On with the Dance," *Baltimore Sun*, November 30, 1897, 10; and Beirne, *Amiable Baltimoreans*, 285–90.

26. Harrison, *There's Always Tomorrow*, 42–43.

27. "Angry with Maine Committee," *New York Times*, July 25, 1901, 3.

28. Harrison, *There's Always Tomorrow*, 38–39.

29. "Personal," *Baltimore Sun*, August 2, 1900, 10.

30. "Society's Fancies," *Baltimore Sun*, October 28, 1898, 12; and "Gay Die Puppenfee," *Baltimore Sun*, January 20, 1899, 10.

31. "An Insane Speculator's Suicide," *New York Times*, February 26, 1885, 1.

32. Louis Gerber, "St. Regis Grand Hotel Rome," *Cosmopolis*, October 3, 2008, http://www.cosmopolis.ch/travel/rome/st_regis_grand_hotel_e0100.htm.

33. "An Interned Turk in Britain," *Ohinemuri Gazette*, September 10, 1917, http://paperspast.natlib.govt.nz/newspapers/OG19170910.2.10.

34. Harrison, *There's Always Tomorrow*, 45–49.

35. "Harrison Succeeds Newcomer," *Baltimore Sun*, January 3, 1901, 7.

36. "Ideal Wedding Day," *Baltimore Sun*, June 6, 1901, 7; and Harrison, *There's Always Tomorrow*, 49.

CHAPTER 3. BONDS OF MATRIMONY

1. Harrison, *There's Always Tomorrow*, 50.
2. Harrison, 51. The 1910 census lists two servants in the Harrison household, Lizzie Stewart and Frances King. Thirteenth Census of the United States, 1910 (NARA microfilm publication T624, 1,178 rolls), Records of the Bureau of the Census, RG 29, NARA, Washington, D.C. Accessed on Ancestry.com, 1910 United States Federal Census (database online).
3. Harrison, *There's Always Tomorrow*, 59–60.
4. "Suburban Personals," *Baltimore Sun*, September 24, 1901, 6.
5. Harrison, *There's Always Tomorrow*, 52.
6. "Furnished House for Rent," *Baltimore Sun*, October 15, 1894, 15.
7. Harrison, *There's Always Tomorrow*, 71.
8. "Juniors in the Dance," *Baltimore Sun*, December 10, 1902, 7.
9. "Society Sees the Horses," *Baltimore Sun*, April 22, 1903, 9; "Going to Chattolanee," *Baltimore Sun*, April 26, 1903, 6; "Dance at Chattolanee," *Baltimore Sun*, July 2, 1903, 6; and "Society News," *Baltimore Sun*, July 17, 1903, 6.
10. "Horse King Again," *Baltimore Sun*, October 14, 1906, 20.
11. "On Moonlight Picnic," *Baltimore Sun*, September 20, 1910, 8.
12. "Huntsmen at Traps," *Baltimore Sun*, September 27, 1903, 9.
13. "Lease Shooting Privilege," *Baltimore Sun*, April 25, 1903, 6.
14. Harrison, *There's Always Tomorrow*, 54–56.
15. Lawrence C. Allin, "The Civil War and the Period of Decline: 1961–1913," in *America's Maritime Legacy: A History of the U.S. Merchant Marine and Shipbuilding Industry since Colonial Times*, edited by Robert A. Kilmarx, 65–110 (Boulder, Colo.: Westview, 1979).
16. "Mr. Baker Returns," *Baltimore Sun*, May 14, 1901, 2.
17. "Mr. B. N. Baker to Retire," *Baltimore Sun*, December 5, 1902, 8.
18. "Society News," *Baltimore Sun*, July 13, 1901, 7; "Telegram Causes Mr. B.N. Baker to Hurry to the Catskills," *Baltimore Sun*, September 7, 1905, 12; "Mrs. B. N. Baker Injured," *Baltimore Sun*, August 13, 1909, 6; and "Society News," *Baltimore Sun*, July 17, 1903, 6.
19. "To Wind Up Affairs," *Baltimore Sun*, April 25, 1903, 7.
20. "Mr. B. N. Baker Elected President," *Baltimore Sun*, April 23, 1903, 7.
21. "Seat on Exchange $4,600," *Baltimore Sun*, November 15, 1904, 7.

22. "Mr. B. N. Baker President," *Baltimore Sun*, January 12, 1905, 7; "Income Holders 'Pat,'" *Baltimore Sun*, March 7, 1905, 12; "United Plan Is Out," *Baltimore Sun*, July 18, 1906, 7; and "Alert for New Trade," *Baltimore Sun*, May 11, 1905, 12.

23. "Offers the City $1,000,000," *Baltimore Sun*, March 31, 1905, 12; and "Subway Plan Dismissed," *Baltimore Sun*, January 2, 1917, 14.

24. "Red Cross Organized," *Baltimore Sun*, April 25, 1905, 12.

25. "Hunting the Elk," *Baltimore Sun*, September 18, 1901, 8; "Home from the Rockies," *Baltimore Sun*, September 21, 1902, 14; and "Protect Animals from Cruelty," *Baltimore Sun*, January 21, 1901, 12.

26. "Mr. Brendan Returns," *Baltimore Sun*, September 29, 1909, 7.

27. "Gives up Horse Shows," *Baltimore Sun*, October 16, 1912, 14; and "Bird Protectors Organize," *Baltimore Sun*, March 20, 1915, 16.

28. "Financier as Farmer," *Baltimore Sun*, September 23, 1915, 7; and "Home to Farmerettes," *Baltimore Sun*, April 21, 1918, 7.

29. "For Moral Education," *Baltimore Sun*, January 11, 1910, 14; and "High Morals the Aim," *Baltimore Sun*, March 29, 1911, 8.

30. "Conservation Our Nation's New Patriotism," *Baltimore Sun*, November 21, 1909, 15; and "For State's Rights," *Washington Post*, September 5, 1910, 1.

31. Harrison, *There's Always Tomorrow*, 61.

32. Degler, *At Odds*, 325.

33. "Protectors of Animals," *Baltimore Sun*, May 5, 1899, 10; and C. P. Remington, *Society Visiting List or "The Blue Book" for the Season of 1898* (Baltimore: Guggenheimer, Weil & Co., 1898), 253.

34. Cynthia Connolly, *Saving Sickly Children: The Tuberculosis Preventorium in America Life, 1909–1970* (New Brunswick, N.J.: Rutgers University Press, 2008), 20–22.

35. "Summer Charities," *Baltimore Sun*, May 25, 1899, 7.

36. "See Orphans at Play," *Baltimore Sun*, May 6, 1903, 6; and "Gifts for the Friendless," *Baltimore Sun*, December 24, 1903, 7.

37. "Vaudeville for Hospital," *Baltimore Sun*, April 14, 1903, 6.

38. "Rebuilding Little Human Wrecks," *Baltimore Sun*, January 22, 1911, L8; "Sang for Worthy Charity," *Baltimore Sun*, March 20, 1907, 6; and "30 Years of Aiding the Crippled," *Baltimore Sun*, May 19, 1935, SF6.

39. "Health for Little Ones," *Baltimore Sun*, August 12, 1907, 8.

40. "Aiding Little Sufferers," *Baltimore Sun*, July 5, 1909, 6.

41. Thirteenth Census of the United States, 1910.

42. "Real Big Show It Was," *Baltimore Sun*, May 22, 1912, 16.

43. "Aid Comes to Cripples," Baltimore *Evening Sun*, December 5, 1910, 7; "To Be Hospital School," *Baltimore Sun*, May 3, 1911, 15; and "Terrapins Will See Show," *Baltimore Sun*, April 12, 1914, 3.

44. "Civic League for Women," *Baltimore Sun*, January 25, 1911, 14.

45. "Civic League for Women," 14.

46. James B. Crooks, "Maryland Progressivism," in *Maryland: A History 1632–1974*, edited by Richard Walsh and William Lloyd Fox (Baltimore: Maryland Historical Society, 1974), 655.

47. Crooks, 662. Maryland did not ratify the Nineteenth Amendment to the Constitution until 1941.

48. Harrison, *There's Always Tomorrow*, 53.

49. William Chafe, *The Paradox of Change*: *American Women in the 20th Century* (New York: Oxford University Press, 1991), 9.

50. "New Head for Trust Co.," *Baltimore Sun*, April 17, 1908, 12; "Mr. B. N. Baker Sued," *Baltimore Sun*, May 10, 1908, 12; "Miss Shearer Caustic," *Baltimore Sun*, January 31, 1908, 12; and "Pat Kirwan's Dog Causes a Feud in Catonsville," *Baltimore Sun*, December 20, 1908, 15.

51. "Ship League Is Formed," *Baltimore Sun*, October. 14, 1909, 9.

52. "Urges Independent Line to Aid Panama," *New York Times*, August 12, 1909, 4.

53. "B. N. Baker to Meet Taft," *Baltimore Sun*, November 1, 1910, 2.

54. "ABC of the Merchant Marine Bill and Its Possible Effect on Baltimore," *Baltimore Sun*, January 28, 1911, 2.

55. "Mr. Rayner Opposes It," *Baltimore Sun*, January 31, 1911, 5.

56. "To Girdle U.S.," *Baltimore Sun*, September 6, 1911, 14.

57. "Ends 11,000 Mile Swing," *Baltimore Sun*, October 4, 1911, 8.

58. "War on Canal Ships," *Washington Post*, November. 17, 1911, 1.

59. "Bar Railroad Owned Ships," *New York Times*, March 13, 1912, 7.

60. "How Mr. Baker Won," *Baltimore Sun*, February 23, 1913, 3.

61. "Scores Shipping Trust," *Baltimore Sun*, April 5, 1915, 7.

62. Harrison, *There's Always Tomorrow*, 58.

63. "Mrs. B. N. Baker Dead," *Baltimore Sun*, February 14, 1915, 16; and "Haste in Ship Trust Inquiry," *Washington Post*, February 17, 1915, 5.

64. "Society News," *Baltimore Sun*, July 27, 1908, 6.

65. "To Tour by Automobile," *Baltimore Sun*, July 9, 1911, WS1.
66. William Lloyd Fox, "Social-Cultural Developments from the Civil War to 1920," in *Maryland: A History 1632–1974*, edited by Richard Walsh and William Lloyd Fox (Baltimore: Maryland Historical Society, 1974), 508.
67. "German Women Aid Red Cross," *Baltimore Sun*, October 31, 1914, 4; and "To Send Germans Aid," *Baltimore Sun*, November 10, 1914, 7.
68. Harrison, *There's Always Tomorrow*, 66–67.
69. Lois Scharf, *To Work and To Wed: Female Employment, Feminism and the Great Depression* (Westport, Conn.: Greenwood, 1980), 11; and Dorothy Schneider and Carl J. Schneider, *American Women in the Progressive Era, 1900–1920* (New York: Facts on File, 1993), 49.
70. Harrison, *There's Always Tomorrow*, 67–68; "News of Society," *Baltimore Sun*, October 29, 1914, 4; and "News of Society," *Baltimore Sun*, March 27, 1915, 4.
71. Neil A. Grauer, *The Special Field: A History of Neurosurgery at Johns Hopkins* (Baltimore: Johns Hopkins University Department of Neurosurgery, 2015), 51–73.
72. Harrison, *There's Always Tomorrow*, 69.

CHAPTER 4. OUT ON A LIMB

1. Harrison, *There's Always Tomorrow*, 12.
2. Harrison, 72.
3. Harrison, 72.
4. Barbara Harris, *Beyond Her Sphere: Women and the Professions in American History* (Westport, Conn.: Greenwood, 1978), 57.
5. Harrison, *There's Always Tomorrow*, 29–30.
6. Harrison, 71–72.
7. Email from Gilman School archivist Johanna Schein to author, January 11, 2018.
8. Harrison, *There's Always Tomorrow*, 72.
9. Harrison, 73.
10. Ishbel Ross, *Ladies of the Press: The Story of Women in Journalism by an Insider* (New York: Harper & Brothers, 1936), 493–94.
11. Williams, *The Baltimore Sun, 1837–1987*, 88.
12. Maurine H. Beasley and Sheila J. Gibbons, *Taking Their Place: A Documentary History of Women in Journalism* (Washington, D.C.: American University Press, 1993), 10, 15.

13. Harrison, *There's Always Tomorrow*, 73–74.
14. Jan Whitt, *Women in American Journalism: A New History* (Urbana: University of Illinois Press, 2008), 38–39.
15. Thomas J. Schlereth, *Victorian American: Transformations in Everyday Life, 1876–1915* (New York: Harper Collins, 1991), 68–69. Exhibited at the 1876 Centennial Exposition, the typewriter helped ease the way for women into the office place because it had no historic ties to either gender the way some "men's machines" in the factories did. Office managers actually preferred female typists believing they possessed greater dexterity than men.
16. Harrison, *There's Always Tomorrow*, 74–75. Harrison recalled that her first news item was an announcement of a bridge party given for a debutante; a search of *Baltimore Sun* articles from this time shows similar stories but none exactly as she describes.
17. Harrison, *There's Always Tomorrow*, 78.
18. "Quartet Gets Ovation," *Baltimore Sun*, December 6, 1916, 4.
19. Harrison, *There's Always Tomorrow*, 79.
20. "Plums Fall for Many," *Baltimore Sun*, May 14, 1916, 14; and "State Boards Named," *Baltimore Sun*, May 30, 1916, 14.
21. Harrison, *There's Always Tomorrow*, 80–81.
22. Garth S. Jowett, "'A Capacity for Evil': The 1915 Supreme Court *Mutual* Decision," in *Controlling Hollywood: Censorship and Regulation in the Studio Era*, edited by Matthew Bernstein (New Brunswick, N.J.: Rutgers University Press, 1999), 18–25.
23. Jowett, 27.
24. First Annual Report, Maryland State Board of Motion Picture Censors, June 1, 1916–May 31, 1917, Accession No. MdHR 785657, Location 2/7/9/31, E13133, Maryland State Archives.
25. "Movie Board Kicks Back," *Baltimore Sun*, July 12, 1917, 12.
26. "Movie Censor Upheld," *Baltimore Sun*, July 11, 1916, 16.
27. Nancy Harrison interview with author, June 14, 2017.
28. Elizabeth Fagg Olds, *Women of the Four Winds* (Boston: Houghton Mifflin, 1985), 160.
29. Brugger, *Maryland*, 451.
30. "Miss Baker a Bride," *Baltimore Sun*, May 19, 1907, 6.
31. Baltimore City Circuit Court No. 2, Equity Papers B, Elizabeth Ritchie versus Albert Ritchie, Box 428, Case No. 15968B, June 8, 1916, Series T57-448, 3/18/12/62, located in the Maryland State Archives.

32. Harrison, *There's Always Tomorrow*, 9, 27.
33. "Sang for Worthy Charity," *Baltimore Sun*, March 20, 1907, 6; "Aid Comes to Cripples," *Baltimore Sun*, December 5, 1910, 7; "Society News," *Baltimore Sun*, July 27, 1908, 7; "Health for Little Ones," *Baltimore Sun*, August 12, 1907, 8; and "Society News," *Baltimore Sun*, September 28, 1907, 6.
34. "Society News," *Baltimore Sun*, May 2, 1912, 8.
35. Frank F. White Jr., *The Governors of Maryland 1777–1970* (Annapolis, Md.: Hall of Records Commission, 1970), 257–63; and "The People's Champion against the Gas Company—Albert C. Ritchie," *Baltimore Sun*, October 13, 1912, LS2.
36. "The People's Champion against the Gas Company."
37. White, *Governors of Maryland*, 259.
38. "To Divorce Mr. Ritchie," *Baltimore Sun*, June 27, 1916, 16.
39. Nancy Harrison interview with author, June 14, 2017.
40. Harrison, *There's Always Tomorrow*, 83. See also "B. N. Baker to Wed Wednesday," *Baltimore Sun*, June 24, 1916, 4.
41. Harrison, *There's Always Tomorrow*, 83.
42. Harrison, 85.
43. Geoffrey Perrett, *America in the Twenties: A History* (New York: Simon and Schuster, 1982), 51.
44. Crooks, "Maryland Progressivism," 665; and Brugger, *Maryland*, 432–43.
45. "Pittsburgh Bars Kreisler," *Baltimore Sun*, November 8, 1917, 2; and "Dr. Hopkinson Discusses the Patriotism of Attending the Fritz Kreisler Concert," *Baltimore Sun*, November 21, 1917, 6.
46. Harrison, *There's Always Tomorrow*, 84–85.
47. "The Lyric: Fritz Kreisler," *Baltimore Sun*, November 23, 1917, 6.
48. "Fritz Kreisler Gives Up," *Baltimore Sun*, November 26, 1917, 1.
49. *War Brides* synopsis, American Film Institute, AFI Catalog of Feature Films: The First 100 Years, 1893–1993, accessed August 13, 2019, https://catalog.afi.com/Catalog/moviedetails/16879.
50. "Reserves Film Decision," *Baltimore Sun*, May 26, 1918, 9. On May 28, 1918, Judge Henry Duffy ruled against the film's owners and prohibited the showing of the movie. "War Brides Film Barred," *Baltimore Sun*, May 29, 1918, 5.
51. David Greenberg, *Republic of Spin: An Inside History of the American Presidency* (New York: Norton, 2016), 107–11.
52. Harrison, *There's Always Tomorrow*, 85.

53. Marguerite E. Harrison, "Red Cross, Greatest of Agents of Mercy," *Baltimore Sun*, June 14, 1917, 8.

54. Marguerite E. Harrison, "Women of the Cabinet and Congress Busy with War Work," Baltimore *Evening Sun*, July 16, 1917, 4.

55. Marguerite E. Harrison, "Mrs. Hoover Talks about Conservation," *Baltimore Sun*, October 27, 1917, 1.

56. Marguerite E. Harrison, "Keenest of 'Eyes' Being Trained for Our Armies," Baltimore *Evening Sun*, September 5, 1917, 1.

57. Marguerite E. Harrison, "Department Stores Can't Get Women Employes [sic] Who'll Stick," *Baltimore Sun*, March 16, 1918, 14.

58. Marguerite E. Harrison, "The Story of a Woman Who Worked a Week in a Shipyard," *Baltimore Sun*, May 18, 1918, 16.

59. Marguerite E. Harrison, "The Record of the First Day's Work in the Shipyard," *Baltimore Sun*, May 9, 1918, 16.

60. Marguerite E. Harrison, "Baltimoreans of German Extraction Give Sons for War," *Baltimore Sun*, July 20, 1918, 16; Marguerite E. Harrison, "German Church Service Flags Show Their Share of Gold Stars," *Baltimore Sun*, July 24, 1918, 14; and Marguerite E. Harrison, "City's Germanic Institutions Show Creditable War Records," *Baltimore Sun*, July 31, 1918, 14.

61. "U.S. Agents Eye on 'Hyphens,'" *Baltimore Sun*, February 3, 1917, 12.

62. "German Consul Here Indicted by U.S. Jury," *Baltimore Sun*, May 9, 1916, 16.

63. "Hun Property in Fire," *Baltimore Sun*, November 2, 1917, 14.

64. Dwight R. Messimer, *The Baltimore Sabotage Cell: German Agents, American Traitors, and the U-Boat Deutschland during World War I* (Annapolis, Md.: Naval Institute Press, 2015).

65. "Calls Husband a Spy," *Baltimore Sun*, December 13, 1917, 8.

66. Nathan Miller, *Spying for America: The Hidden History of U.S. Intelligence* (New York: Paragon, 1989), 199.

67. Gilbert, *World War I*, 89–90.

68. "Society News," *Baltimore Sun*, May 15, 1907, 6.

69. Ralph H. Van Deman, *The Final Memoranda*, edited by Ralph E. Weber (Wilmington, Del.: Scholarly Resources Imprint, 1988), 84.

70. Marguerite Harrison File, P-47767, Central Archive of the Federal Security Bureau, Moscow, Russia.

71. Harrison, *There's Always Tomorrow*, 86.

72. Harrison, 84.

CHAPTER 5. IN THE WEB

1. Nancy Harrison interview with author, June 14, 2017.
2. Harrison, *There's Always Tomorrow*, 101–2.
3. Harrison, 103.
4. Van Deman, *The Final Memoranda*, 84–85.
5. Harrison, *There's Always Tomorrow*, 104.
6. Marguerite E. Harrison, "Two Baltimore Base Hospitals Only Cheery Places in Vosges," *Baltimore Sun*, January 22, 1919, 1; Marguerite E. Harrison, "Prussian Officers Hoping to See Kaiserism Reinstated," *Baltimore Sun*, January 23, 1919, 1; and Marguerite E. Harrison, "Russia's Deposed President Urges Allies to Intervene Now," *Baltimore Sun*, January 29, 1919, 1.
7. Marguerite E. Harrison, "Home Boys See Smiles," *Baltimore Sun*, January 9, 1919, 1.
8. Harrison, *There's Always Tomorrow*, 107.
9. "Crazy over Smiles," *Baltimore Sun*, February 28, 1919, 16.
10. Otto Friedrich, *Before the Deluge: A Portrait of Berlin in the 1920s* (New York: Harper & Row, 1972), 46.
11. Harrison, *There's Always Tomorrow*, 110–13.
12. Gilbert, *World War I*, 32, 117–18.
13. Harrison, *There's Always Tomorrow*, 137, 139.
14. Germany report, undated, File 124-160-4, RG 165 (War Department General Staff), Military Intelligence Division General Correspondence, 1917–1941, Box 143, NARA, College Park, Md.
15. Thomas M. Johnson, *Our Secret War: True American Spy Stories, 1917–1919* (Indianapolis: Bobbs-Merrill Co., 1929), 303.
16. Van Deman, *The Final Memoranda*, xviii.
17. Harrison, *There's Always Tomorrow*, 130.
18. Johnson, *Our Secret War*, 194–99, 254.
19. Johnson, 301.
20. Friedrich, *Before the Deluge*, 56.
21. Harrison, *There's Always Tomorrow*, 118.
22. Harrison, 135.
23. Harrison, 135.
24. Harrison, 178.
25. Harrison, 148.
26. Harrison, 149.

27. Marguerite E. Harrison, "Rich Germans 'Hogging' Food While Poor Starve to Death," *Baltimore Sun*, April 3, 1919, 1; and Marguerite E. Harrison, "Wages High in Socialized Germany, but Workmen Go Hungry," *Baltimore Sun*, April 4, 1919, 1.

28. Marguerite E. Harrison, "Socialized German Government as Funny as Comic Opera," *Baltimore Sun*, April 9, 1919, 1.

29. Marguerite E. Harrison, "Soviet of Munich Dictates Smallest Details of Man's Daily Life," *Baltimore Sun*, May 4, 1919, 16.

30. Marguerite E. Harrison, "Germans Kill Each Other with Zest Worthy of Battlefield," *Baltimore Sun*, April 27, 1919, 1.

31. Harrison, *There's Always Tomorrow*, 163.

32. Melanie King, *The Lady Is a Spy* (London: Ashgrove, 2019), 35.

33. King, 41–42.

34. Käthe Kollwitz, *The Diary and Letters of Kaethe Kollwitz*, edited by Hans Kollwitz, translated by Richard and Clara Winston (Evanston, Ill.: Northwestern University Press, 1955), 6.

35. King, *Lady Is a Spy*, 42.

36. Mina Loy, *The Lost Lunar Baedeker: Poems of Mina Loy* (New York: Farrar, Straus and Giroux, 1996), 46.

37. Harrison, *There's Always Tomorrow*, 163.

38. Harrison, 164.

39. Harrison, 163–65.

40. Stan Harding, *Underworld of State* (London: George Allen & Unwin, 1925), 61.

41. Harrison, *There's Always Tomorrow*, 172–73.

42. Harrison, 178–90.

43. Untitled report written by Marguerite Harrison concerning Robert Minor investigation, October 19, 1919, File PF-39205, RG 165 (War Department General Staff), Military Intelligence Division, Box 607, NARA, College Park, Md.

44. Harrison, *There's Always Tomorrow*, 196–98.

45. Joseph North, *Robert Minor, Artist and Crusader; An Informal Biography* (New York: International, 1956), 112–16.

46. Harrison, *There's Always Tomorrow*, 205.

47. Edward Davis to Marlborough Churchill, August 5, 1919, in File PF-39205, RG 165 (War Department General Staff), Military Intelligence Division, Box 607, NARA, College Park, Md.

48. Edward Davis to Director of Military Intelligence, July 30, 1919, in File PF-39205, RG 165 (War Department General Staff), Military Intelligence Division, Box 607, NARA, College Park, Md.
49. Marguerite E. Harrison, "Germany Today Is Sane, Normal, Full of Fight; World Trade Her Goal," *Baltimore Sun*, August 31, 1919, 1.
50. Harrison, *There's Always Tomorrow*, 207; and Marguerite E. Harrison, "Mercier Lands in New York," *Baltimore Sun*, September 10, 1919, 1.
51. Harrison, *There's Always Tomorrow*, 210.
52. Harrison, 209.
53. From Director of Military Intelligence to Military Attaché, Warsaw, Poland, October 22, 1919; Marlborough Churchill to Edward Davis, Sept. 2, 1919, and Edward Davis to Washington, September 25, 1919; Sherman Miles, Military Intelligence Division General Staff to Military Attaché American Embassy, Paris, October 22, 1919 in File PF-39205, RG 165 (War Department General Staff), Military Intelligence Division, Box 607, NARA, College Park, Md.

CHAPTER 6. AGENT B

1. David S. Foglesong, *America's Secret War against Bolshevism* (Chapel Hill: University of North Carolina Press, 1995), 114–25.
2. Foglesong, 114–25.
3. Harrison, *There's Always Tomorrow*, 39.
4. Harrison, 210–11.
5. Ross, *Ladies of the Press*, 110–12.
6. Oliver Gramling, *AP: The Story of News* (Port Washington, N.Y.: Kennikat, 1940), 290.
7. Gilbert, *World War I*, 212–17.
8. Bruce W. Bidwell, *History of the Military Intelligence Division, Department of the Army, General Staff, 1775–1941* (Frederick, Md.: University Publications of America, 1986), 110, 258.
9. Dorothy M. Brown, *Setting a Course: American Women in the 1920s* (Boston: Twayne, 1987), 3.
10. "Sailor Shoots Flag Insulter," *Daily Herald* (Chicago), May 9, 1919, 1.
11. Office of MID, Customhouse, N.Y. to Acting Director of Military Intelligence Division, March 6, 1919; and Marlborough Churchill to Assistant

Chief of Staff, May 16, 1919, File 102997-331, RG 165 (War Department General Staff), Military Intelligence Division, Box 607, NARA, College Park, Md.

12. Perrett, *America in the Twenties*, 51–59.

13. Harrison, *There's Always Tomorrow*, 212–13.

14. Harrison, 212.

15. Harrison, 70.

16. *Cynosure*, Gilman School yearbook, 1919, 38.

17. Nancy Harrison interview with author, June 14, 2017.

18. Report filed by "B" on Julius Hecker, October 28, 1919, File 11010-1475 Record Group 165, Military Intelligence Division Correspondence, 1917–1941, Box 2807; and Julius Hecker to R. C. Bannerman, January 23, 1920, File PF-32905, RG 165 (War Department General Staff), Military Intelligence Division, Box 607, NARA, College Park, Md.

19. Robert Collins to Marguerite Harrison, November 12, 1919, in Marguerite Harrison File, P-47767, Russian Federal Security Bureau Archives, Moscow, Russia.

20. Advertisement, *The Queen Newspaper Book of Travel* (London: Horace Cox, 1905), 360.

21. Julie Wheelwright, *The Fatal Lover: Mata Hari and the Myth of Women in Espionage* (London: Collins & Brown, 1992), 53.

22. Marguerite E. Harrison, "How Lady Astor Won Seat in Parliament over Two Men," Baltimore *Evening Sun*, December 3, 1919, 1; Marguerite E. Harrison, "France First to Recover Balance in Race for National Rebuilding," *Baltimore Sun*, December 7, 1919, 1; Marguerite E. Harrison, "Exiled King Expects to Rule Greece Again," *Baltimore Sun*, December 14, 1919, 1; and Marguerite E. Harrison, "German Prince to Visit U.S. to Publish His Book on War," *Baltimore Sun*, December 8, 1919, 7.

23. Harrison, *There's Always Tomorrow*, 220.

24. Marguerite E. Harrison, "Vienna on the Verge of Starvation While Country Districts Have Plenty," *Baltimore Sun*, December 30, 1919, 1.

25. Harrison, *There's Always Tomorrow*, 223–24.

26. Marguerite E. Harrison, "Baltimoreans Help Poland in Crisis," *Baltimore Sun*, December 31, 1919, 1.

27. Marguerite E. Harrison, "Ledochoswski Tells of Father's Murder," *Baltimore Sun*, January 1, 1920, 1.

28. Harrison, *There's Always Tomorrow*, 224; Marguerite E. Harrison, "Paderewski's Fall Partially Due to Wife," *Baltimore Sun*, January 7, 1920, 3; and Marguerite E. Harrison, "Glad Paderewski Is Out of Politics," *Baltimore Sun*, January 30, 1920.

29. Harrison, *There's Always Tomorrow*, 243; and untitled report, December 23, 1919, File PF-32905, RG 165 (War Department General Staff), Military Intelligence Division, Box 607, NARA, College Park, Md.

30. W. F. H. Godson to Marlborough Churchill, December 8, 1919, File PF-32905, RG 165 (War Department General Staff), Military Intelligence Division, Box 607, NARA, College Park, Md.

31. Marlborough Churchill to Military Attaché, Berne, Switzerland, January 20, 1920, File PF-32905, RG 165 (War Department General Staff), Military Intelligence Division, Box 607, NARA, College Park, Md.

32. Marguerite Harrison letter to Friend, December 27, 1919, File PF-32905, RG 165 (War Department General Staff), Military Intelligence Division, Box 607, NARA, College Park, Md.

33. Harrison, *There's Always Tomorrow*, 230.

34. Harrison, 230.

35. Harrison, 232.

CHAPTER 7. INTO RUSSIA

1. Harrison, *There's Always Tomorrow*, 238–39.

2. Robert K. Murray, *Red Scare: A Study of National Hysteria, 1919–1920* (New York: McGraw-Hill, 1955), 213; and Perrett, *America in the Twenties*, 61.

3. Harrison, *There's Always Tomorrow*, 246–47.

4. Marguerite E. Harrison, "Poland's Women Soldiers Win Country's Admiring Respect," *Baltimore Sun*, March 4, 1920, 6.

5. Marguerite E. Harrison, "Polish Refugees from Russia Well Fed and Well Dressed," *Baltimore Sun*, February 23, 1920, 1; and Marguerite E. Harrison, "Polish Soldiers Facing Reds Endure Hardships Like Spartans," *Baltimore Sun*, March 7, 1920, SM4.

6. Harrison, *There's Always Tomorrow*, 252.

7. Harrison, 253–55.

8. Lt. Col. E. E. Farman to the Director of Military Intelligence Division, February 7, 1920, File PF-32905, RG 165 (War Department General Staff), Military Intelligence Division, Box 607, NARA, College Park, Md.

9. Marguerite E. Harrison, *Marooned in Moscow: The Story of an American Woman Imprisoned in Russia* (New York: George H. Doran, 1921), 11–44; and Harrison, *There's Always Tomorrow*, 259–73.

10. Harrison, *There's Always Tomorrow*, 273–75.

11. Marina Tsvetaeva, *Earthly Signs, Moscow Diaries, 1917–1922*, edited by Jamey Gambrell (New Haven, Conn.: Yale University Press, 2002), xii, 83.

12. Francis McCullagh, *A Prisoner of the Reds: A Story of a British Officer Captured in Siberia* (New York: Dutton, 1922), 188–92.

13. McCullagh, 198.

14. Harrison, *There's Always Tomorrow*, 275.

15. Harrison, 276–77.

16. George Leggett, *The Cheka: Lenin's Political Police* (Oxford: Clarendon, 1981), 100.

17. Harrison, *There's Always Tomorrow*, 278.

18. Harrison, 291.

19. Leggett, *The Cheka*, 250–54.

20. Leggett, 187.

21. Leggett, 198.

22. Victor Serge, *Memoirs of a Revolutionary, 1901–1941*, translated and edited by Peter Sedgwick (London: Oxford University Press, 1963), 99.

23. Harrison, *There's Always Tomorrow*, 285.

24. Marguerite E. Harrison, "Baltimore Woman in Russia Welcomed by Soviet Officers," *Baltimore Sun*, May 23, 1920, 1; and Marguerite E. Harrison, "Bolsheviki Amiable to Woman Who Entered Moscow for News in Violation of Their Rules," *Baltimore Sun*, May 30, 1920, ED2.

25. Harrison, *There's Always Tomorrow*, 299.

26. Harrison, 294.

27. McCullagh, *Prisoner of the Reds*, 279.

28. McCullagh, 233–47.

29. McCullagh, 307.

30. Harrison, *There's Always Tomorrow*, 294.

31. Harrison, 297.

32. Harrison, 299.

33. Harrison, *Marooned in Moscow*, 72; see also McCullagh, *Prisoner of the Reds*, 252–53.

34. Harrison, *There's Always Tomorrow*, 308.

35. Harrison, 309–10.

36. McCullagh, *Prisoner of the Reds*, 279.

37. Marlborough Churchill Memorandum for MI-4, December 8, 1921, File PF-32905, RG 165 (War Department General Staff), Military Intelligence Division, Box 607, NARA, College Park, Md. In her autobiography Harrison writes that the Russians also had seen an article in *Army and Navy Journal* that described her work in helping catch Robert Minor. However, despite attempts by several researchers, no such article has been found.

38. W. F. Godson to Military Staff, March 15, 1920, File PF-32905, RG 165 (War Department General Staff), Military Intelligence Division, Box 607, NARA, College Park, Md.

39. Harrison, *There's Always Tomorrow*, 310–13.

CHAPTER 8. DOUBLE TROUBLE

1. Giles Milton, *Russian Roulette: How British Spies Thwarted Lenin's Plot for Global Revolution* (New York: Bloomsbury, 2013), 78–84.

2. British Secret Services Report, April 17, 1920, File PF-32905, RG 165 (War Department General Staff), Military Intelligence Division, Box 607, NARA, College Park, Md.

3. Marguerite Harrison File, P-47767, 1920, Russian Federal Security Bureau Archives, Moscow, Russia.

4. Davis to Military Staff, April 15, 1920, File PF-32905, RG 165 (War Department General Staff), Military Intelligence Division, Box 607, NARA, College Park, Md.

5. E. E. Farman to Marlborough Churchill, February 28, 1920, File PF-32905, RG 165 (War Department General Staff), Military Intelligence Division, Box 607, NARA, College Park, Md.

6. Alexander B. Coxe to W. L. Hurley, April 16, 1920; File PF-32905, RG 165 (War Department General Staff), Military Intelligence Division, Box 607, NARA, College Park, Md.

7. Marguerite Harrison File, P-47767, Russian Federal Security Bureau Archives, Moscow, Russia.

8. Marlborough Churchill memorandum for M.I. 4, December 8, 1921. File PF-32905, RG 165 (War Department General Staff), Military Intelligence Division, Box 607, NARA, College Park, Md.

9. Davis to Washington, April 14, 1920, and April 15, 1920, File PF-32905, RG 165 (War Department General Staff), Military Intelligence Division, Box 607, NARA, College Park, Md.

10. Harrison, *There's Always Tomorrow*, 329–30.

11. Melvin J. McKenna to Assistant Chief of Staff for Military Intelligence, October 6, 1920, File PF-32905, RG 165 (War Department General Staff), Military Intelligence Division, Box 607, NARA, College Park, Md.

12. McCullagh, *Prisoner of the Reds*, 283, 307. McCullagh and Harrison also give different accounts of what happened to Dr. Karlin. McCullagh wrote that she remained locked in solitary confinement when he left Russia three weeks after his release. McCullagh, 205. Marguerite wrote that Karlin was "detained several days" and then released to take a post as a doctor in the Red Army. Harrison, *There's Always Tomorrow*, 314.

13. British Secret Service Report, May 1, 1920, File PF-32905, RG 165 (War Department General Staff), Military Intelligence Division, Box 607, NARA, College Park, Md.

14. British Secret Service Report, May 1, 1920.

15. "Mrs. Harrison Believed to Be Safe," *Baltimore Sun*, May 18, 1920, 24; see also "Baltimore Woman in Russia Welcomed by Soviets," *Baltimore Sun*, May 23, 1920, 1.

16. Letter from Harold Carlson to an American Representative, August 18, 1920, File PF-32905, RG 165 (War Department General Staff), Military Intelligence Division, Box 607, NARA, College Park, Md.

17. Hurley to Winslow, May 15, 1920, Oscar Solbert to Washington, May 27, 1920, File PF-32905, RG 165 (War Department General Staff), Military Intelligence Division, Box 607, NARA, College Park, Md.

18. F. M. Begoum [John P. Dimmer Jr.], "Observations on the Double Agent," *Studies in Intelligence* 6 (Winter 1961): 13-21-5, available at http://cryptome.info/0001/double-agent.htm.

19. Begoum.

20. Harrison, *There's Always Tomorrow*, 315–16.

21. Harrison, 324.

22. Harrison, 324.

23. Harrison, 319.

24. Harrison, 336.

25. Bertrand Russell, *Autobiography of Bertrand Russell, 1914–1944*, vol. 2 (Boston: Little, Brown, 1951), 141.

26. Russell, 142.

27. Russell, 143.

28. Russell, 151.

29. Russell, 141–44, 151.

30. Russell, 151.

31. Harrison, *There's Always Tomorrow*, 337; and Russell, *Autobiography*, 150.

32. Harrison, *There's Always Tomorrow*, 165.

33. Harding, *Underworld of State*, 47.

34. Harding, 48. See also Victor Madeira, *Britannia and the Bear: The Anglo-Russian Intelligence Wars* (Woodbridge, U.K.: Boydell, 2014), 194; Kollwitz, *The Diary and Letters of Kaethe Kollwitz*, 6, 45; Susan Wintsch Churchill, *The Little Magazine Others and the Renovation of Modern American Poetry* (Burlington, Vt.: Ashgate, 2006), 219; and Stan Harding Butyrka Prison questionnaire, State Archive of Russian Federation, GARF, F. 8419, op. 1, d. 266, page 42, available at http://pkk.memo.ru/letters_pdf/000425.pdf.

35. Harding, *Underworld of State*, 49.

36. Harding, 54.

37. Harding, 57–59.

38. Harding, 64.

39. Harrison, *There's Always Tomorrow*, 341.

40. Harrison, 341.

41. Harrison, 341–42.

42. Harding, *Underworld of State*, 64–65.

43. Harding, 104.

44. Harrison, *There's Always Tomorrow*, 345.

45. Harding, *Underworld of State*, 91.

46. Harrison, *There's Always Tomorrow*, 338.

47. Harrison, *Marooned in Moscow*, 191.

48. Harrison, 202.

49. Harrison, 203.

50. Harrison, *There's Always Tomorrow*, 346–48.

51. Harrison, 349.

52. Harrison, 349–50.

53. Mark Cotta Vaz, *Living Dangerously: The Adventures of Merian C. Cooper, Creator of King Kong* (New York: Villard, 2005), 69–70.

54. Harrison, *Marooned in Moscow*, 221.

55. Granville Hicks, *John Reed: The Making of a Revolutionary* (New York: Macmillan, 1936), 390.

56. Mary V. Dearborn, *Queen of Bohemia: The Life of Louise Bryant* (Boston: Houghton Mifflin, 1996), 167.

57. Richard B. Spence, "John Reed, American Spy? Reed, American Intelligence, and Weston Estes' 1920 Mission to Russia," *American Communist History* 13, no. 1 (2014): 54, http://dx.doi.org/10.1080/14743892.2014.896642.

58. Weston B. Estes, "Russian Experiences," *Long Island Medical Journal* 15, no. 12 (December 1921): 411.

59. Statement of John Flick, Bolshevism—Negative, August 15 1921, File 2070-2119/12, RG 165 (War Department General Staff), Military Intelligence Division, microfilm 1443, NARA, College Park, Md.

60. Hicks, *John Reed*, 390–400.

61. Harrison, *Marooned in Moscow*, 222.

62. Richard O'Connor and Dale L. Walker, *The Lost Revolutionary: A Biography of John Reed* (New York: Harcourt, Brace & World, 1967), 301–3.

63. Harrison, *There's Always Tomorrow*, 351–53.

CHAPTER 9. THROUGH DIFFICULTIES TO THE STARS

1. McCullagh, *Prisoner of the Reds*, 272–74.

2. Harding, *Underworld of State*, 80.

3. Marguerite B. Harrison File, P-47767, 1920, Russian Federal Security Bureau Archives, Moscow, Russia.

4. McCullagh, *Prisoner of the Reds*, 274.

5. Harrison, *There's Always Tomorrow*, 360–61.

6. Harrison, 358–61.

7. Harrison, 363.

8. McCullagh, *Prisoner of the Reds*, 282.

9. McCullagh, 279.

10. Harrison, *There's Always Tomorrow*, 365.

11. Harding, *Underworld of State*, 82.

12. Harrison, *There's Always Tomorrow*, 366.

13. Harrison, 367.

14. Harding, *Underworld of State*, 187.

15. McCullagh, *Prisoner of the Reds*, 283.

16. Harrison, *There's Always Tomorrow*, 366. One must ask whether Marguerite's feelings for Mogilevsky reflected a case of Stockholm syndrome, in which prisoners become enamored of their captors. Although not a recognized psychological disorder, numerous examples have been recorded since the syndrome first received the name in 1973 when hostages in a bank robbery in Stockholm, Sweden, refused to testify against the defendants.

17. Maria Karikh, "Intentional Air Crash: Beria Never Allowed Anyone to Look into His Past," *Military Industrial Courier* (March 23–29, 2005): 11, https://vpk-news.ru/sites/default/files/pdf/issue_77.pdf.

18. Marguerite B. Harrison File, P-47767, 1920, Russian Federal Security Bureau Archives, Moscow, Russia.

19. Harrison, *There's Always Tomorrow*, 367.

20. Harrison, 368.

21. Harrison, 381–82.

22. Harrison, 381–82; Marguerite Harrison, "Unfinished Tales," *Cosmopolitan*, October 1922, 165. In the *Cosmopolitan* magazine article, Harrison called the woman Tasya.

23. Leggett, *The Cheka*, 181.

24. Hershell Walker to Post Wheeler, September 11, 1920, 164–334, RG 165, Classified Correspondences and Receipts, 1917–1941, Military Intelligence Division, Box 2807, NARA, College Park, Md.

25. "Mrs. M. E. Harrison Held by Bolsheviki," *Baltimore Sun*, November 28, 1920, 26.

26. Albert C. Ritchie to Bainbridge Colby, November 29, 1920, 316.1121H24, RG 59 (State Department Decimal File, 1910–1929), Box 4325, NARA, College Park, Md.

27. "Mrs. Harrison Held in Prison by Bolsheviki," *Baltimore Sun*, December 16, 1920, 1.

28. Service report 10783 from England-8, January 11, 1921, File PF-39205, RG 165 (War Department General Staff), Military Intelligence Division, Box 607, NARA, College Park, Md.

29. Tommy Harrison to Marguerite Harrison, December 20, 1920, Marguerite B. Harrison File, P-47767, 1920, Russian Federal Security Bureau Archives, Moscow, Russia.

30. Harrison, *There's Always Tomorrow*, 384–89.
31. Marguerite Harrison to Albert Ritchie, January 16, 1921, Marguerite B. Harrison File, P-47767, 1920, Russian Federal Security Bureau Archives, Moscow, Russia.
32. Marguerite Harrison to Albert Ritchie, undated, Marguerite B. Harrison File, P-47767, 1920, Russian Federal Security Bureau Archives, Moscow, Russia.
33. Harrison, *There's Always Tomorrow*, 398.
34. Frank Kent to Joseph Ames, January 24, 1921, File PF-39205, RG 165 (War Department General Staff), Military Intelligence Division, Box 607, NARA, College Park, Md.
35. Joseph Ames to Marguerite Harrison, May 6, 1921, Marguerite B. Harrison File, P-47767, 1920, Russian Federal Security Bureau Archives, Moscow, Russia.
36. "Mrs. Harrison Is Freed from Russian Prison," *Baltimore Sun*, January 21, 1921, 18; "Communists Call Lenin a Betrayer," *New York Herald*, April 17, 1921, 2; "Americans Marked for Soviet Cruelty," *New York Times*, April 18, 1921, 12; and "Reds Withhold Food Sent Mrs. Harrison," *New York Times*, April 19, 1921, 3.
37. Associated Press, "Americans in Soviet Prisons Reported in Desperate Plight," *Baltimore Sun*, June 6, 1921, 1.
38. Merian C. Cooper to Hugh Gibson, undated, included in memorandum from Gibson to Secretary of State, May 9, 1921, 316.1121H24/23, RG 59 (State Department Decimal File, 1910–1929), Box 4325, NARA, College Park, Md.; and Harry T. Mahoney and Marjorie L. Mahoney, *American Prisoners of the Bolsheviks: The Genesis of Modern American Intelligence* (Bethesda, Md.: Academica, 2001), 329, 342.
39. "Senator France Acts to Aid Mrs. Harrison," *Baltimore Sun*, April 21, 1921, 3.
40. "Moscow Denies Mrs. Harrison Is Ill-Treated," *Baltimore Sun*, April 27, 1921, 20.
41. Marguerite Harrison to Albert Ritchie, May 4, 1921, Marguerite B. Harrison File, P-47767, 1920, Russian Federal Security Bureau Archives, Moscow, Russia.
42. Harrison, *There's Always Tomorrow*, 395.
43. Harrison, 405–6.
44. Harrison, 403–15.
45. Vladimir I. Lenin to Georgy Chicherin, July 15, 1921, in Vladimir Lenin, *Complete Collection of Works*, vol. 53, *Letters: Second Half of July 1921*, accessed

August 16, 2019, https://leninism.su/works/39-tom-53/245-letters-jul-212
.html#.D0.93._.D0.92._.D0.A7.D0.98.D0.A7.D0.95.D0.A0.D0.98.D0.9D
.D0.A3_4.

46. Harrison, *There's Always Tomorrow*, 416–22.

CHAPTER 10. "A LADY WITH A MYSTERIOUS PAST"

1. Dennis Nolan to Joseph Ames, July 27, 1921, File PF-39205, RG 165 (War Department General Staff), Military Intelligence Division, Box 607, NARA, College Park, Md.
2. Harrison, *There's Always Tomorrow*, 424.
3. Harrison, 425.
4. Hollyday to Director of Military Intelligence Division, August 4, 1921, File 164-334-116, RG 165 (War Department General Staff), Military Intelligence Division, Correspondences 1917–41, NARA, College Park, Md.
5. Stan Harding, "Returns to England Broken from Harrowing Experiences," *Philadelphia Inquirer*, February 27, 1921, 1; Stan Harding, "Mrs. Harding Meets Mme. X; Is Trapped," *Philadelphia Inquirer*, February 28, 1921, 20; and Stan Harding, "Woman in Fear of Reds' Stupidity," *Philadelphia Inquirer*, March 1, 1921, 2.
6. Hollyday to Marlborough Churchill, September 22, 1921, File 10110, RG 165, Military Intelligence Division Classified Correspondences and Receipts, 1917–1941, Box 2821, NARA, College Park, Md.
7. Associated Press, "Jailers Were Kind Says Mrs. Harrison," *New York Times*, August 1, 1921, 2.
8. United Press, "Mrs. Harrison, Held Prisoner in Russia, Longed for Cigarets [sic]," *News-Herald* (Oil City, Pa.), August 30, 1921, 1.
9. "150,000 Prisoners in Red Jails, Kilpatrick Declares," *Washington Post*, September 6, 1921, 5; and "Released American's First Story of Russia; Terror Worse than Ever; What Caused Famine," *New York Times*, August 12, 1921, 1.
10. "Estes Describes His Prison Life," *New York Times*, August 14, 1921, 2.
11. Frank E. Mason, "Tells Story of Years in Soviet Jail," *Decatur Herald*, August 21, 1921, 12.
12. Associated Press, "Americans Released, Now Leaving Russia," *New York Times*, August 5, 1921, 3.

13. Harrison, *There's Always Tomorrow*, 426.

14. Mark S. Watson, "Mrs. Harrison Is Much Better than Physicians Hoped to Find," *Baltimore Sun*, August 5, 1921, 1.

15. Harrison, *There's Always Tomorrow*, 427.

16. Watson, "Mrs. Harrison Is Much Better."

17. Associated Press, "Mrs. Harrison Goes A-Shopping Immediately upon Reaching Berlin," *Baltimore Sun*, August 4, 1921, 1.

18. Report 2190, "Russia: Current Conditions by B," August 10, 1921, File 2070-2117, RG 165 (War Department General Staff), Military Intelligence Division, microfilm 1443, NARA, College Park, Md.

19. Harrison, *There's Always Tomorrow*, 428.

20. Marguerite E. Harrison, "Mrs. Harrison Recounts in Detail Experiences During Stay in Russia," *Baltimore Sun*, August 6, 1921, 1.

21. Marguerite E. Harrison, "Soviet Rule Will Stand Despite Famine Crisis, Asserts Mrs. Harrison," *Baltimore Sun*, August 9, 1921, 1.

22. Marguerite E. Harrison, "Names Gorky as Relief Hope," *Baltimore Sun*, August 14, 1921, 1; Marguerite E. Harrison, "Famine Relief May Modify Present Russian Government," *Baltimore Sun*, August 25, 1921; and Marguerite E. Harrison, "Strength of the Communist Party in Russia Explained," *Baltimore Sun*, August 26, 1921, 1.

23. Harold E. West, "Mrs. Harrison Shows Benefit of Sea Voyage," *Baltimore Sun*, August 27, 1921, 1.

24. West, 1.

25. "Mrs. Harrison Reaches Home after 2 Years," *Baltimore Sun*, August 31, 1921.

26. "Compares Mrs. Harrison with the Apostle Paul," *Baltimore Sun*, August 29, 1921, 5.

27. Marguerite Harrison, "Ten Months in Prison Described by Mrs. Harrison," *Baltimore Sun*, September 25, 1921, 1.

28. Harrison, *There's Always Tomorrow*, 428–29.

29. "Mrs. Harrison to Appear," *Baltimore Sun*, September 1, 1921, 9; and "Life in Russian Prison Told by Mrs. Harrison," *Baltimore Sun*, September 3, 1921.

30. "Life in Russian Prison."

31. "Mrs. Marguerite E. Harrison Addresses Educational Society," *Baltimore Sun*, November 12, 1921, 14; "Tells of Russian Leaders," *Baltimore Sun*, October 9, 1921, 14; "Will Lecture on Europe," *Baltimore Sun*, November 9, 1921, 8; and "Praises Russian Women," *Baltimore Sun*, October 6, 1921, 9.

32. Harrison, *There's Always Tomorrow*, 429.
33. Marlborough Churchill, Memorandum for M.I.4., December 8, 1921, File 10110-1475/10, RG 165, Military Intelligence Division 1917–1941, Box 2807; Marlborough Churchill, Memorandum for Hurley, December 14, 1921, File 10110-1475/12, RG 165, Military Intelligence Division 1917–1941, Box 2807; J. V. McConville, Memorandum for File, October 15, 1921, File 10110-1475/8, RG 165, Military Intelligence Division 1917–1941, Box 2807, NARA, College Park, Md.
34. Harrison, *There's Always Tomorrow*, 430.
35. Harrison, 431.
36. Harrison, 436–38.
37. Harrison, 435–37.
38. "Woman Says She Stole Expecting Victim to Die," *Baltimore Sun*, November 18, 1921, 9; "Woman Faces Theft Charge," *Baltimore Sun*, November 21, 1921, 5; and "Jury Refuses to Hear Attorneys at Trial," *Baltimore Sun*, January 11, 1922, 20.
39. "Mrs. Harrison on Russia," *New York Times*, March 13, 1922, 2.
40. Harrison, *There's Always Tomorrow*, 432–34.
41. Report made by William E. Dunn, September 26, 1921, investigative case files of the Bureau of Investigation, 1908–1922, Case #202600-2593-1, M1085 boi_section_875-955_0017, https:www.fold3.com/image/5084253.
42. Special Informant W. March 1, 1922, 10110-2461 RG 165 (War Department General Staff), Military Intelligence Division, Correspondences 1917–41, NARA, College Park, Md.
43. Col. J. R. Proctor to Assistant Chief of Staff, War Department, March 13, 1922, File PF-39205/30, RG 165 (War Department General Staff), Military Intelligence Division, Box 607, NARA, College Park, Md.
44. Bidwell, *History of the Military Intelligence Division*, 264.
45. Marguerite Harrison to Marlborough Churchill, April 14, 1922, File PF-39205/32, RG 165 (War Department General Staff), Military Intelligence Division, Box 607, NARA, College Park, Md.
46. Marlborough Churchill to Marguerite Harrison, April 26, 1922, File PF-39205/33, RG 165 (War Department General Staff), Military Intelligence Division, Box 607, NARA, College Park, Md.
47. C. F. Cox to Chief of Staff, G-2, "Report of Conversation with Marguerite Harrison," March 5, 1923, File PF-39205, RG 165 (War Department General Staff), Military Intelligence Division, Box 607, NARA, College Park, Md.

48. "Mrs. Harrison's Friends Feared She Would Try to Re-enter Russia," *Baltimore Sun*, December 8, 1922, 2.

49. Marlborough Churchill to Wallace C. Philoon, assistant military attaché to China, Canton, China; Marlborough Churchill to Lt. Col. Charles Burnett, military attaché, Tokyo, Japan; Marlborough Churchill to Colonel Sherwood Chaney, military attaché, Peking, China; Marlborough Churchill to Major Philip Faymonville, Military Observer, Chita, Far Eastern Republic, all letters May 25, 1922, File PF-39205, RG 165 (War Department General Staff), Military Intelligence Division, Box 607, NARA, College Park, Md.

50. Churchill to Philoon et al., May 25, 1922.

51. Harrison, *There's Always Tomorrow*, 442.

CHAPTER 11. "A VERY CLEVER WOMAN"

1. Dewitt Poole to Alvey Adee, November 28, 1922, File 361.1121, Marguerite Harrison, RG 59, Department of State Decimal File, 1910–1929, NARA, College Park, Md.

2. Marguerite E. Harrison, *Red Bear or Yellow Dragon* (New York: George H. Doran, Co., 1924), 205.

3. Bernard Baker Estate, Baltimore County Register of Wills, Estate Papers, C356-55, File 3787; and File 3189, Baltimore County Register of Wills, Estate Papers, C-356-47, Maryland State Archives.

4. Harrison, *There's Always Tomorrow*, 445.

5. Harrison, *Red Bear or Yellow Dragon*, 25–26.

6. Harrison, 29.

7. "Princess Oyama," *Vassar Encyclopedia*, accessed August 24, 2019, http://vc encyclopedia.vassar.edu/alumni/princess-oyama.html.

8. Harrison, *Red Bear or Yellow Dragon*, 30.

9. Harrison, 30.

10. Harrison, *There's Always Tomorrow*, 450–51.

11. Harrison, *Red Bear or Yellow Dragon*, 34.

12. Harrison, 34.

13. Harrison, 34.

14. Charles Burnett to Colonel Stuart Heintzelman, August 13, 1922, PF-39205, RG 165 (War Department General Staff), Military Intelligence Division, Box 607, NARA, College Park, Md.

15. Burnett to Heintzelman.
16. Burnett to Heintzelman.
17. Burnett to Heintzelman.
18. Harrison, *There's Always Tomorrow*, 458.
19. Harrison, 479.
20. Harrison, 462.
21. American Consulate in Siberia to Secretary of State, "Gold Mining Opportunities in Eastern Siberia," November 8, 1922, File 861A.6341, RG 59, State Department Records Related to the Internal Affairs of Russia and the Soviet Union, 1910–29, M 316 Roll 175, NARA, College Park, Md.
22. Harrison, *There's Always Tomorrow*, 464.
23. Harrison, *Red Bear or Yellow Dragon*, 106.
24. Harrison, 107.
25. Harrison, *There's Always Tomorrow*, 470–74.
26. Harrison, 485.
27. Harrison, 485.
28. Document file note from Warren, September 6, 1922, File 861a.01/327, RG 59, State Department Records Related to the Internal Affairs of Russia and the Soviet Union, 1910–29, M 316 Roll 175, NARA, College Park, Md.
29. Harrison, *There's Always Tomorrow*, 482.
30. "The Case of Mrs. Stan Harding," *Guardian*, August 21, 1922, 6.
31. "Mrs. Harrison Called Red Agent," *Japan Advertiser* (Tokyo), August 24, 1922, 1.
32. D.C. Poole to William Phillips, August 31, 1922, File 361.1121, Marguerite Harrison, RG 59, Department of State Decimal File, 1910–1929, NARA, College Park, Md.
33. Gray to Secretary of State, September 4, 1922, File 811.91261/115, RG 59, Department of State Central Decimal File, 1910–29, NARA, College Park, Md.
34. (William) Phillips to Peking, September 4, 1922, File 811.91261/115, RG 59, Department of State Central Decimal File, 1910–29, NARA, College Park, Md.
35. Col. Stuart Heintzelman to Lt. Col. Charles Burnett, September 13, 1922, PF-39205, RG 165 (War Department General Staff), Military Intelligence Division, Box 607, NARA, College Park, Md.
36. Harrison, *There's Always Tomorrow*, 491.
37. Harrison, *Red Bear or Yellow Dragon*, 157.

38. Harrison, 159–70.
39. Harrison, *There's Always Tomorrow*, 498.
40. Telegram from Genrickh Yagoda and Prokofiev to Belsky, October 9, 1922, Marguerite Harrison File 28578, Russian Federal Security Bureau Archives, Moscow, Russia.
41. Harrison, *There's Always Tomorrow*, 499.
42. Harrison, *Red Bear or Yellow Dragon*, 187.
43. Harrison, 200.
44. Harrison, *There's Always Tomorrow*, 516.
45. Harrison, *Red Bear or Yellow Dragon*, 209.
46. Harrison, 212.
47. Harrison, *There's Always Tomorrow*, 529.
48. Harrison, *Red Bear or Yellow Dragon*, 235.
49. Harrison, 238.
50. Harrison, 240.
51. Harrison, *There's Always Tomorrow*, 536.

CHAPTER 12. RETURN TO RUSSIA

1. Harrison, *There's Always Tomorrow*, 536.
2. Marguerite Harrison File, File 2857, Russian Federal Security Bureau Archives, Moscow Russia.
3. Thomas to Secretary of State, November 27, 1922, File 316.112, Marguerite Harrison File, RG 59, Department of State Decimal File, 1910–1929, NARA, College Park, Md.
4. Harrison, *There's Always Tomorrow*, 537.
5. Harrison, 538.
6. Harrison, 539.
7. Harrison, 540.
8. Thomas to Secretary of State, November 27, 1922, File 316.112, Marguerite Harrison File, RG 59, Department of State Decimal File, 1910–1929, NARA, College Park, Md.
9. Dewitt C. Poole to Alvin Adee, November 28, 1922, File 316.112, Marguerite Harrison File, RG 59, Department of State Decimal File, 1910–1929, NARA, College Park, Md.
10. Poole to Adee.

11. Harrison, *There's Always Tomorrow*, 540–41.

12. Harrison, 541–42.

13. Harrison, *Red Bear or Yellow Dragon*, 269–71.

14. Harrison, *There's Always Tomorrow*, 551.

15. Marguerite Harrison File, File 28578, Russian Federal Security Bureau Archives, Moscow, Russia.

16. Sergei Burkorsky, "Spy by Nationality," October 30, 2014, v.kursk.com, accessed August 24, 2019, http://vkurske.com/society/99866/.

17. Karikh, "Intentional Air Crash," 11.

18. Olds, *Women of the Four Winds*, 195.

19. Joseph Ames to Christian Herter, November 28, 1922, American Relief Administration, Russian Operational records, Box 324, Folder 11, Hoover Institution Archives, Stanford University.

20. Albert C. Ritchie to Christian Herter, January 13, 1923, American Relief Administration, Russian Operational records, Box 324, Folder 11, Hoover Institution Archives, Stanford University.

21. Christian Herter to Edgar Rickard, November 29, 1922, American Relief Administration, Russian Operational records, Box 324, Folder 11, Hoover Institution Archives, Stanford University.

22. Edgar Rickard to Christian A. Herter, December 1, 1922, American Relief Administration, Russian Operational records, Box 324, Folder 11, Hoover Institution Archives, Stanford University.

23. "Says Mrs. Harrison Called Her a Spy," *New York Times*, February 15, 1923, 2.

24. "Pays Mrs. Stan Harding," *New York Times*, August 22, 1923, 3.

25. Herbert C. Rideout, "British Journalists Are Stirred Up by Mrs. Stand Harding Charges," *Editor and Publisher*, September 23, 1922, 14.

26. "Denies Betrayal by Mrs. Harrison," *Baltimore Sun*, December 16, 1922, 20.

27. "Gov. Ritchie Declares Charges Untrue," *Baltimore Sun*, December 1, 1922, 1.

28. Joseph Ames to Marlborough Churchill, December 29, 1922, PF-39205, RG 165 (War Department General Staff), Military Intelligence Division, Box 607, NARA, College Park, Md.

29. Dewitt Poole to Christian Herter, February 13, 1923, American Relief Administration, Russian Operational records, Box 324, Folder 11, Hoover Institution Archives, Stanford University.

30. Harrison, *There's Always Tomorrow*, 557–58.

31. Harrison, 559.

32. W. B. Cox to Assistant Chief of Staff, March 6, 1923, PF-39205, RG 165 (War Department General Staff), Military Intelligence Division, Box 607, NARA, College Park, Md.

33. Harding, *Underworld of State*, 92–94.

34. William Haskell to Christian Herter, February 19, 1923, American Relief Administration, Russian Operational records, Box 324, Folder 11, Hoover Institution Archives, Stanford University.

35. Joseph Ames to Dewitt Poole, February 25, 1923, File 316.112 Marguerite Harrison File, RG 59, Department of State Decimal File, 1910–1929, NARA, College Park, Md.

36. Joseph Ames to Christian Herter, March 28, 1923, American Relief Administration, Russian Operational records, Box 324, Folder 11, Hoover Institution Archives, Stanford University.

37. Marguerite Harrison File, File 28578, Russian Federal Security Bureau Archives, Moscow, Russia.

38. Harrison, *Red Bear or Yellow Dragon*, 272–73.

39. Harrison, *There's Always Tomorrow*, 561.

40. Harrison, 561.

41. Harrison, 562.

42. Frederick W. B. Coleman to Secretary of State, March 2, 1923, File 316.112 Marguerite Harrison File, RG 59, Department of State Decimal File, 1910–1929, NARA, College Park, Md.

43. C. F. Cox to Assistant Chief of Staff, March 5, 1923. PF-39205, RG 165 (War Department General Staff), Military Intelligence Division, Box 607, NARA, College Park, Md.

44. Harrison, *There's Always Tomorrow*, 563.

45. "Mrs. Marguerite Harrison Back from Sojourn in Russian Prison," *Baltimore Sun*, March 23, 1923, 3.

46. "Little Depends on Lenine [*sic*], Mrs. Harrison Believes," *Baltimore Sun*, March 24, 1923, 3.

47. Marguerite Harrison File, File 4467, Russian Federal Security Bureau Archives, Moscow Russia.

48. Undated document, Marguerite Harrison File, File 28578, Russian Federal Security Bureau Archives, Moscow Russia.

49. "American Agent Accused," *Los Angeles Times*, February 16, 1923, 5.

50. Marlborough Churchill to Col. William Naylor, March 29, 1923, PF-39205, RG 165 (War Department General Staff), Military Intelligence Division, Box 607, NARA, College Park, Md.

51. Col. William Naylor to Marlborough Churchill, April 2, 1923, PF-39205, RG 165 (War Department General Staff), Military Intelligence Division, Box 607, NARA, College Park, Md.

52. Statement by Marguerite Harrison, April 14, 1923, PF-39205, RG 165 (War Department General Staff), Military Intelligence Division, Box 607, NARA, College Park, Md.

53. "An Unhappy Incident," *Manchester Guardian*, May 7, 1923, 1.

54. Bernard Baker estate papers, Baltimore County Register of Wills, Estate 3189 and 3787, Maryland State Archives.

55. Joseph Ames to Christian Herter, March 28, 1923, American Relief Administration, Russian Operational records, Box 324, Folder 11, Hoover Institution Archives, Stanford University.

56. Joseph Ames to Dewitt Poole, February 25, 1923, File 316.112, Marguerite Harrison File, RG 59, Department of State Decimal File, 1910–1929, NARA, College Park, Md.

57. Harrison, *There's Always Tomorrow*, 565.

58. Harrison, 564.

59. Merian Cooper to Maj. J. L. Collins, undated, RG 165, Military Intelligence Division Correspondences, 1917–1941, 164–334, NARA, College Park, Md.

60. Lt. Col. M. E. Locke to Merian Cooper, September 6, 1922, RG 165, Military Intelligence Division Correspondences, 1917–1941, 164–334, NARA, College Park, Md.

CHAPTER 13. DESERT DRAMA

1. Bahman Maghsoudlou, *Grass: Untold Stories* (Costa Mesa, Calif.: Mazda, 2009), 154.

2. Harrison, *There's Always Tomorrow*, 566–67.

3. Kevin Brownlow Collection, Tape 3, July 1971, Special Collections and Manuscripts, Harold B. Lee Library, Brigham Young University, Provo, Utah.

4. Ernest B. Schoedsack, "Grass: The Making of an Epic," *American Cinematographer*, February 1983.

5. Vaz, *Living Dangerously*, 112.

6. Merian Cooper to Gen. Sherman Miles, November 19, 1940, File 164-334, 133, RG 165, Military Intelligence Division 1917–1941, NARA, College Park, Md.

7. Kevin Brownlow Collection, Tape 3, July 1971, Special Collections and Manuscripts, Harold B. Lee Library, Brigham Young University, Provo, Utah.

8. Kevin Brownlow Collection, Tape 3, July 1971.

9. Harrison, *There's Always Tomorrow*, 573.

10. Vaz, *Living Dangerously*, 45–46.

11. Vaz, 112.

12. Harrison, *There's Always Tomorrow*, 572.

13. Harrison, 571–72.

14. Priya Satia, *Spies in Arabia: The Great War and the Cultural Foundations of Britain's Covert Empire in the Middle East* (New York: Oxford University Press, 2008), 184–85.

15. "Four Liners Carry Tourists to Europe," *New York Times*, August 4, 1923, 13.

16. Schoedsack, "Grass," 44.

17. Harrison, *There's Always Tomorrow*, 578.

18. Harrison, 578.

19. Harrison, 582.

20. Harrison, 582.

21. Merian C. Cooper, *Things Men Die For* (New York: G. P. Putnam's Sons, 1927), 73.

22. Schoedsack to Kevin Brownlow, cited in Maghsoudlou, *Grass*, 173.

23. Harrison, *There's Always Tomorrow*, 589.

24. Satia, *Spies in Arabia*, 50.

25. Harrison, *There's Always Tomorrow*, 592.

26. Marguerite E. Harrison, "Gertrude Bell a Desert Power," *New York Times*, July 18, 1926, XX12; and Harrison, *There's Always Tomorrow*, 592.

27. Gertrude Lowthian Bell, *The Letters of Gertrude Bell*, vol. 2, *1921–1926* (New York: Boni and Liveright, 1927), 787.

28. Schoedsack, "Grass," 109.

29. John Randolph to Secretary of State, March 7, 1924, File 867.404/83, RG 59, State Department Records Relating to the Internal Affairs of Turkey 1910–1919, M353 Roll 49, NARA, College Park, Md.

30. Marguerite E. Harrison, "Mosul Oil Still Lies in the Ground," *New York Times*, April 5, 1925, SM5.

31. Harrison, *There's Always Tomorrow*, 595.

32. Harrison, 605–6.

33. Merian C. Cooper, *Grass* (New York: G. P. Putnam's Sons, 1925), 97.

34. Harrison, *There's Always Tomorrow*, 608.

35. Maghsoudlou, *Grass*, 192.

36. Harrison, *There's Always Tomorrow*, 612.

37. Bethany Lane, "The Women Who Shook It Up and Made It Happen," University of Glasgow Library, reposted by Sammaddra on March 8, 2015, accessed August 28, 2019, https://universityofglasgowlibrary.wordpress.com/2015/03/08/the-women-who-shook-it-up-made-it-happen-by-bethany-lane/.

38. Cooper, *Grass*, 167; and Harrison, *There's Always Tomorrow*, 615.

39. Harrison, *There's Always Tomorrow*, 617.

40. Harrison, 635.

41. Cooper, *Grass*, 59.

42. Harrison, *There's Always Tomorrow*, 642.

43. Merian C. Cooper, "Col. Cooper Describes Fight for Persian Oil," *New York Times*, July 17, 1924, 3.

44. Tim Carroll, *The Dodger: The Extraordinary Story of Churchill's American Cousin, Two World Wars, and The Great Escape* (Guilford, Conn.: Lyons Press, 2013), 88–90.

45. Marguerite E. Harrison, "Soldierly Dictator of Persia Is a Gracious Host at Tea," *New York Times*, December 6, 1925, SM4.

46. Charles Evans Hughes to (Maxwell) Blake, May 26, 1923, RG 59, State Department General Records Central Decimal File 1910–1929, 123 Imr1, Box 1448, NARA, College Park, Md.

47. Louise Bryant to Charles Evans Hughes, July 12, 1923, RG 59, State Department General Records Central Decimal File 1910–1929, 123 Imr1, Box 1448, NARA, College Park, Md.

48. Cooper, *Things Men Die For*, 118.

49. Cooper, *Grass*, 12.

50. Michael Zirinsky, "Blood, Power and Hypocrisy: The Murder of Robert Imbrie and American Relations with Pahlavi Iran, 1924," *International Journey of Middle Eastern Studies* 18 (1986): 275–92.

51. Zirinsky, 275–92.
52. Katherine Imbrie to Secretary of State Charles Hughes, August 14, 1924, RG 59, State Department General Records Central Decimal File 1910–1929, 123 Imr1/255, Box 1448, NARA, College Park, Md.
53. Zirinsky, "Blood, Power and Hypocrisy," 275–92.
54. Cooper, *Grass*, xii.
55. "Imbrie's Death Laid to Persian Politics," Baltimore *Evening Sun*, September 30, 1924, 3.
56. Harrison, *There's Always Tomorrow*, 646.
57. Harrison, 647.
58. "Grass," *New York Daily News*, March 24, 1925, 137.
59. "The Russian Aeroplane Accident," (London) *Times*, March 25, 1925, 13.

CHAPTER 14. EBB TIDE

1. Harrison, *There's Always Tomorrow*, 554.
2. "The Russian Aeroplane Accident," (London) *Times*, March 25, 1925, 13.
3. Karikh, "Intentional Air Crash," 11; and Valdimir Antonov, "The Mystery of the Death of Solomon Mogilevsky," *Nezavisimaya Gazeta*, September 24, 2010, accessed September 1, 2019, http://nvo.ng.ru/spforces/2010-09-24/12 _mogilevsky.html.
4. Quoted in "Lavrenty Palych Beria Came to Visit Us," Algorithm Publishing House, August 22, 2012, https://algoritm-izdat.ru/2012/08/22/beriya/.
5. Harrison, *There's Always Tomorrow*, 554.
6. Mildred Spain, "Grass Hailed as Film Epic," *New York Daily News*, March 1, 1925, 17.
7. Harrison, *There's Always Tomorrow*, 648.
8. Harrison, 650.
9. Harrison, 650.
10. Harrison, 651.
11. Harrison, 652.
12. Enclosure titled "Some of the Stage Roles Played by 'Arthur Middleton' Blake," Merian C. Cooper Papers, MSS 2008, Box 32, Folder 5, Harold B. Lee Library, Brigham Young University, Provo, Utah.
13. Harrison, *There's Always Tomorrow*, 660.
14. Harrison, 656–59.

15. Harrison, 660.
16. Harrison, 664.
17. H. Earle Russell to Secretary of State, August 2, 1927, 881.404/1, RG 59, State Department General Records Central Decimal File 1910–1929, NARA, College Park, Md.
18. Johnson, *Our Secret War*, 303.
19. "Mr. and Mrs. Blake Gone to New York," *Baltimore Sun*, January 19, 1930, 68.
20. Letters from Merian Cooper to Walter Wanger, Irving Thalberg, David O. Selsnick, Jesse Lasky, and Ernest Lubitech, July 23, 1935, Merian C. Cooper Papers, MSS 2008, Box 32, Folder 5, Harold B. Lee Library, Brigham Young University, Provo, Utah.
21. "Former Baltimoreans Book Made Grounds for Libel Suit," *Baltimore Sun*, April 21, 1938, 26.
22. Marguerite Harrison Blake to Merian C. Cooper, January 22, 1938, Merian C. Cooper Papers, MSS 2008, Box 32, Folder 5, Harold B. Lee Library, Brigham Young University, Provo, Utah.
23. Merian C. Cooper to Marguerite Harrison Blake, March 6, 1942, Merian C. Cooper Papers, MSS 2008, Box 32, Folder 5, Harold B. Lee Library, Brigham Young University, Provo, Utah.
24. William Grimes to Merian Cooper, September 6, 1967, Merian C. Cooper Papers, MSS 2008, Box 32, Folder 5, Harold B. Lee Library, Brigham Young University, Provo, Utah.
25. Marguerite Harrison file, archives of the Society of Woman Geographers, Library of Congress.
26. John Edgar Hoover to Special Agent in Charge, Los Angeles, August 23, 1941, and November 26, 1941, FBI File, 100-HQ-40298, NARA, College Park, Md.
27. Report by Special Agent D. W. Magee, May 19, 1942, FBI File, 100-HQ-40298, NARA, College Park, Md.
28. Report by Special Agent D. W. Magee, August 22, 1942, FBI File, 100-HQ-40298, NARA, College Park, Md.
29. Report by K. A. Vosburgh, December 13, 1941, FBI File, 100-HQ-40298, NARA, College Park, Md.
30. R. B. Hood to J. Edgar Hoover, April 8, 1942, FBI File, 100-HQ-40298, NARA, College Park, Md.
31. Nancy Harrison interview with author, June 14, 2017.

32. Susan Richards, *Chosen by a Horse: How a Horse Fixed a Broken Heart* (New York: Soho Press, 2006), 163–64.

33. Nancy Harrison interview with author, June 14, 2017.

34. Baltimore City Register of Wills, Estate Papers No. 92,476, MSA T-1018-1703, Maryland State Archives; Baltimore City Register of Wills, vol. LCS 317, pp. 13–16, MSA CM219-383, Maryland State Archives.

35. Baltimore City Health Department Bureau of Vital Statistics, Certificate of Death No. 67 6813, Marguerite E. Blake, July 16, 1967, MSA CE502-456.

AFTERWORD

1. Society of Woman Geographers, accessed September 1, 2019, http://www .iswg.org/about/history.

BIBLIOGRAPHY

ARCHIVES

American Relief Administration, Russian Operational Records, Hoover Institution Archives, Stanford University

Central Archive of the Federal Security Bureau, Moscow, Russia

Kevin Brownlow Collection, Harold B. Lee Library, Brigham Young University, Provo, Utah

Maryland Historical Society, Baltimore, Maryland

Maryland State Archives, Annapolis, Maryland

Merian C. Cooper Papers, Harold B. Lee Library, Brigham Young University, Provo, Utah

National Archives and Records Administration (NARA), College Park, Maryland

Society of Woman Geographers, Library of Congress, Washington, D.C.

U.S. Army Heritage and Education Center, Carlisle, Pennsylvania

PUBLISHED WORKS

Adams, Amanda. *Ladies of the Field: Early Women Archaeologists and Their Search for Adventure*. Vancouver: Greystone, 2010.

Allen, Frederick Lewis. *Only Yesterday: An Informal History of the Nineteen-Twenties*. New York: Harper & Row, 1931.

Allin, Lawrence C. "The Civil War and the Period of Decline: 1961–1913." In *America's Maritime Legacy: A History of the U.S. Merchant Marine and Shipbuilding Industry since Colonial Times*, edited by Robert A. Kilmarx, 65–110. Boulder, Colo.: Westview, 1979.

Balabanoff, Angelica. *My Life as a Rebel*. 3rd ed. New York: Greenwood Press, 1968.

Balsan, Consuelo Vanderbilt. *The Glitter and the Gold: The American Duchess— In Her Own Words*. New York: Harper & Bros., 1952.

Baram, Phillip J. *The Department of State in the Middle East, 1919–1945*. Philadelphia: University of Pennsylvania Press, 1978.

Beasley, Maurine H., and Sheila J. Gibbons. *Taking Their Place: A Documentary History of Women in Journalism*. Washington, D.C.: American University Press, 1993.

Beirne, Francis F. *The Amiable Baltimoreans*. Hatboro, Pa.: Tradition, 1968.

Bell, Gertrude Lowthian. *The Letters of Gertrude Bell*, vol. 2, *1921–1926*. New York: Boni and Liveright, 1927.

Bernstein, Carl. "The CIA and the Media." *Rolling Stone*, October 20, 1977. http://www.carlbernstein.com/magazine_cia_and_media.php.

Berry, Helen. "Gertrude Bell: Pioneer, Anti-Suffragist, Feminist Icon?" In *Gertrude Bell and Iraq: A Life and Legacy*, edited by Paul Collins and Charles Tripp, 127–54. Oxford: Oxford University Press, 2017.

Bidwell, Bruce. *History of the Military Intelligence Division, Department of the Army General Staff, 1775–1941*. Frederick, Md.: University Publications of America, 1986.

Blanton, Casey. *Travel Writing: The Self and the World*. New York: Twayne, 1997.

Bradley, Patricia. *Women and the Press: The Struggle for Equality*. Evanston, Ill.: Northwestern University Press, 2005.

Brooks, Neal A., and Eric G. Rockel, and William C. Hughes. *A History of Baltimore County*. Towson, Md.: Friends of the Towson Library, 1979.

Brown, Dorothy M. *Setting a Course: American Women in the 1920s*. Boston: Twayne, 1987.

Bruche, Eleanor. "The Industrialization of Maryland, 1860–1914." In *Maryland: A History 1632–1974*, edited by Richard Walsh and William Lloyd Fox, 471. Baltimore: Maryland Historical Society, 1974.

Brugger, Robert J. *Maryland: A Middle Temperament 1634–1980*. Baltimore: Johns Hopkins University Press, 1988.

Burkorsky, Sergei. "Spy by Nationality," October 30, 2014. http://vkurske.com/society/99866/.

Carroll, Tim. *The Dodger: The Extraordinary Story of Churchill's American Cousin, Two World Wars, and The Great Escape*. Guilford, Conn.: Lyons Press, 2013.

Chafe, William H. *The Paradox of Change: American Women in the 20th Century*. New York: Oxford University Press, 1991.

Chalabi, Tamara. "Fragments of a Mirror: The Writing of Gertrude Bell." In *Gertrude Bell and Iraq: A Life and Legacy*, edited by Paul Collins and Charles Tripp, 155–84. Oxford: Oxford University Press, 2017.

Churchill, Susan Wintsch. *The Little Magazine Others and the Renovation of Modern American Poetry*. Burlington, Vt.: Ashgate, 2006.

Connolly, Cynthia. *Saving Sickly Children: The Tuberculosis Preventorium in America Life, 1909–1970*. New Brunswick, N.J.: Rutgers University Press, 2008.

Cooper, Merian C. *Grass*. New York: G. P. Putnam's Sons, 1925.

———. *Things Men Die For*. New York: G. P. Putnam's Sons. 1927.

Craig, Patricia, and Mary Cadogan. *The Lady Investigates: Women Detectives and Spies in Fiction*. New York: St. Martin's Press, 1981.

Crooks, James B. "Maryland Progressivism." In *Maryland: A History, 1632–1974*, edited by Richard Walsh and William Lloyd Fox, 590–671. Baltimore: Maryland Historical Society, 1974.

Crozer, Emmett. *American Reporters on the Western Front, 1914–1918*. New York: Oxford University Press, 1959.

Davidson, Isobel. *Real Stories from Baltimore County History*. Hatboro, Pa.: Tradition, 1967.

Dearborn, Mary V. *Queen of Bohemia: The Life of Louise Bryant*. Boston: Houghton Mifflin, 1996.

Degler, Carl N. *At Odds: Women and Family in America from the Revolution to the Present*. Oxford: Oxford University Press, 1980.

Desmond, Robert W. *Crisis and Conflict: World News Reporting between Two Wars 1920–1940*, Iowa City: University of Iowa Press, 1982.

Dole, Gertrude Evelyn. *Vignettes of Some Early Members of the Society of Woman Geographers in New York*. New York: Society of Woman Geographers, 1978.

Dulles, Foster Rhea. *Americans Abroad: Two Centuries of European Travel*. Ann Arbor: University of Michigan Press, 1964.

Edwards, Julia. *Women of the World: The Great Foreign Correspondents*. Boston: Houghton Mifflin, 1988.

Erb, Cynthia Marie. *Tracking King Kong: A Hollywood Icon in World Culture*, Detroit: Wayne State University Press, 2009.

Estes, Weston B. "Russian Experiences." *Long Island Medical Journal* 15, no. 12 (December 1921): 411.

Foglesong, David S. *America's Secret War against Bolshevism*. Chapel Hill: University of North Carolina Press, 1995.

Fox, William Lloyd. "Social-Cultural Developments from the Civil War to 1920." In *Maryland: A History, 1632–1974*, edited by Richard Walsh and William Lloyd Fox, 499–589. Baltimore: Maryland Historical Society, 1974.

Frederick, Bonnie, and Susan McLeod. *Women and the Journey: The Female Travel Experience*. Pullman: Washington State University Press, 1993.

Friedrich, Otto. *Before the Deluge: A Portrait of Berlin in the 1920s*. New York: Harper & Row, 1972.

Fussell, Paul. *Abroad: British Literary Traveling between the Wars*. Oxford: Oxford University Press, 1980.

Gerber, Louis. "St. Regis Grand Hotel Rome." *Cosmopolis*, October 3, 2008. http://www.cosmopolis.ch/travel/rome/st_regis_grand_hotel_e0100.htm.

Gerson, Leonard D. *The Secret Police in Lenin's Russia*. Philadelphia: Temple University Press, 1976.

Gilbert, James L. *World War I and the Origins of U.S. Military Intelligence*. Lanham, Md.: Scarecrow, 2012.

Goldman, Emma. *My Life*. New York: Alfred A. Knopf, 1931.

Gramling, Oliver. *AP: The Story of News*. Port Washington, N.Y.: Kennikat, 1940.

Grauer, Neil A. *The Special Field: A History of Neurosurgery at Johns Hopkins*. Baltimore: Johns Hopkins University Department of Neurosurgery, 2015.

Greenberg, David. *Republic of Spin: An Inside History of the American Presidency*. New York: Norton, 2016.

Gregory, Alexis. *Families of Fortune: Life in the Gilded Age*. New York: Rizzoli International, 1993.

Griggs, Catherine. "Beyond Boundaries: The Adventurous Life of Marguerite Harrison." PhD dissertation (unpublished), George Washington University, 1996.

Harding, Stan. *Underworld of State*. London: Allen & Unwin. 1925.

Harris, Barbara J. *Beyond Her Sphere: Women and the Professions in American History*. Westport, Conn.: Greenwood, 1978.

Harrison, Marguerite. "Marguerite Harrison's Tales of Russian Nights Unfinished Stories." *Cosmopolitan*, November 1922, 47–49, 114–20.

———. *Marooned in Moscow: The Story of an American Woman Imprisoned in Russia*. New York: George H. Doran, 1921.

———. "More of Marguerite Harrison's Unfinished Stories." *Cosmopolitan*, October 1922, 82–86, 162–66.

———. *Red Bear or Yellow Dragon*. New York: George H. Doran Co., 1924.

————. *There's Always Tomorrow: The Story of a Checkered Life*. New York: Farrar & Rinehart, 1935.

————. "Unfinished Stories." *Cosmopolitan*, September 1922, 32–35, 165–171.

Hayden, Joseph R. *Negotiating in the Press: American Journalism and Diplomacy, 1918–1919*. Baton Rouge: Louisiana State University Press, 2010.

Heilbrun, Carolyn G. *Writing a Woman's Life*. New York: Norton, 1988.

Hicks, Granville. *John Reed: The Making of a Revolutionary*. New York: Macmillan, 1936.

Hollihan, Kerrie Logan. *Reporting under Fire: 16 Daring Women War Correspondents and Photojournalists*. Chicago: Chicago Review Press, 2014.

Ind, Allison. *A Short History of Espionage*. New York: David McKay, 1963.

Jelinek, Estelle C. *The Tradition of Women's Autobiography: From Antiquity to the Present*. Boston: Twayne, 1986.

Johnson, Thomas M. *Our Secret War: True American Spy Stories, 1917–1919*. Indianapolis: Bobbs-Merrill, 1929.

Jowett, Garth S. "'A Capacity for Evil': The 1915 Supreme Court *Mutual* Decision." In *Controlling Hollywood: Censorship and Regulation in the Studio Era*, edited by Matthew Bernstein. New Brunswick, N.J.: Rutgers University Press, 1999.

Karikh, Maria. "Intentional Air Crash: Beria Never Allowed Anyone to Look into His Past." *Military Industrial Courier* (March 23–29, 2005): 11. https://vpk-news.ru/sites/default/files/pdf/issue_77.pdf.

King, Melanie. *The Lady Is a Spy*. London: Ashgrove, 2019.

Kinghorn, Jonathan. *Atlantic Transport Line, 1881–1931*. Jefferson, N.C.: McFarland, 2012.

Knightley, Phillip. *The First Casualty: The War Correspondent as Hero and Myth-Maker from the Crimea to Kosovo*. Baltimore: Johns Hopkins University Press, 2004.

Kollwitz, Käthe. *The Diary and Letters of Kaethe Kollwitz*, edited by Hans Kollwitz, translated by Richard and Clara Winston. Evanston, Ill.: Northwestern University Press, 1955.

Lane, Bethany. "The Women Who Shook It Up and Made It Happen." University of Glasgow Library blog, reposted by Sammaddra on March 8, 2015. https://universityofglasgowlibrary.wordpress.com/2015/03/08/the-women-who-shook-it-up-made-it-happen-by-bethany-lane/.

Leggett, George. *The Cheka: Lenin's Political Police*. Oxford: Clarendon, 1981.

Lenin, Vladimir. *Complete Collection of Works*. Vol. 53, *Letters: Second Half of July 1921*. https://leninism.su/works/39-tom-53/245-letters-jul-21-2.html#.D0.93._.D0.92._.D0.A7.D0.98.D0.A7.D0.95.D0.A0.D0.98.D0.9D.D0.A3_4.

Loy, Mina. *The Lost Lunar Baedeker: Poems of Mina Loy*. New York: Farrar, Straus and Giroux, 1996.

Lutes, Jean Marie. *Front-Page Girls: Women Journalists in American Culture and Fiction, 1888–1930*. Ithaca, N.Y.: Cornell University Press, 2006.

Madeira, Victor. *Britannia and the Bear: The Anglo-Russian Intelligence Wars, 1917–1929*. Woodbridge, Suffolk, U.K.: Boydell, 2014.

Maghsoudlou, Bahman. *Grass: Untold Stories*. Costa Mesa, Calif.: Mazda, 2009.

Mahoney, Harry Thayer, and Marjorie Locke Mahoney. *American Prisoners of the Bolsheviks: The Genesis of Modern American Intelligence*. Bethesda, Md.: Academica, 2001.

Mahoney, M. H. *Women in Espionage: A Biographical Dictionary*. Santa Barbara, Calif.: ABC-Clio, 1993.

Mayo Clinic. "Graves Disease." N.d. https://www.mayoclinic.org/diseases-conditions/graves-disease/symptoms-causes/syc-20356240.

McCausland, Christianna. *St. Timothy's School: A History from 1882–2000*, edited by Leslie Lichtenberg. Parkton, Md.: Neustadt Creative Marketing, 2008.

McCullagh, Francis. *A Prisoner of the Reds: The Story of a British Officer Captured in Siberia*. New York: Dutton, 1922.

McKenna, Marthe. *I Was A Spy! The Classic Account of Behind-the-Lines Espionage in World War I*. Oxford: Pool of London Press, 2015.

Mencken, H. L. *A Gang of Pecksniffs and Other Comments on Newspaper Publishers, Editors and Reporters*. New Rochelle, N.Y.: Arlington House, 1975.

———. *Thirty-five Years of Newspaper Work*, edited by Fred Hobson, Vincent Fitzpatrick, and Bradford Jacobs. Baltimore: Johns Hopkins University Press, 1994.

Messimer, Dwight R. *The Baltimore Sabotage Cell: German Agents, American Traitors, and the U-Boat Deutschland during World War I*. Annapolis, Md.: Naval Institute Press, 2015.

Miller, Nathan. *New World Coming: The 1920s and the Making of Modern America*. New York: Scribner, 2003.

———. *Spying for America: The Hidden History of U.S. Intelligence*. New York: Paragon, 1989.

Milton, Giles. *Russian Roulette: How British Spies Thwarted Lenin's Plot for Global Revolution*. New York: Bloomsbury, 2013.

Murray, Robert K. *Red Scare, A Study of National Hysteria, 1919–1920*. New York: McGraw-Hill, 1964.

North, Joseph. *Robert Minor: Artist and Crusader; An Informal Biography*. New York: International, 1956.

O'Connor, Richard, and Dale L. Walker. *The Lost Revolutionary: A Biography of John Reed*. New York: Harcourt, Brace & World, 1967.

Olds, Elizabeth Fagg. *Women of the Four Winds*. Boston: Houghton Mifflin, 1985.

Perrett, Geoffrey. *America in the Twenties: A History*. New York: Simon and Schuster, 1982.

Proctor, Tammy M. *Female Intelligence: Women and Espionage in the First World War*. New York: New York University Press, 2003.

Richards, Susan. *Chosen by a Horse: How a Horse Fixed a Broken Heart*. New York: Soho Press, 2006.

Rideout, Herbert C. "British Journalists Are Stirred Up by Mrs. Stand Harding Charges." *Editor and Publisher*, September 23, 1922.

Ross, Ishbel. *Ladies of the Press: The Story of Women in Journalism by an Insider*. New York: Harper & Brothers, 1936.

Russell, Bertrand. *Autobiography of Bertrand Russell, 1914–1944*. Vol. 2. Boston: Little, Brown, 1951.

Satia, Priya. *Spies in Arabia: The Great War and the Cultural Foundations of Britain's Covert Empire in the Middle East*. New York: Oxford University Press, 2008.

Scharf, Lois. *To Work and To Wed: Female Employment, Feminism and the Great Depression*. Westport, Conn.: Greenwood, 1980.

Schlereth, Thomas J. *Victorian American: Transformations in Everyday Life, 1876–1915*. New York: Harper Collins, 1991.

Schneider, Dorothy, and Carl Schneider. *American Women in the Progressive Era, 1900–1920*. New York: Facts on File, 1993.

Schoedsack, Ernest. "Grass: The Making of an Epic." *American Cinematographer*, February 1983.

Schudson, Michael. *Discovering the News*. New York: Basic Books, 1978.

Serge, Victor. *Memoirs of a Revolutionary, 1901–1941*, translated and edited by Peter Sedgwick. London: Oxford University Press, 1963.

Showalter, Elaine, ed. *These Modern Women: Autobiographical Essays from the Twenties*. Old Westbury, N.Y.: Feminist Press.

Spence, Richard B. "John Reed, American Spy? Reed, American Intelligence, and Weston Estes' 1920 Mission to Russia." *American Communist History* 13, no. 1 (2014): 54. http://dx.doi.org/10.1080/14743892.2014.896642.

Tsvetaeva, Marina. *Earthly Signs, Moscow Diaries, 1917–1922*, edited by Jamey Gambrell. New Haven, Conn.: Yale University Press, 2002.

Van Deman, Ralph. *The Final Memoranda*, edited by Ralph E. Weber. Wilmington, Del.: Scholarly Resources Imprint, 1988.

Vaz, Mark Cotta. *Living Dangerously: The Adventures of Merian Cooper, Creator of King Kong*. New York: Villard, 2005.

Ward, Stephen J. A. *The Invention of Journalism Ethics: The Path to Objectivity and Beyond*. Montreal: McGill-Queen's University Press, 2004.

Wheelwright, Julie. *The Fatal Lover: Mata Hari and the Myth of Women in Espionage*. London: Collins & Brown, 1992.

White, Frank F., Jr. *The Governors of Maryland 1777–1970*. Annapolis, Md.: Hall of Records Commission, 1970.

Whitt, Jan. *Women in American Journalism: A New History*. Urbana: University of Illinois Press, 2008.

Williams, Harold A. *The Baltimore Sun, 1837–1987*. Baltimore: Johns Hopkins University Press, 1987.

Wynn, Neil A. *From Progressivism to Prosperity: World War I and American Society*. New York: Homes & Meier, 1986.

Zirinsky, Michael. "Blood, Power and Hypocrisy: The Murder of Robert Imbrie and American Relations with Pahlavi Iran, 1924." *International Journey of Middle Eastern Studies* 18 (1986): 275–92.

INDEX

seizure by, 189; *Miles of Smiles* showing to Maryland troops in, 64, 65–66
France, Joseph I., 136, 140–41, 143–44, 145, 148, 149–50, 154, 184
Frick, Henry Clay, 111
Fuller, George, 204

gambling, 224
Gannett, Lewis, 155
geishas, 160, 162, 163
Germany: American agents working in, 69–70; economic and political conditions in, 64, 66–67, 68–72, 75; food aid to, 72; intelligence mission to with *Miles of Smiles* reporting as cover, 13–14, 64; missions of Marguerite in, 4, 68–76, 130; pro-German spies and saboteurs in Baltimore, 4, 6, 59–62, 130; punishment for war, 70, 75; reparation obligations and Ruhr valley seizure by French, 189; sympathies with workers in, 189; U.S. declaration of war on, 55, 56; Weimar National Assembly election and meeting, 68, 72; women voting in, 68; WWI outbreak and support for, 41. *See also* Berlin
Gillett, Nancy, 19
Godson, W. F., 85, 87
Goldman, Emma, 82, 111, 122
Grass (Cooper), 214
Grass (film): bravery of Marguerite while filming, 196; completion and production of, 217; conflicting stories about decision to film, 194–96; criticism of Marguerite by Cooper and Schoedsack while filming, 196–98; decision for Marguerite to join, 196; filmmaking knowledge of team and realistic cover for operation, 197; funding for, 194, 195, 196, 215; intelligence gathering as true purpose of, 194–95, 217; oil concessions for U.S. companies as reason for making, 196, 229; premier of and advertisement for, 215, 217; reviews of, 217. *See also* Bakhtiari tribe
Great Britain: Asian trade strategy of, 162; Atlantic Transport Line cargo and passenger service to London, 17; delegation to explore trade with Russia, 112–14; hospital ship donation to, 24–25; intelligence missions of Harding for, 73–74; oil interests of, 204, 210–11; socializing during vacations in, 18–19; socializing with royalty in, 24–25; Soviet Russian trade with, 162; summer vacations to, 18–19; use of women as spies by, 8

Haidar, 206–9
Harbin, 169–70
Harding, Constance "Stan": apology and compensation demand from for allegations of betrayal, 118, 184–85, 189, 191, 222; arrest, imprisonment, and solitary confinement of,

117–18, 125, 128, 129–30, 133, 145; double agent proposal from Mogilevsky, 117, 129–30; early life and marriage of, 73; identification as foreign agent by Marguerite, 117–18, 130, 145, 167, 189–91, 229; intelligence and journalist career of, 73–74, 116–18, 133, 189–90, 191; Kharitonyesky guesthouse housing of, 116–17; meeting in Berlin and relationship with Marguerite, 73–75, 140, 191; Mogilevsky description by, 129; political leanings of, 74; rescue of Marguerite from Russia, 116; suspicion of being a spy by Mogilevsky, 117; travel to Russia as journalist, 114–16
Harding, Warren, 134, 152–53
Hari, Mata, 7, 8, 9, 85
Harrington, Elizabeth, 188
Harrison, Margery D. Andrews, 214
Harrison, Marguerite: accuracy of and conflicting stories about life and adventures of, x–xii, 177, 182–84, 186–87, 188–89, 191–92; adventurous spirit of and compulsion to travel by, 10, 18, 29, 58, 62, 83, 159, 192, 214–15, 226–27; affair with Ritchie, 51, 52, 226; Afghanistan delegate proposal to, 119; alienation from people and values once dear, 152–53; ambitions of mother for marriage to royalty by, 8–9, 24–27, 233n7; appearance of, 7, 225; *Asia Reborn*, 222; author and lecturer career of, 77, 150–51, 153, 154–55, 159, 191–92, 215, 217–18, 221–23, 224; autobiography of, x, 9; balance of single mother responsibilities with desire for work and adventure, 83; birth, family, and early life of, 8, 15–16, 18–25; chameleon self-description of, 104; character of, 15, 109–10, 225, 226–27; charitable and civic interests of, 7, 15, 24–25, 35, 36–38; Christmas celebration in Turkey, 200–201; clothes shopping in Berlin, 147; credit and respect for accomplishments of, 217–18; death and scattering of ashes of, ix, 227; death of and repayment of loan to Cooper, 223; death of father and settlement of estate, 64–65, 153–54, 160, 191; death of husband of, ix, 4, 43; debut to society of, 23–24; difficult delivery of son and family-size decision, 31; disarray of life after Tom's death, 43; domestic help for, 31, 236n2; early life of, x; edge-of-scandal behavior of, 15; education of, 19, 20–23; engagement and marriage to Tom, 4, 25–28, 34; engagement while at Radcliffe, 22–23; estate of, 227; expenses after death of Tom, 44, 45; failure to find contentment in U.S., 156, 159–60; fashion sense of, 25, 32; FBI investigation of, 223–25; final years of, 226–27; financial struggles of, 40, 42, 153–54, 222–23, 224–25; health of during and after imprisonment, 136, 138, 139, 141, 143, 147, 184, 187, 189; high-society ambitions of mother for, 15–16,

ABOUT THE AUTHOR

ELIZABETH ATWOOD is a former newspaper reporter and editor who worked for more than twenty years at the *Baltimore Sun*, where she first learned about Marguerite Harrison, the newspaper reporter turned double agent. Atwood is an associate professor of journalism at Hood College in Frederick, Maryland. Her research focuses on the ways in which journalists contribute to social and political revolutions.